D1593850

FREE
ADMISSIONS

JONATHAN KALB

FREE

ADMISSIONS

Collected Theater

Writings

Limelight Edition   New York   1993

First Edition, November 1993
Copyright © 1986, 1987, 1990, 1991, 1992, 1993 by Jonathan Kalb
All rights reserved under International and Pan-American Copyright Conventions. Published
in the United States by Proscenium Publishers Inc., New York, and simultaneously in
Canada by Fitzhenry & Whiteside, Limited, Toronto.

Library of Congress Cataloging-in-Publication Data
Kalb, Jonathan.
Free admissions : collected theater writings / Jonathan Kalb. —
1st Limelight ed.
p. cm.
Includes bibliographical references and index.
ISBN 0-87910-169-5. — ISBN 0-87910-168-7 (pbk.)
1. Theater—United States—History—20th century. 2. Theater—
Germany—History—20th century. 3. Theater—New York (N.Y.)—
Reviews. I. Title.
PN2266.5.K36 1993
792′.0973′09045—dc20   93-25358
                                                          CIP

Manufactured in the United States of America

FOR OLIVER

Contents

Introduction

There are jobs and there are jobs. Not all of them require cosmic justification, but here's a stickler for a dead sage with some time on his/her hands: why does anyone ever become a theater critic? The question used to hover in my head during those particularly baleful nights of theater that leave you with a lingering black mood unless you occupy yourself with more serious issues. I was never forced actually to formulate a response, though, until last year when several interviewers directly asked me after I was given an award for my theater criticism. The unanswerability of it is what preoccupies me now.

No one starts out wanting to be one; that much is clear. No callow youngster yearns for dramaturgical training in order to figure out girls or the engine of a Camaro. Early experiences in the theater are invariably anti-critical, the product of passions and habits difficult to reconcile with the intellect. My earliest theater memory is a trauma. At eight years old I watched my father "die" as the King in an amateur production of *The King and I* and retched on the spot, that grave "Something Wonderful" refrain swelling round me like a monstrous, musical poultice. My mother hastened to reassure me, even producing the living man (as "frown'd he once") to support her case. But I hadn't confused fact with fiction, as everyone assumed. The problem was that I felt betrayed. I *knew* it was all make-believe, and it wrenched my feelings anyway. Who knows? Maybe the child really did need to spend his next three decades taking apart the toy that upset him, and other toys like it.

As an undergraduate I wrote four excessive plays and directed them myself. The more I learned about dramatic literature and theater history, though, the more dissatisfied I became with what I had written. One of my kindlier English professors said I was "too smart to be a playwright," which discouraged me despite being well intended. The message that successful American dramatists in the mold of O'Neill generally played the naif, generally read less and not more as their commitment to the craft grew stronger, was more enervating than the prospect of lifelong financial insecurity. Perhaps I really did have the wrong temperament for it. If (as I strongly doubt) a desire to see the insides of the great dramatic toys necessarily impedes one's ability to build good ones, then I am guilty as charged. In any case, my critical career began in my mind as a hiatus from playwriting, prompted first of all by a need to write myself out of an obsession with Samuel Beckett.

Free Admissions is, in the spirit of Oscar Wilde's quip that criticism "is the only civilised form of autobiography," the best answer I can offer to the question of how I came to this profession. It is a collection of essays, reviews, interviews and other writings spanning the period 1984-1992 and previously published in *American Theatre, Theater, Performing Arts Journal, Theater Three, The Threepenny Review, The Michigan Quarterly Review* and other publications acknowledged below. For approximately half of that period I was a regular reviewer for *The Village Voice*, and the section "On the Front Line" is a selection of *Voice* pieces that seem to me of continuing interest. In general I have resisted the urge to emend my stylistic peculiarities, though I have done some tinkering, making cuts to avoid redundancy and removing, say, the odd adverb chosen hastily in the enthusiasm of the moment. Also, text originally cut due to space limitations has been replaced and numerous copy-editor's improvements repaired. The one exception is the essay "Maya-kovsky's Tragic Comedy," which appears here in a substantially revised version.

One piece has not been published before, "German Theater after the *Wende*," first given as a talk at a 1990 conference at the University of Michigan. That conference, on recent changes in Germany (entitled *"Gegenwartsbewältigung*—Coming to Terms with the Present," a pun on the old propaganda term *Vergangenheitsbewältigung*—coming to terms with the past, a post-World War II pomade), was one of many events I attended in the year following the fall of the Berlin Wall in an attempt to come to terms myself with the bewilderingly sudden upheaval that was occurring in a place I had lived for two years (in 1986-87 and 1988-89). The book's opening section, *"Deutschland Deutschland,"* which is not exclusively about the theater, chronicles my experiences in Germany during the strange transitional period when unification was still uncertain and thousands still worked toward the continued existence of a reformed GDR. "German Theater after the *Wende"* is a report on a colloquium held in Berlin in May 1990, but it is also a snapshot of a historical moment, the likes of which will not come again soon, when the cultural elites of East and West, with their variously leftist idealisms, had their noses briefly rubbed in realpolitik.

The topic of Germany recurs in the other sections of *Free Admissions* as well: "Head Shots," a selection of interviews and interview-essays, and "Ends and Odds," miscellaneous texts, three of which happen to deal with Beckett, the intellectual first love I still have not quite escaped. As for Germany, I might forestall some confusion by admitting right away that the deeper preoccupation is really with "Germany," not so much a geographically locatable place as a mental place, a locus for a sort of aberrant idealism. I am aware that the tone of some of my statements leaves an impression of idealizing conditions (particularly relating to state subsidy) that, in actuality, have as many deleterious as beneficent effects. There is a "Germany" of my mind, though, basic to my continuing interest in the theater, that has come to stand as a figure for the kind of rigorous artistic investment and probity of thought I search for and need, wherever I am. The phenomenon is hardly new. Others have had other figures—a dramaturg/translator I know searches perpetually for a "Russia" that both does and doesn't correspond to what she sees during regular trips to Moscow. "Germany" is my cache of ideas about what the theater *can* be, without which I couldn't write a word about it. And the truth is, somewhere between the cerebralism of the German theater and the anti-intellectualism of the American theater is a benign middle ground for both cultures, though doubtless not the same one.

In addition to Germany and Beckett, the book contains a third recurrent theme: distrust of directors. Several friends have offered opinions about the source of this fixation of mine. One traces it to my third year at the Yale School of Drama, when I found sixteen pages from my Dramaturg's Protocol, the product of six months' hard labor, unquoted and unattributed, in the first draft of a directing student's Masters Thesis. (This director has gone on to a remarkably successful career on and off Broadway, and much of what I know about cronyism, vacuous charisma, and the cataract-mechanisms of hype comes from his example.) An instructor at the same institution reminds me of another experience in which an obnoxious Swedish director assigned to me as a "master-teacher" at the Yale Repertory Theater repeatedly crumpled up my earnestly delivered dramaturgical notes and, with a haughty sneer, tossed them into the garbage can in front of me. Not to deny the impact of these memories, the theme has a sounder basis than personal rancor.

My mental preset regarding directors is an outgrowth of hundreds of theatergoing experiences as a critic. Far more often than not I have come away from productions that were devoid of nourishment for mind or belly, saying to myself that the emptiness onstage had nothing to do with deficiencies in the writing or performing but rather with ideas and behaviors imposed in the name of "subjective vision" or "conceptual unity." (My reviews, both those collected here and not, will serve as examples.) Certainly, this was not always the case, and perhaps it was a coincidence of my reviewing assignments, but it happened with enough frequency that I eventually acquired an impression of a general and generally destructive syndrome: a once restorative and fruitful theory—that all creative decisions in the theater ought to be controlled by a single auteur figure—had become vitiated and shopworn, an intellectual mask for worship of authority for its own sake. Most Americans who work in the theater know at least one director who doesn't even really *like* the job of staging plays, let alone demonstrate any special ability at it, but who nevertheless continues because of the mystique and the power of the position. A critic encounters such practitioners several dozen times a year. Unfortunately, it has been half a century since the ends justified the means on this score, except in isolated cases such as Richard Foreman and Robert Wilson. The principle of absolute autonomy for the *Regisseur* has come full circle in this century to being responsible for enslaving the theater to old ideas—a realization that, now and then, has brought me dangerously close to a return to playwriting.

Most members of that tiny, forsaken group known as the American theater intelligentsia will now expect me to launch into a disquisition on the need for dramaturgs. Alas, others will have to fight that fight—although, as should be abundantly clear, I do agree that the typical production in this country cries out for feedback from someone who reads a bit more than the director does. Nor will I succumb to another powerful temptation: expatiating on the culture industry, which encourages and protects most of what is reprehensible in our arts, including moribund, Napoleonic directors and certain editorial policies of the *Village Voice*. As for the latter topic, whatever I have to say publically about it is included in the two-part piece "Why I Write for the *Village Voice*"—with the exception of one important acknowledgement. Erika Munk and Ross Wetzsteon, the two editors I have principally worked with at the paper, both of whom have also suffered under the conditions I describe, have my gratitude for making my complaining possible.

The burden of that reckless, not to say desperate, piece was to make clear that theater criticism survives today in increasingly strangulated circumstances. The depth of analysis in even some of my own pieces from a few years ago—say, "Krapp at the Palast," or "Homo, Fuge!" and "Chez Ubu" for that matter—is no longer possible in the *Voice* or any other American publication that appears while the productions it covers are still running. If this collection (whose title I freely admit was suggested by Stanley Kauffmann) succeeds in persuading some fence-sitters that that is indeed regrettable, it will have served a far nobler purpose than the autobiographical one.

January 1993

DEUTSCHLAND, DEUTSCHLAND

Berlin by Metaphor

Friends and I used to joke that flying to West Berlin by way of Tegel Airport was cheating. You had to drive or take the train, preferably the night train, if you wanted a first impression that didn't deceive. The slow, clanking diesel engine that sometimes ground to a stop with long, unbearable squeals, sitting still for twenty minutes, or thirty, for no apparent reason; the blue- and green-uniformed men who periodically snapped on the compartment lights and gleefully barked "*Fahrkarten, bitte!*" and "*Pässe, bitte!*," like SS-officers turned housewives, spacing out their visits as if to ensure that you didn't get more than an hour's uninterrupted sleep; the GDR soldiers with machine-guns, German Shepherds, and *really* bad attitudes sniffing around outside the windows for a half-hour before the train entered the city at sunrise; that was the true paradigmatic journey from West to East to West—overlong, exhausting, infuriating, anachronistic. Anything else was either a lie or a euphemism.

Since the *Wende*, or turning point, it's hard to talk about such difficulties without seeming to be gloating or condescending. Lest we forget, though, there was one western city that had to deal with them on a daily basis for over four decades, and ultimately accepted them as commonplace. Some Berliners have even gone through a sort of withdrawal from them over the past year, complaining that they miss the Wall, that makeshift yet endless palimpsest, that public yet private message-board equally amenable to the most radical political *Schrei* and the most insular love proclamation. The sentiment may sound strange—it certainly evokes little enough sympathy among "*Wessies*" from other places, or "*Ossies*" from anywhere—but having lived in this city for two years, I confess that I share it. As its residents never tire of explaining, West Berlin was not just another western metropolis before and is not about to become one now with the incorporation of its "lost" half. Despite the profusion of new corporate offices in the West and Day-glo Camel-cigarette café umbrellas in the East—which appeared overnight, as instantaneously as the Wall once did—that rarified, alienated condition known as "Berliner" (formerly "West Berliner") will continue to exist and will likely remain deeply resonant to outsiders for a good, long while.

Now and then during the time I lived here, I considered earning a little money by writing a travel essay on Berlin in the spirit of *Baedeker* and *Blue Guide*, but I eventually gave up the idea after realizing that such a "guide" would be even more pointless than it is in other places—not only because of the city itself but also because of the preconceptions people bring to it. Guides are for stable things, timeless objects that have already been eulogized, laid to rest in a way that enables tourists to relax, the job of thinking already done for them. Anyone who comes here on a pilgrimage to the front of the Cold War, or for any other reason, soon sees that the job isn't finished and, as a compensation, quickly acquires an arsenal of metaphors, loaded and ready to fire. There's no avoiding the impulse to understand Berlin this way. It's why visitors always found the Wall so irresistible. Didn't it symbolize the bankruptcy of so-called Communism, political hypocrisy in general, the wages of German nationalism, man's inability to conquer his aggressiveness? More, didn't its symbolism also encompass our private pathos, all those difficulties that self-help books try to ameliorate: the barriers between parent and child, men and women, you and your mother, your father, your girlfriend, the pigeons you fed in the park on Sundays?

It was the perfect epitome of a city that could be all things to all people, and its effective disappearance one day last November didn't change the obliging nature of the place. Berlin still repays the tourist's expense and trouble with a confirmation for every prejudice. In fact, the Wall's disappearance turns out to be as metaphorically provocative as the Wall itself. Think about it: Orwellian sanitation of history, denial of the fascist past, the triumph of the will to freedom, to capitalism. *Plus ça change, plus c'est la même chose*, with one important caveat. In this city, *la même chose*, the thing that never changes, is an abstract idea, a permanent condition of ephemerality, and anyone really interested in understanding the changes now occurring here must first understand that preexisting fact. There is no such thing as a durable iconic image in Berlin.

Native Berliners have always held particular scorn for those who come and gawk and leave, or, worse, those who come and work and attempt to stay; and such feelings have been especially prevalent since throngs of *Ossies* arrived for orgies of free-market consuming. To see that scorn as something more than contempt for the vulgar tourist or the poor cousin, however—a variation on the superficial local pride encountered in any large city—takes a certain induced toughness of mind. It takes a resistance to metaphor, or rather, since resistance is ultimately futile, a self-consciousness about why the mind keeps rushing to comparison. Before you succumb, consider where you are: a place where the nature of truth isn't just relative, as everywhere, but exceptionally temporary. Metaphors, like guides, are for stable objects; comparison can actually encumber thought about the unstable. A perfectly upstanding, hard-working metaphor can suddenly appear lazy in Berlin, a poor substitute for the ebb and flow of events, for endless talk in smoke-choked *Kneipen*—bars—where nothings hangs on the walls and the patrons all show up in black clothing.

Of course, the black is just style, isn't it? Just a uniform for the spoiled middle-class teenagers from West Germany who once flocked to Berlin in order to avoid military service or to find comrades for their various murky rebellions. Their motto: "No future!" Yes, on one level, that's what it is: the black pirate-flag in a make-believe sea battle, the ideal badge for a dilettant-ish flirtation with anarchy. On another level, though, it's as thoroughly Prussian as the great Friedrich himself, obligatory, manipulative, disposed to coerce mood, delimit conversation (Shall we talk about death today?), and inspire the same imperious pride as did the blue in Friedrich's coat. Or the shiny point on Bismarck's helmet. Or the polished barrels of Ulrike Mein-hof's guns . . .

You see, that's just how it happens. The metaphors slip in without your noticing. You can't really help it. And it doesn't only occur with foreigners. Recently, a well-known German choreographer named Johann Kresnik won the coveted director's prize at the Theatertreffen, Berlin's annual invitational theater festival, for a dance-theater piece that used Meinhof's biography as a metaphor for the *Wende* and postwar German history in general. The piece treated Meinhof as *only* a victim—she commits no terrorist acts herself and is raped again and again by various symbolic and non-symbolic characters— which is as skewed a view of history as that which sees her *only* as a terrorist. In Berlin, though, where having a strong opinion is far more important than being right, the oversimplification was seen as profound, the elisions a small price to pay for the forcefulness of the sledgehammer imagery.

Of course, there's nothing inherently wrong with comparison per se but rather with the way it tends to mitigate the truth, distract from the facts.

Ulrike Meinhof, *directed and choreographed by Johann Kresnik, Theater der Freien Hansestadt, Bremen, Germany, 1990.*

After all, Berlin isn't like Prussia; it *is* Prussia, neither a forgotten place nor an obsolete concept. (Look up the number of the *Staatsbibliothek* some time in the Berlin phone book; you won't find it under "S," or even "B," but rather "P" for *Preussischer Kulturbesitz—*Prussian Cultural Property.) Berlin is the thing itself, still the actual or symbolic nexus of countless strands of imperialist influence and domination, its history a conglomeration of facts about power politics so cold and hard that the propaganda of appearances— made as adroitly here as anywhere—can hardly cover them up. Berlin is the original, the rarity. Its isolated and divided condition was a literal expression of, and not a metaphor for, the conditions of modern imperialism: at once doggedly persistent and fearfully precarious. And the same is true of its reunified condition: a reflection of the new imperialism, monodirectional, self-satisfied, oblivious. Berlin isn't like other places, they are like aspects of it, and when I am asked to explain why I've spent so much time here, I always return to this point about centrality.

Beyond cheap thrills, what is the attraction of a place in which the weight of history is so immediate and oppressive it makes the most disciplined mind feel itself to be scrambling in a frenzy for explanations? The answer lies in the double challenge that Berlin poses to the onlooker: not only to get behind its reality of shifting appearances but also to perceive the significance of that shifting. The former challenge applies almost anywhere, but the latter is unique to Berlin, where superficiality is a sort of religion and doesn't always indicate insignificance. To gain insight into that religion is to feel that you are at least scrambling to a purpose.

This is a city of surfaces, a city of padded shoulders, chartered libertinism, a city unashamed to value texture above color, shape above function, style for style's sake, means at the expense of meaning. What other city would support Robert Wilson to the extent that this one does? What other city would find ways actually to build structures from so many "postmodern" architectural designs? What other place would become home to a movement called *Neue Wilde* whose painters really believe that a surfeit of red goo can still represent a rent body or a bludgeoned spirit? Where else would some people risk arrest in order to decorate and desecrate a heavily guarded international border fortification, only to contend with neighbors who insist that it be respected and kept clean? In May 1990, when demolition of the Wall was already in full swing, I actually saw two East German workmen whitewash over new graffiti that had appeared on their side of the Wall for the first time. The experience was surreal, as if I'd seen someone washing and waxing an abandoned car, but I've learned not to judge absurdity too fast here.

Especially in the city's western half, you can make friends fairly easily if you let people express their surfaces, so to speak. Ask someone where she likes to drink, dance, bowl, but don't ask her not to smoke in your bedroom, and don't open the door the *Kneipe* to let any oxygen in. Ask a person where he buys his black clothes, what his opinion on the census boycott is, but wait a while to ask more than superficially about his work, his love troubles, or he'll lose interest in you. You won't have much luck trying to see through a Berliner, as American friends play guru and try to see through to the core even at a first meeting, largely because the German language doesn't provide the proper tools for those urbane games of pop-psychologizing—all that jargony, circumlocutionary stuff that allows English-speakers to keep up the appearance of going deeper while in fact giving their neuroses free play. For forty-five years, the city's best kept secret has been that it isn't cosmopolitan in that sense; its a blown-up *Dorf*, a village that enjoyed flattering itself with the image of a metropolis cut in half.

The fact is, Berlin, like many other cities, really was originally an amalgamation of *Dörfer* that, over centuries, gathered into a single municipality with the palatial structures along the Spree and the wide avenue Unter den Linden at its center. That center lay entirely in the East, however, and after the erection of the Wall, West Berlin had to pretend to be a coherent *Grossstadt* when in fact it regressed to its earlier identity as a collection of contiguous villages. Officially, the villages became city districts, like the boroughs of New York, but they retained their small-town mentalities to a surprising degree, each acting independently to suppress "difference" and enforce mindless adherence to a peculiar provincial ideal of order. West Berlin always displayed an extremely puzzling resistance to blending these various attitudes; it preferred to preserve the state of parallel narrow-mindedness, despite the fact that, for practical purposes such as mass transit, it did function as a large city.

This narrowness appeared to apply everywhere, as much to Kreuzberg, the supposedly enlightened haven for the avant-garde, as to stuffy suburban districts like Zehlendorf and Mariendorf. To have met a thirteen-year old who was so isolated and over-protected that he never even heard of the city magazines *Tip* and *Zitty*—he believed that "everything you could want is right here in Zehldendorf"—wasn't so surprising; it was like an eighth-grader in Staten Island never having heard of the *Village Voice*. But to see *Autonomen* (literally "the autonomous ones") in Kreuzberg smashing windows and torching cars right in their own neighborhood was shocking to the point of bewilderment. The *Bezirk*, or district, constituted the limits of even the revolutionary imagination: too drunk or high or unorganized to go down to Kurfürstendamm ("Ku'damm" to the locals) to register a louder voice, they rationalized the soiling of their own nest as a sort of generic protest. There was no parallel with the suicidal violence that convulses American ghettoes, a truly urban phenomenon born of real deprivation, where home base represents a socio-economic prison imposed from without. The parallel was with the "bad boys" from the high schools of New Rochelle, New York or Milpitas, California or a thousand other suburbs, who get suspended for fighting and then run away to make trouble in the nearby city pool hall until they're bored enough to buckle down and join Daddy's business. Kreuzberg was West Germany's pool hall.

Now that Berlin is whole again, though, it is being wrenched back into its cosmopolitanism with a vengeance. Soon it will once again enjoy the dirt, the violent crime, the confusion, all those aspects of modern urbanism from which its long, provincial beauty sleep, to an amazing extent, spared it; and no one is asking whether the people also can change so suddenly and convulsively. Imagine, if you can, a western metropolitan subway system in which overcrowding and graffiti became problems for the first time in 1989. Imagine the instantaneous appearance of futuristically dense crowds in the city center, a babel of languages in the banks and shops, fierce competition for apartments, for used cars, for university places. The full scope of the new reality will take as many years to sink in here as it will in the East. Most of what the stunned West Berliners feel is a vague first-time realization of how good they had it before.

It's a shame that no one who travels here from now on will be able to see the peculiar detached attitude the locals used to take toward the Ku'damm area. Ku'damm, the ersatz downtown of the West, was supposed to be exceptional, a bastion of true urbanity; in fact, the neon was as indigenous to the city as tacos. The whole avenue was imported, a collection of pre-fab objects and images whose main purpose was to serve tourists. Ku'damm was an alien phenomenon, an outgrowth of military occupation, as foreign to the Berliner's mindset as the concept of fashion, its dozens of designer shops notwithstanding. Yes, that's right, there was no such thing as indigenous fashion here. How could there be? Fashion is a combination of innovativeness and perceptiveness about beauty and self, beauty in relation to self. The typical Berlin villagers possessed the former in superfluity but were so estranged from the latter that they hadn't even the slightest notion what it was. The city's anti-health ethic was the telling backdrop in this regard: the ubiquitous smoking, the drinking, the sedentariness. It's as if entrapment inside a concrete cage had caused some sort of chronic alienation from the body, as if the full experience of physical presence was, over a lifetime in Berlin, more than anyone could bear.

For Americans this could be extremely hard to understand. We didn't want to understand it because we didn't want to be disappointed. We preferred to interpret the lights of Ku'damm as real *Donner* and *Blitzen*, a foreign brand of authentic excitement, rather than as a replica of what we just came from, perfunctorily pasted onto another culture like a "SOLD" sign. The longings that underlie our own urbanity, the yearnings for security disguised as stimulation, are what we hope to escape in Europe, and Berlin did allow a kind of escape; it wore its garish coat so awkwardly that the effect was sometimes one of self-mockery. Ultimately, though, you couldn't help recognizing that the Berliners were deeply indifferent to the whole affair. They were thankful for the money the businesses brought them, but the place remained irrelevant to their self-image. I remember being initially fooled, for instance, by the crowds of what looked like American kids wearing football jerseys (from supposedly American teams—the Cleveland Bears?) and drinking

Coca-Cola on the steps of the Kaiser Wilhelm Memorial Church: only when I stopped to listen did I learn that their chatter in heavy Berlinese was a distended harangue on American vulgarity, arrogance, and imperialism, pieced together from clichés half-heard during weekend nights in Kreuzberg.

The point is, this unimpressibility wasn't a weakness; it actually demonstrated a strength of character of which we and the West Germans could only dream. Like most foreigners, we were blinded by the configuration of our basic needs and fears, especially our assumption that everyone faced with precariousness must cling to something solid. Berlin, able to survive economically only because of huge subsidies from the West German government, a land-locked island inside a totalitarian state, possibly the most dangerous place in the world to be in the event of an East/West conflict—how could the people in such a place resist clinging to the name brands, the ad-speak and cheap media images that offered us at least the illusion of security? That was precisely the peculiarity of the Berliner's self-image, though. In a culture with a long history of embracing arrant abstractions, it was actually possible to cling to precariousness itself.

Now, however, the precariousness is gone, and the Berliners have no choice but to start believing in that mantle of glitziness so dearly bought for them over four decades. Fashion will now return, on the way to spread its terrorism through the East, and Ku'damm will again become an indigenous phenomenon, though perhaps not the one everyone expects. In these first transitional months there are wonderfully telling scenes, as mobs of shoppers suffocate the downtown area in violent, starved embrace, seeing there the source of all things good. Good is a point of view, though, and these mobs aren't buying Bendel originals or Gucci shoes, but rather Japanese electronics and Lipton iced-tea mix by the case. In other words, they're worshipping the wrong gods according to Western standards, patronizing all the peripheral shops whose parasitic growth on Augsburgerstrasse and the other side-streets always poignantly reflected the Berliners' lack of respect for Ku'damm as a city center. Through all its practical difficulties over the years, West Berlin was prepared for many eventualities, including, under certain circumstances, to be plundered like a jewelry shop in a poor neighborhood. It was never prepared, however, for what actually happened, for the East to call the West's bluff, transforming the place overnight into something it never was or wanted to be, a team player, an obedient soldier. Now all it can do is sit there, in its chronic bad mood, passively observing its own draft induction.

The shock to East Berlin is even more acute, and more upsetting. A people to be pitied: unlike the majority of their countrymen, they voted for the Social Democrats as if to protect themselves from their own naiveté, and their instincts were right. No one there even *sees* the corporate advance men as they claim vast physical and mental territories with advertising before a single individual has a chance to exercise his or her new right to conduct private enterprise. Unfortunately, I'm all too familiar with this sort of benevolent strongarming: it's my culture's preferred method of filling power vacuums. Sometimes, against the ubiquitous grey, the swatches of high-tech color in the cigarette umbrellas and billboards resemble party-pins on giant suit-lapels, *Western* party-pins. Other times they leave an impression of spores, which is of course figuratively what they are, seeds for a system that's meant to grow like a weed. The advertising isn't only meant to sell things to the *Ossies* but also to reassure us *Wessies*, makes us feel safe in the knowledge that somewhere in this former "desert" someone is not giving a sucker an even break.

Alas, instead of being reassured, I'm alternately furious and ashamed. How do you explain to people who've never been allowed to travel to New York that the idiotic carousel constantly spinning sights and sounds round your head there, without your blessing or permission, may not be wholly benevolent? How do you explain the conspiracy to steal attention, to inter-pret every minute of your waking life as an opportunity to sell you some-thing, to people enraptured by the conspiracy's most perfect instruments, television and the disorienting environments of the Europa Center and other shopping malls? The answer is, you don't. Like Americans, they'll only insist on learning for themselves, and when that carousel starts gathering momen-tum, they won't have the slightest idea what hit 'em.

I don't stay furious or ashamed for long, though, because as soon as I start to relax all those metaphors start jumping out at me again from behind every sewer grate and tree stump. Comparison is an easy form of reflection, and inasmuch as the shifting of realities becomes a commonplace here, you become a believer in the value of approximate and temporary similarity, convinced of the pointlessness of demanding permanence of any truth. Ber-lin, everything in it, and everything that happens in it strike you as epitomes, and as the images and associations start to swarm, you make the only decision left you and allow the swarm to run its course.

Look at the Teufelsberg, highest point in the city, literally a pile of rubble from bombed-out buildings, carried in buckets to the northern edge of the Grunewald after the war, almost entirely by women. The logical thing would be to pile it still higher with pieces from the demolished Wall after Berlin is triumphantly declared *Mauerrein*—that is, the pieces not stored away in museums alongside the torahs, talises, and other Jewish treasures that sur-vived another November 9 not long ago. Objectivity in this place means a view from rubble overgrown with pretty grass.

Look at the Berliner Ensemble, the theater founded by Bertolt Brecht—which couldn't fill its seats if not for American tourists—once the standard-bearer for ideals of immediacy in performance and egalitarianism backstage, now administrator of a waxworks repertory and a star-system as ruthless as that of New York or Los Angeles. Its work before the *Wende* bore approxi-mately the same relation to Brecht as the GDR's political system did to Communism, and today it gropes along that same moribund path, hoping the new political reality will magically endow it with fresh significance. On countless fronts, keeping up appearances will now replace all deep reflection and self-scrutiny.

Recall the woman saved from drowning in the Landwehrkanal in 1920, claiming to be the Grand Duchess Anastasia, pampered and humored for years by opportunistic Germans and Americans with eyes on her family's fortune. How long, I used to ask myself, could the Federal Republic be expected to tolerate, feed, and nurse West Berlin, its problem child, in the desperate hope it would prove an authentic relic from a lost world? Now, suddenly, the lost world has been regained through an opportunism so intense it devalues even further our notions of authenticity. Anastasia is no longer relevant; this week's new icon is the *Ossie* with his newly acquired free enterprise, who chisels at a slab of concrete that he's just spray-painted because he knows he can charge more money for colored "relics of the true Wall."

Ponder the Reichstag, the world's most useless building, atrociously re-stored as a dull museum. How touching it was all these years, that its engraved proclamation of democracy (DEM DEUTSCHEN VOLKE) faced not eastward like a reproof but westward like a warning light on a control panel. ("*Achtung!* You are leaving the American Sector!!") Its function was to wait endlessly, a petrified Didi or Gogo, its noblest purpose, to be wrapped as a Christo sculpture. Poor giant edifice, all it can do is loom again now, a dumb sponge for hopefully obsolete fears about the future, its waiting no more resonant than an affianced debutante's.

The mind goes on and on until exhausted. Nothing is exempt, not the tree branch outside your window that resembles an expressionist wood-cut more than a living plant, not the relentlessly dark and brutal winter that lasts from October until June and leaves you permanently scarred, or should I say branded, with frostbite acquired on ordinary trips to the corner store. History makes you edgy when it's written too plainly on your environment, especially if you're an American.

In the end, you have to admit the truth to yourself, though: that you haven't in fact been overwhelmed but have been struggling all along to make sense of the swarm, to project sense onto it if need be. After all, you're not a Berliner but an outsider with a privileged vantage point. Searching for themes and motifs, you find them almost too easily by indulging in the old intellectual sport of analyzing the Teutonic personality. Is that wrong, un-fair? Perhaps, but it's also common and inevitable, a sort of involuntary act of mental hygiene when you live here for any length of time. I never lost interest, during my stay, in the question of why I was fascinated by Berlin, but as time went on I did become more and more inclined to differentiate it, understand it in light of the other undeniable fact that the idea of spending a year or two in any other German city repulsed me.

"Berlin isn't Germany as New York isn't America," goes the saying, and there is truth in it. With its multitude of bullet- and shrapnel-pocked facades and cheap, grey-stucco, non-designed buildings, Berlin is the only western German city that doesn't look as if the war never happened—a sort of visual frankness that warms the foreigner's heart. There is no self-consciousness in the cleaned-up landscape of, say, Frankfurt, where you almost believe that the engraving on the Alte Oper, DEM WAHREN SCHOENEN GUTEN ("To Truth, Beauty, and Goodness") extends to its neighboring network of happy corporate logos—ALLIANZBASFDEUTSCHEBANKDRESD-NERBANKHOECHSTBMW—as well as to all other potent symbols of the "economic miracle." Also, despite its lack of real tolerance for alternative behavior and ideas, Berlin, like New York, has a flourishing cultural scene and a huge "visiting" population that give it an appearance of tolerance that no other German city can rival.

It's easy to miss the point, though. Berlin would have none of its metaphorical resonance if not specifically for its Germanness. It still retains its age-old identity as showcase for exceptions that prove rules about the culture. How appropriate, for instance, that a city eighty percent flattened in war and then shorn of its identity as a capital—the capital of a people who themselves search perpetually for identity—should first scrape the ornamentation from the facades of its surviving buildings in an effort to wipe out all vestiges of German folk tradition, and then become foster parent to an architectural movement—"postmodernism"—that it didn't help create and that isn't really even a movement.

In the apartments by Hans Hollein, Rob Krier, and others in the Tiergartenviertel, built from winning designs in the *Internationale Bau-Ausstellung*, hybridity becomes a metaphor for identity-crisis, identity as a pastiche of other identities. Some of these buildings are quite beautiful, all are whimsical and risky, there are a thousand interesting points to be made about them, but in Berlin what impresses first is the deep-rooted diffidence of the "postmodern" in general, the ridiculous arrogance of calling it a style at all. The humor of the various pastiches draws distrust like an inadvertent smile—especially now that the Wall is gone and the eye can take in the frivolously new and the appallingly dilapidated old in a single glance. It's both the ideal stage set for the *Wende* and the ideal architecture for a city that banks on the world's uncertainty about its imperialistic future.

The monstrous, futuristic *Internationales Congress Centrum*, one of the city's most famous buildings, may be the most comprehensive example. In it, excess becomes a metaphor for an age-old form of German self-deception: the quixotic attempt at reification. The gaudy overdecoration in Bavarian and Austrian churches, where every piece of gilt molding, every cherub and angel, had to be depicted in brightly colored plaster relief, reflected an effort to encourage belief by making heaven more "real," and the ICC's icy metal tubes and phony "modularity" constitute a similar effort to enhance belief in the heaven of machines and technology. The Bavarians, blinded by their *horror vacui*, could never see that the Italian *trompe-l'oeil* frescoes painted on plain pillars and unadorned walls, which their churches tried to imitate and "top," were ultimately more tasteful and more convincing, and the Berliners, blinded by their drive to be *au courant*, again don't quite "get it": that you can't just plunk down a huge, steel behemoth in the middle of nowhere next to an Autobahn interchange and expect it to make the same kind of contextual sense as the Pompidou Centre does in the middle of the Beaubourg.

This is the famous spectacle of the Germans trying too hard, and over the past year it has come to represent all that is most feared about this people and its culture. Even those of us who usually maintain a pretense of harmlessly observing *Kultur* have lately found it impossible to resist direct commentary on the society. My own usual field of view is the theater, which, as is well known, both German governments support to an astounding degree. (The Federal Republic, for instance, now spends over 2 billion Marks, or 1.2 billion dollars, annually on theater, seven times more than the United States spends on all the arts combined.)* And Berlin has remained the theater capital of the German-speaking world—some twenty houses receive substantial public support and hundreds of "Off" theaters survive on their own—even through twenty-eight years when it couldn't draw audiences from a wide commuter belt.

All in all, the subsidy is wonderful, the sort of historical accident that melts through cynicism. Since the *Wende*, however, you also can't help noticing that it serves the same sort of authoritarian power structure that has proved ruinous to countless other German institutions, including the state of East Germany. The authority of the director has become absolute, he (almost never she) tolerates few serious challenges from playwrights and other "minions," and one of the commonest results is blind perpetuation of the paternalistic "bashing aesthetic," the attitude that sees the theater's Enlightenment function as a process of chastising audiences—choose your own examples, from Sturm und Drang, through Expressionism, right up to Heiner Müller. The other common results are elitism and aestheticism, which reach their logical culmination in the Theatertreffen, an event attended almost exclusively by "insiders" and consisting of productions such as Achim Freyer's *Woyzeck* or Katharina Thalbach's *Mann ist Mann*, chosen on the basis of "purely aesthetic criteria" and disdainful of the very idea that theater should remain accessible to first-time viewers.

If only one could point to a few intrepid souls who actively fight against this system. At a recent colloquium in Berlin entitled "Opportunities and Hazards for the Theater in the GDR," however, a large, diverse panel of artists and critics spent two and a half hours discussing the coming budget crunch in East Germany without anyone even mentioning the idea of interpreting adversity as opportunity and returning to fundamentals, making theater with less money, or none. Of course, poverty and unemployment aren't to be wished on anyone, but has *all* interest in grassroots work and avant-gardism here, even among artists, been completely overpowered by the craving to become a cog in a well-oiled machine? Is it really true that the goal of *every* young German director today is to become an assistant in a Staatstheater and then climb up the ladder of that corporate-style institution?

Of course, these issues are more complicated than I'm making them seem.

Perhaps all I'm really saying is that 1990 was a bad year for theatergoing, a bad time for representation in general. The theater couldn't compete with the drama outside on the streets—a point that was driven home pungently for me one night after seeing Maxim Gorky's *The Last Ones* at the Theatertreffen. Actually, I saw very little of *The Last Ones* because of the infuriating narrowness of the stage set, but I did *hear* the gist of the story. It was about a corrupt and cruel police chief who destroys his family through lies and self-deception, four hours of hypertrophied psycho-pummeling that paled by comparison with events outside the theater that night. Audience members strolling toward Ku'damm after the show encountered a real riot by a rowdy crowd that had just come from forming a 300-square-yard "living swastika" in the middle of Alexanderplatz.

It's one of the great post-war challenges: to recognize that the really difficult task is to characterize the Germans as human, to see and admit to yourself what is all too human in them, without glossing the facts. Berlin is one of the few places where this is possible, for it's still, even without the Wall, the only German city capable of both enraging and allowing distance from your rage. The distance comes from the ironies, which don't exist elsewhere. It's not ironic when an average German pedestrian waits for a traffic light on a deserted corner at 2:00 a.m., but it is when a punker does, replete with safety-pin earrings and purple-sprayed hair. Cigarette advertising isn't in itself ironic, but when seen against a landscape drained of all other color, it is. Right-wing radicalism isn't in itself ironic either, but it appears so in a city run by a coalition of Socialist and Green parties. Berlin offers a footing, a vantage-point, a time-space in which to contemplate the obvious: that the whole Teutonic melodrama, and in particular the badly redundant sub-plot about authority, has something deeply to do with you.

Project whatever meanings you like onto the swarm of metaphors; the city itself will ensure that your reflections reach beyond German-bashing. Think about who's to blame for the success of the Republikaner party, or the now victorious Federal Republic never having been properly denazified, and try to keep your thoughts from wandering toward the United States, Klaus Barbie's postwar protector and employer. Try looking at bullet-ridden facades and not-yet-demolished war bunkers day in and day out without recalling that America's bombs were too precious to drop on even one rail connection to Auschwitz. Laugh all you want at the soon-to-be-shipped-out GIs without high-school diplomas racing their mag-wheeled Camaros down Clayallee, yelling and tossing beer cans at pedestrians; your mirth might just succeed at blocking out the thought that Germany isn't the only place where certain people have found the failures of the Enlightenment terribly convenient.

There are no innocents in Berlin. To come here is to be forced, until recently at gunpoint, to see some larger context. And to live here is to be constantly reminded that all the really pressing questions can be posed as German questions, and that very few German questions have only to do with Germany.

(1990)

Notes on the Last Cold-War Theatertreffen (1989)

The high point of every theater season in West Berlin is the Theatertreffen, the annual festival of "roughly ten remarkable productions" from throughout the German-speaking world. Over the years, many have forgotten that the Theatertreffen was originally a product of the Cold War, a direct result of the building of the Berlin Wall. Having been deprived of its identity as a state capital, West Berlin went to extraordinary lengths after 1961 to form a new identity for itself as a cultural and artistic center, and the theater festival was part of that effort. Like so much high and popular culture in West Germany, though, it also became an opulent advertisement for the higher standard of living and cultural subsidy in the West, and the German Democratic Republic boycotted it until 1989.

Why the GDR chose to participate suddenly last year is still a matter of public speculation. Only in a very distant way can the decision have been a harbinger of the coming upheaval. Some cited the election in West Berlin of a socialist *Bürgermeister* who enjoyed better relations with the East than his Christian Democratic predecessor. Others cited the gradual loosening of censor restrictions in recent years—a phenomenon now completely overshadowed by the much more significant freedoms that followed the breaching of the Wall. To be sure, the fundamental character of the festival will now change, but last year it retained, perhaps for the last time, its Cold War background. Rightly or not, each of the three plays that came from the GDR was received by West Berlin audiences as the petition of a brave, oppressed writer for a more open society, and performances were cheered like a national anthem.

In one case, this was undeserved: Horst Hawemann's production of Nikolai Erdman's *Der Selbstmörder* (*The Suicide*) from the Mecklenburgisches Staatstheater in Schwerin was inept. The night I attended, the audience didn't laugh once during the first act, and I spent the entire time reflecting on the myriad subtle ways in which the German language undermines comedy, making punch lines fussy with indirect objects and reflexive pronouns, for instance. As the much belated GDR premiere of a play about Stalinism from the early Stalin era, though, Hawemann's production qualified as an event almost regardless of its quality, and its invitation to the festival was probably ensured by that and by the jury's desire to include at least one GDR *Provinz-theater* (invariably a condescending term, to the German ear). In the other two cases, the acclaim was earned.

Heiner Müller's production of his own 1956 play *Der Lohndrücker* (*The Scab*) from the Deutsches Theater in East Berlin was as much a new playwriting achievement as a directorial achievement. Based on the true historical case of Hans Garbe, a worker who became a hero in the GDR's early years by risking his life to rebuild a broken circular kiln before it was fully cooled down—also the subject of several novels by GDR authors and of a planned play by Brecht—*Der Lohndrücker* depicts Balke (Müller's Garbe surrogate) as an *"Aktivist"* whom the other workers hate because the effect of his "heroism" is to depress the wages of those who don't want to work as hard as he does. As Marc Silberman discusses in an informative article on this production (*Theater*, Fall 1988), the play has almost always been produced as psychological realism, which Müller believes deprives it of power and affect by simplifying it into a parable with a clear moral.

As he says in an interview published in the program: "That's the misunderstanding about a play like *Lohndrücker*, that the people are always seeing politics and ideology where it's actually only a question of behavior of laboratory animals who have to conduct themselves under specified conditions which they haven't specified themselves . . . And every ideological view of that is a false view and prevents seeing what's really there." Müller, obviously drawing heavily on his erstwhile collaborations with Robert Wilson, did all he could to deemphasize illusionism and easily recognizable psychologies by making numerous cuts, inserting additional texts such as the entirety of another play of his called *The Horatian* and, in Silberman's words, "fracturing even more the chronology or continuity of the already laconic sequence of scenes in the printed text."

The action was thus sharpened and the nature of the parable muted to the point where its moral was no longer clear—it was never nearly as simple and clear as some have thought, anyway—and the deeper questions in the text had a chance to emerge as main issues. For instance: how is the German worker to reconcile the fact that his or her famed efficiency is really an asocial force, nurtured under fascism and then appropriated by the socialists in time of need? Isn't denying or sacrificing the self for the good of an abstraction such as "the Party" a fascist idea, and thus inconsistent with the socialist notion of workers striving consciously to build a utopia whose benefits they understand? Moreover, is the process by which society creates heroes necessarily contaminated by these asocial forces, and, if so, how is achievement to be rewarded? If all these questions were relevant, even urgent, for both Eastern and Western audiences before the breaching of the Wall on November 9, 1989, they are even more so now.

Surprising as it was to see *Der Lohndrücker* in the GDR theatre schedule, it was even more so to see Volker Braun's *Die Übergangsgesellschaft* (*The Transitional Society*), directed by Thomas Langhoff at the Maxim Gorki Theater in East Berlin. Written expressly in response to a Langhoff production of *The Three Sisters* that had been in the Gorki Theater repertory for a decade, this play deserves an article in itself. Writing in a willfully discontinuous, disjunctive style that owes much to Müller and that seemed calculated to make it impossible for the censor bureau to understand—a character speaks at one point of "a play that survived the censor . . . and now forbids itself"—Braun applied the sense of *Auswegslosigkeit* (no-way-out-ness) he felt in Chekhov to the contemporary GDR, depicting a group of people who've been yearning for another place for so long that their very capacity to dream is dying.

In a prologue played in a junk-strewn garden, a man in a service cap, Franz, tries to intimidate an old man named Wilhelm as he sits reading the GDR party newspaper; like Lucky in *Waiting for Godot*, however, Franz loses potency when his hat is taken away. Meanwhile, various characters from *The Three Sisters* emerge from plastic cocoons (gauze coverings in the original text) and speak overlapping speeches from Chekhov. In the play proper, the three sisters, deathly bored, lounge about in their GDR apartment, which may or may not be up for rent, with or without their knowledge, and wait for their brother, Walter, a middle-level *apparatchik* who apparently makes all important family decisions. When at the prompting of visitors, the sisters begin to rise out of their lassitude, to reverie and then to open discussion of dreams of flight, Walter ends the ebullience abruptly with a fierce Stalinist outburst. He seizes control of the situation and then, among other things, forbids anyone to watch Western television or listen to Western radio. In the end, the house burns down under mysterious circumstances, and Franz delivers the last words as he runs across stage snickering: "It wasn't me. It wasn't me."

The play offered a spectacle not only of heroic utterance of truths under truth-repressing circumstances but also of the uselessness of that heroism under the imagination-destroying circumstances of day-to-day life in the GDR. At one point a character says, quoting Peter Weiss' *Ästhetik des Widerstands* (*Aesthetic of Resistance*), "If we don't liberate ourselves, it'll remain without consequences for us." Braun dispenses quickly with what Mother Courage might have called his "short rage," anger about the absence of particular freedoms, and proceeds immediately to deeper questions: e.g., what use is the freedom to speak openly when the scope of people's dreams, personal secrets and private desires is so perversely limited and distorted by their narrow horizons? As Walter's outburst shows, it may no longer be possible, for some, to define "freedom" as anything more than what is gained by rising to the top of the ladder of totalitarian authority.

Braun's vision is extremely dark, and the ending of his play seemed to me heartbreakingly pessimistic even before the recent political events, which neither Braun nor anyone else could possibly have foreseen. After Wilhelm says, more or less heroically, "The revolution can't reach its goal as dictator," he dies, and no one is left onstage to measure up to his ideals, no one who's ever had the chance to live out idealism in any form. For all the heartbreak in Chekhov's plays, none of them end on such a bleak note of hopelessness, and for that and other reasons, Braun's analogy ultimately struck me more for its cleverness than its profundity. Quibbles aside, though, *Übergangsgesellschaft* was prescient of a great deal and will doubtless find its place in history for that reason alone.

These two GDR productions provided far more food for the mind than any of the western entries. Protests and bomb threats before the opening at the Burgtheater in Vienna notwithstanding, Thomas Bernhard's swan song, *Heldenplatz*, turned out to be a weak treatment of an extremely important subject, the resurgence of Austrian anti-semitism. The Bremer Theater production of *Der arme Vetter* (*The Poor Cousin*) by Ernst Barlach, the expressionist sculptor-writer, directed by Günter Krämer, was what publicist love to call "a visual feast"—scene after scene of flawless *tableaux vivants* that contained few clues as to why this tired, whiny and predictable text needed to be revived. In the Berlin Schaubühne's production of Botho Strauss' *Die Zeit und Das Zimmer* (*The Time and the Room*), the first-rate direction (Luc Bondy) and one extraordinary performance (Libgart Schwarz) saved a mediocre text from seeming mediocre. No such luck for Strauss, alas, in Dieter Dorn's production of *Besucher* (*Visitor*) from the Münchner Kammerspiele which, for all its painstaking photorealistic drops and other facile devices inviting facile reflections on illusion and reality, couldn't help revealing the author as the half-realized talent he is. Briefly: nearly every Strauss play in recent years has been disappointing to me after its first scene, sinking into too-clever repartee or airy generalization. They come off as TV-sketches with an existential aftertaste.

One West German production superseded these others in my mind, however, partly because the fact that it was invited to the festival spoke volumes about the manner in which the ten "remarkable productions" are selected each year. A jury of well-known critics, working under the auspices of a government-funded organization called the Berliner Festspiele, chooses the productions and guarantees that the state has nothing to do with the choices. It also seems to guarantee that the choices have little to do with playwrights, however. At the back of the 480-page jubilee book published by the Festspiele in 1988 to commemorate the Theatertreffen's first twenty-five years are a series of tables pedantically quantifying and correlating the participants over the years: one table for jurors, another for theaters, another for directors, set designers, costume designers, even one for dramaturgs. No table for playwrights, though; apparently their part in the collaborative process isn't important enough to contribute to "remarkableness."

Let me begin by conceding that my reaction to the mini-scandal provoked by Alexander Lang's production of Bernard-Marie Koltès' *Rückkehr in die Wüste* (*Le retour au desert—Return to the Desert*) was emotional. Actually, the scandal was one of those pathetic affairs begun by hearsay denunciations that makes the public suspect both sides of disingenuousness. Now that tempers have all too literally died down and questions of censorship no longer apply, however, a few words about non-legal matters are in order.

Lang was originally scheduled to direct the German premiere of *Rückkehr in die Wüste* at the Thalia Theater in Hamburg shortly after Patrice Chereau directed the world premiere in Paris. When Chereau's production was postponed, Lang's became the world premiere and attracted more attention than usual. Through friends, Koltès heard of a number of Lang's directorial decisions, grew infuriated, and asked his agent to take legal action to stop the premiere. His chief grievance at the time was that Lang had cast a white actor for a role written for a black man.

Koltès, who died of AIDS in April and was ill during this entire episode, hadn't any idea how insignificant that casting choice looked next to Lang's other excesses. For those us who knew and admired his writing, and thus cared for his feelings, there was some harsh solace in knowing that he never saw a performance. His position became widely known in Germany after an interview with him was published in *Der Spiegel* (Oct. 24, 1988):

> I'd like to beseech the German public and the German critics to satisfy themselves that they have still never seen my plays. I beg the German public, the critics, to wait until a decent director produces my plays. I can't recognize productions like the one in Hamburg; I feel totally betrayed. The public and the critics are now about to judge a play that has nothing to do with me.

Comments like that were hardly calculated to win critical hearts in a country where directorial autonomy is defended as if by constitutional right. The production went on as planned.

Two months later, in the December issue of *Theater heute*, Michael Merschmeier (one of the Theatertreffen jurors) published a 4000-word article, ostensibly comparing Lang's and Chereau's productions, whose real object was to defend Lang and discredit the *Spiegel* interview. Referring to

Rückkehr in die Wüste (Return to the Desert) by Bernard-Marie Koltès, directed by Alexander Lang, Thalia Theater, Hamburg, Germany, 1988. From left to right, Mathilde's daughter Fatima (Martina Schiesser), Mathilde (Elisabeth Schwarz), Adrien's deceased first wife Marie (Angelika Thomas).

"promptings disguised as questions," Merschmeier wrote that the interviewers had "seduced" Koltès into "diverse imprudent statements. They let their conversation partner walk into a knife, although they knew he was blind." And in the festival program, which went to press as Koltès lay dying, Ulrich Schreiber, another juror, repeated Merschmeier's allegations and then compared, in one breath, Koltès' opinions with Beckett's and Brecht's heirs', as if the difference between living and dead authors had temporarily escaped him. To me, statements like this one from the very beginning of the conversation seem neither blind nor naive nor coerced: "Let's not forget, when a play is produced in another country for the first time, then it's the responsibility of those directing, the dramaturgs, to perform the play as it was written." The inability to see that the wishes of a dying author concerning a premiere ought to be respected, on the other hand—now, that I call blindness.

Rückkehr in die Wüste was, along with *Der Lohndrücker* and Kleist's *Das Kätchen von Heilbronn* (*Kitty from Heilbronn*—which I didn't see), among the most substantial pieces of writing in the festival. It tells the story of a woman, Mathilde, who was driven from her home in provincial France at the end of World War II, ostensibly for the crime of sleeping with an enemy soldier. After fifteen years in Algeria, she returns, determined to reclaim the house she left in her corrupt brother Adrien's hands. Since Koltès' earlier plays did not stress narrative, this one has been widely praised as his first step toward wide popularity. But skillful though the storytelling is, it's only a small part of the play's uniqueness. Koltès' language asserts itself before anything else, in reading or spectating. Rhythmic, enlarged, fabulously blunt, it presents a tortuous translation problem which Simon Werle solved astonishingly well in his German version.

The characters enter and jump into battle like giants, larger than life from their first utterances, word-swords drawn like those of Strindberg's sundry titanic "creditors." The opening scene has the grand contours of myth about it, dispensing with petty ambitions such as building atmosphere, or justifying expository information within a believable realism. And events in the family drama go on to unfold against the political background of France's imperialistic involvement in Algeria, creating a double-tiered structure in which each tier functions as a metaphor for the other. In fact, the character whose casting Koltès disputed, The Great Black Paratrooper, is a symbolic focus for this structure: the military as both the source of the bourgeoisie's security and the representation of its philistinism. In the end, when Mathilde's daughter gives birth to black twins, the implication is that the paratrooper raped her.

Imagine Strindberg and Caryl Churchill collaborating on a farce and you have some idea of the tension of antipodes at work in this quietly enraged play. Then imagine a director who cannot or will not see past the farce because he knows that's the only genre in which he can slip his trademark fidgetings past the critics, and you have some idea of Lang's production. The set is a tent-like structure made of orange-pink fabric stretched between tall poles, continuing onto the floor and over the forestage in irregular gathers and whirls that look like sand dunes—a gorgeous evocation of a desert landscape that succeeded in confusing me for two hours about the location of the action. With the costumes also very colorful and non-European, I had to read the play to find out what the cultural conflict in it was. Lang was so bent on literalizing the title's obvious implication—provincial France is also a sort of desert—that he forgot to evoke France.

The production does contain some extraordinary acting—mostly by Elisabeth Schwarz and Christian Grashof as Mathilde and Adrien—but it can be seen only in the soliloquies, where Lang seems to have left them to their own very considerable resources. Whenever more than one actor is onstage, movement and speech are aggressively stylized, including marionette-like gestures that don't even create believable puppet characterizations, long freezes in which actors growl like animals or declaim like Hyde Park stumpers, and extremely gymnastic fights full of acrobatic tumbling that invariably end up in slapstick—as if Koltès wrote this familial battle as nothing more than a driftless clown act. And Lang has no compunction about changing or ignoring Koltès' text if the action is too psychological for his farcical styling, as when a tender scene calls for intimate business with a bedroom closet and he uses grand gestures with a large, scenic house door.

Only when you know about all this, and about the innumerable other gratuitous gags and stylizations—e.g., designer blood stains on a midwife's smock, exotic animals occasionally rolling across stage on a conveyer belt— can you begin to see the rhetorical question Merschmeier asks in its true context: who even noticed that the paratrooper wasn't black? Well, I'll admit that I didn't. I was too preoccupied trying to understand the appearance of the black babies as something more than a tasteless non sequitur. And I was too disgusted at the thought that the zeal of objecting to censorship and the atavistic inclination to defend directorial freedom could blind some of Germany's foremost critics to this sort of arrant superficiality.

Perhaps, ultimately, there was something premonitory in last year's Theatertreffen: the fact that the two most publicized Western entries were a toothless Austrian political play (*Heldenplatz*) and a French family drama whose political background had been emasculated (*Rückkehr in die Wüste*), whereas the two most significant GDR entries could hardly have been more *engagé*. For years, Heiner Müller has been asserting that contemporary West German writing is largely "muttering"; i.e., that it avoids fundamental questions about history and politics, despite its formal complexity. Whatever we may think of this assessment, we must acknowledge that a great many Germans, particularly in the East, see much more than a grain of truth in it, and the next several years will doubtless bring on a cultural clash, even a culture-shock, with unforeseeable results. In literature and theatre, as in politics, the "German question" must now be reformulated: will GDR writers use their newly won freedoms to join in the muttering, or will they continue to resist and challenge it in the socialist spirit of their "gentle revolution"?

Berlin Stories 1990 (Theatertreffen 1990)

The 200-year-old tradition of enormous state support for the theater in Germany has always been one of those wonderfully bizarre accidents of history that even hardened Germanophobes have trouble bashing. Numbers prove nothing, of course, but at a time when the NEA's budget of $171 million, for *all* the arts, is acutely endangered, comparisons are irresistible. West Germany now spends 2.04 billion Deutsche marks (1.28 billion dollars) annually on the theater alone—constitutionally guaranteed free of censorship—and East Germany, where bananas and iced-tea mix are considered luxuries, boasts the world's highest per capita theater subsidy (firm numbers are still elusive but the best guesses are well over half a billion marks). Good or bad, theater in the land of Lessing is taken seriously.

It wasn't the riches, though, that sent me back to West Berlin in May to see what I suspected might be the last Theatertreffen. It was a desire to find out how the theater was dealing with the new social and political realities brought on by the *Wende* last November. This was the second year East Germany participated and, sure enough, the productions were more topically pointed than ever. With the streets overrun with Poles, Romanians, and other *Ossies* frantically caught up in the orgy of free-market consuming, however, the real problem was keeping my mind on business, which is to say, plays.

In fact, the 3.5 million mark (2.2 million dollar) Theatertreffen appears to be in some distress these days. Not for lack of money, heaven knows, but for lack of reasons to continue existing in its present form. Like countless other subsidized cultural events in West Berlin, the twenty-seven-year-old festival was originally designed to help shore up the city's new identity as a cultural center (as opposed to a state capital). Tickets were scarce, performances attended mostly by "insiders," and the whole affair had the air of an elite convention whose unacknowledged function was to show off to the East. By the 1980s, this couldn't have been more ridiculous. The GDR theater was hardly a poor cousin, hardly a "Trabant-theater," as one journalist put it, using the tiny, cardboard-bodied East German cars as a metaphor for cheapness, and the needlessness of boycotting the Theatertreffen apparently became clear to Honecker's government even before the *Wende*. Now, suddenly, the pressing issue is redundancy. The GDR has long had its own "competing" festival called the Berliner Festtage, which, in all likelihood, will soon be merged with its former "enemy"—like the currency, the police, and the train system.

But some things never change. The day of the first production, Botho Strauss' 1987 play *Visitor* from the Thalia Theater in Hamburg, someone defaced the graves of Bertolt Brecht and Helene Weigel in East Berlin with spraypaint—"JUDEN RAUS/SAU JUD" (Jews get out/Jew swine)—and the papers ran the usual modest stories regretting, as one of them put it, "these isolated acts of a few unteachable idiots." In *Visitor*, an arrogant, egomaniacal West German star with a Nazi past, Karl Joseph, condescends to appear as a "guest" at a provincial theater and encounters a young, alcoholic actor named Max, recently displaced from the GDR, whom he loathes but who forces him into shop-talk discussions about realism and authenticity.

Last year's Theatertreffen included another production of this same play in which a real West German star, Heinz Bennent, played the leading role as a parody of actor Bernhard Minetti—a reference immediately recognizable to German audiences as stressing the character's Nazi background. This year in Hamburg, Karl Joseph was played by Will Quadflieg, the actor whose published memoirs provided much of Strauss' dialogue but who originally declined the role because he thought it "repulsive." "Play it repulsively then," retorted Strauss, paraphrasing a line from the play, and it seems his argument finally held sway. The Hamburg production—in which Max is played by a real GDR transplant, Christian Grashof—places the emphasis squarely where it belongs: on the questions about mendaciousness in acting, which are, by extension, also questions about how the public is manipulated by false, tranquilizing messages in all media.

Perhaps I should mention in passing that *Visitor* is in no way a great piece of writing. Nor did the festival's second offering—an obsessively overwritten attack on the Russian middle class by Maxim Gorky called *The Last Ones* (1908)—strike me as an unduly neglected classic. In Berlin, though, particularly these days, such literary judgements quickly come to seem effete and irrelevant. Gorky's four-hour play, produced as a tour-de-force melodrama by the Schauspielhaus Bochum, tells the story of a corrupt and cruel police chief who, after being forced to retire, has nowhere to focus his evil except on his family and eventually manages to return to public service. As if led by the ghost of Julian Beck, this heavy-handed drama, directed by Andrea Breth with bulldozer subtlety, continued on the street after the performance. Audience members strolling toward Kurfürstendamm encountered what has become, for Berliners, a familiar sight: hundreds of policemen in riot gear, without name or number tags—*Western* policemen—roughing up bystanders and sealing off the road from onlookers.

Only the next day was it clear exactly what had happened: the police were

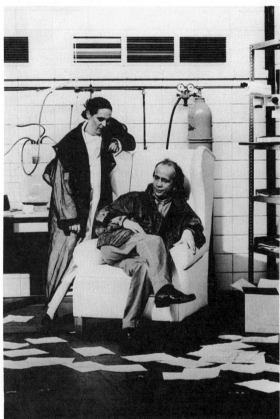

Besucher (Visitor) *By Botho Strauss, directed by Wilfrid Minks, Thalia Theater, Hamburg, Germany, 1989. Charlotte Schwab as "Lena, a rich young woman" and Christian Grashof as the actor Maximilian Steinberg.*

*Stage setting for Act Three of **Visitor,** designer Wilfred Minks.*

"protecting the public" from a rowdy, drunken crowd that had attended a championship soccer game that afternoon and then formed a "living swastika" in the middle of Alexanderplatz. (Another spontaneous, isolated act, no doubt.) It couldn't have been contrived as a more perfect prelude to the festival's third event and only GDR entry: George Tabori's 1987 play *Mein Kampf*, which the Maxim Gorky Theater in East Berlin had inserted into its repertory in March, postponing another production, as a direct response to resurgent right-wing radicalism.

Mein Kampf depicts a fictional encounter in a Viennese men's shelter, circa 1909, between an uncouth, shamelessly bigoted hillbilly named Adolf Hitler and a wise Jewish bible salesman named Schlomo Herzl. Herzl, who thinks Hitler can be shown by example how to love thy neighbor as thyself, takes the youth under his wing, mothering him devotedly, abjectly, and, in the end, futilely: woe to those whom a born suicide loves as himself. Since its premiere two years ago in Vienna, German critics have been dutifully respectful of this strange, provocative allegory—which is replete with searing Jewish humor—

Mein Kampf by George Tabori, directed by Thomas Langhoff, Maxim Gorki Theater, Berlin, Germany, 1990. Klaus Manchen as Schlomo Herzl and Gundula Köster as Gretchen Globuschek.

Mann ist Mann (Man is Man) *by Bertolt Brecht, directed by Katharina*
Thalbach, Thalia Theater, Hamburg, Germany, 1989.

but it's clear between the lines of their reviews that the praise is often disingenuous. Heiner Müller, for instance, once dismissed it as mere *"Kabaret."* In fact, as a critic, I'd also concede that *Mein Kampf* is no play-of-the-century. As a human being and a Jew, however, I'd go on to point out that it's also a literary object no German could ever produce, tacitly challenging Germans to try to understand its genesis beyond the level of ideas. Tabori, who lived for many years in America, is a Hungarian Jew whose family was almost completely annihilated by the Nazis. For him, the writing of such a Hitler character, the very effort of imagining what kind of adolescent could have grown into the adult monster, represents an act of love worthy of Schlomo Herzl. It bears reiterating: the really difficult task is to portray the Nazi as all too human.

Not every festival production was so topical. Indeed, the one whose text most explicitly strained toward topicality—Katharina Thalbach's version of Brecht's *Man is Man* from Hamburg's Thalia Theater—was the furthest out in left field. Like the author and her own father (director Benno Besson) before her, Thalbach sidestepped the problem of textual deficiencies in this hopelessly simpleminded play, staging it as a human puppet-show. Similarly, Achim Freyer, although working with a much more substantial text, all but abdicated interpretive responsibilities in his production of Büchner's *Woyzeck* at the Burgtheater in Vienna, staging it as a series of slow-moving visual images, purged of psychology, on a lighted parallelogram free-floating in a black void. Freyer subsequently announced he was giving up theater to spend the next decade painting.

The winner of the festival's directing prize was a dance-theater piece from the Bremer Theater entitled *Ulrike Meinhof*, created in December and January by Johann Kresnik, who is as prominent in Germany as Pina Bausch. Kresnik's response to the *Wende* was to use the biography of the co-founder of the Baader-Meinhof terrorist group as a metaphor for postwar German history, and his piece has caused quite a stir in the popular press. *Ulrike Meinhof* would be far more timeless, though, if he'd thought less about provocation and more about clarifying his metaphor. The dominant, repeated imagery involves passive, obedient women being raped by agents of simplistically symbolic forces—for instance, makers of fast food, owners of fur coats, and, lest we miss the facile historiography, Nazi officers. Inconveniently, the social forces behind Meinhof's fate are complex, as are those behind the *Wende*, and nothing is served by oversimplifying them—except, perhaps, the popular press.

The high point of the festival was a gloriously irreverent production of Lessing's 1755 bourgeois tragedy *Miss Sara Sampson*, from the Bayerisches Staatsschauspiel in Munich, directed by an East German named Frank Castorf whose work was barely known in the West before last year. Why glorious? Well, if you'd seen the Medea-esque fury on the face of the woman beside me as she booed at the top of her lungs during the curtain call, you'd understand at once. That a *play* could be held so sacred, could be *known* so

Mann ist Mann (Man is Man) *by Bertolt Brecht, directed by Katharina Thalbach, Thalia Theater, Hamburg, Germany, 1989.*

well by an audience, made me teeth-grindingly envious. Four-fifths of the text was cut, the action was spiced with flagrant fillips such as a sing-along to "Why Don't We Do it in the Road?" yet the final result was strangely respectful of Lessing. It's as if Castorf thought the original text, with its insistent moralizing and polarized characterizations, was tongue-in-cheek, and had sought a modern equivalent for the 18th-century affectation.

Envy, of course, is a common emotion for a Third World tourist, which is exactly what we Americans are when we visit the German theater. Perhaps this year it was just a bit more acute than usual, given the vision Berlin provided of *Kultur* doing its best to bring the lessons of the past to bear on a fearful present.

Fairy Tales
(Theatertreffen 1991)

"Learning from the Federal Republic means learning to conquer," said Heiner Müller in his 1990 interview collection *On the State of the Nation*. The pithy provocation becomes more like an axiom every day. In a thousand areas of German social and political life unification is proving a euphemism for conquest. From housing administration to job security to television programming to book and magazine editing to the hugely subsidized theater, Western ways have invariably prevailed after perfunctory nods to "GDR priorities." Artistic life, alas, is no exception.

A year ago I speculated that the 1990 Theatertreffen might be the last of its kind. At that time there was much talk about a possible merger with the Berliner Festtage, the longtime competing festival in the not-yet-abolished GDR. As it turned out, the talk was just that, and the sordid story of this year's festival really begins last fall, when the Festtage was simply canceled and the unaltered Theatertreffen, begun twenty-eight years ago as an occasion for Western strutting, became the dominant regular theater gathering in reunified Germany.

For a foreigner, attending Theatertreffen '91 was a lot like intruding on a family squabble. In March, Claus Peymann, director of Vienna's Burgtheater, wrote a furious letter to the press after learning that six of the twelve productions (one from the Burgtheater) originated in Berlin, "the navel of the world." "That's more than laughable," Peymann wrote. "It's strategy and cultural politics. The weaknesses of the Berlin theaters are supposed to be concealed, and we're supposed to get the impression of a thriving theater metropolis that in reality doesn't exist."

Internecine pleasantries aside, Peymann's comments touch on some difficult truths. The champagne drinking on the Wall is over now—necessarily, since the structure has disappeared so completely from downtown it's hard to tell it was ever there—and suddenly the pressing issue is redundancy of institutions. Both Germanys pumped billions into the city's *Kultur* over four decades, the East in order to have a world-class capital, the West to keep its alluring jewel polished. Thus, newly unified Berlin awoke after its wedding bash to find itself with more publicly funded stages than any other city in

Europe, requiring an outlay of roughly one and a half times the entire NEA budget.

Something has to give, and from the look of things, it's not going to be the Berlin Senate. Erich Honecker's government never wavered in drawing pride from the size of its theater subsidy, but West Berlin politicians grew increasingly impatient in recent years with the insatiable thirst of stages like the Freie Volksbühne, which set a new German record in 1990-91 by receiving 340 Deutsche Marks ($186) from taxpayers for every ticket sold (average price 25 Marks). Who will get the ax now and who the candy?

While local professors study the problem (prompted by a government commission), the battle has already been joined, in arts journalism, casting and technical meetings, shouting matches during curtain calls, and murmured comments in lobbies. Not only in Berlin but everywhere even one state theater is endangered, Darwinian behavior is ubiquitous, most crudely perhaps in the palpable condescension to *Ossies* encountered at panel discussions—little murderous digs, spoken and not, about their vulgar habits, acquisitiveness, and inferior skills. Sides have been drawn for what promises to be a brutal fight between rich uncles and poor cousins in which the superficial issue may be the survival of this or that ensemble, but the essential question will be the acceptance of GDR experience as a legitimate part of any pan-German cultural identity.

How satisfying it would be to be able to report that the festival productions from the former GDR clearly exhibited a mature, unique aesthetic that proved too profound for Western pinheads to appreciate. The two that I saw (of three), however, both Ibsen plays coincidentally, were conspicuously immature and smacked strongly of tokenism—as if the frustrated jury had looked long and hard for something to include from *"drüben"* ("over there") and finally decided that driftless provocation was the only means of avoiding more serious embarrassment.

The biggest newsmaker was a version of *A Doll's House* from Weimar staged by Leander Haussmann, whom one tabloid dubbed "the director-discovery of the year." In his nightmarish vision, Nora hasn't been so much trapped by a repressive lifestyle as driven to distraction by what amounts to a madhouse. Played with manic precision by Steffi Kühnert, she is an overwound toy who speaks too fast and moves in jerky fits that eventually establish a pattern for the whole cast. Everyone seems to walk around suppressing energy bubbles that pop out at inopportune moments like behavioral farts.

To be fair, Haussman had an interesting idea: to play the domestic characters as ghouls and giants living at the pitched of frayed nerves—Ibsen-as-Strindberg. Making it work, though, required a much more heavily adapted text than he had. The script as is just doesn't contain enough of the serio-comic bile that propels Strindberg's plays through their involuted melodramatic tunnels, and after three hours the actors seem desperate to become either more satirically self-conscious or less. Haussman probably sensed some deficiency, because he capped the evening off with a monumentally

ANNELIESE HEUER

John Gabriel Borkman by Henrik Ibsen, directed by Frank Castorf,
*Deutsches Theater, Berlin, Germany, 1990. Axel Wandtke as Erhart, Katrin
Klein as Fanny Wilton, and Bärbel Bolle as Mrs. Borkman (on floor).*

wrongheaded *coup*: Torvald, having prevented Nora from leaving, grapples
gymnastically with her and then shoots her to death, after which the set
rotates to reveal the backs of flats, stage machinery, and eavesdropping
actors. In case you didn't get it, both worlds—even the one behind the
"wall"—are mendacious and maddening.

That sort of facile, overblown topicality also cramped the work of a
director I'd grown to admire lately, last year's press-discovery and enfant
terrible, Frank Castorf, whose production of *John Gabriel Borkman* from the
Deutsches Theater in Berlin also featured animalistic grunting and grappling
in lieu of verbal argument. Castorf apparently started from the assumption
that nowadays no intelligent spectator could possibly be seduced by Ibsen's
plot-making. Thus, every moment in which the gears of storytelling show—
and heaven knows there are enough of them—is transformed into a distended, irritating shtick: sudden, inexplicable screams that go on and on, say,
or an actor holding a colleague upside-down for an entire scene.

Again, what is left to explode after three hours of this stuff? The most

Bernhard Minetti telling Grimms' fairy tales in **Märchen in Deutschland** *(***Fairy Tales in Germany***), Schiller Theater, Berlin, Germany, 1990.*

interesting question of the evening is why the hell Castorf chose to direct this play, and ultimately, as with Haussmann, the answer is unforgivably obvious. Borkman, son of a miner, was a gifted working-class youth corrupted by greed in the big, bad capitalist world. For all its pseudo-avant-garde trappings, this production—the last hour of which is dominated by the image of the two old sisters clutching fur coats—tells an oversimplified fable about the bankruptcy of materialism.

   Which brings me to the dominant theme, surely inadvertent, of the five Western productions I saw. Eighty-five-year-old Bernhard Minetti seemed to establish festival guidelines with his delightfully gruesome one-man show at Berlin's Schiller Theater, *Fairy Tales in Germany*, in which he sat downstage for seventy-five minutes, in a wizard's outfit, magisterially reciting weird stories from the brothers Grimm. Peter Handke borrowed heavily from the Grimms' style in his new, wonderfully laconic translation of Shakespeare's *The Winter's Tale*, directed by Luc Bondy across town at the Schaubühne. Shakespeare's fairy tale about the jealous King Leontes is half tragedy, half comedy, and—cultural clichés be damned—Bondy and designer Erich Wonder really were brilliant at the former and inept at the latter. The Sicily set, for instance, a fantastically disorienting backward rake descending toward an earthen floor and hanging, blue-velour walls, provided a perfect, ambiguous environment for startlingly original scenes such as III, ii, in which the word of the Delphic oracle arrives on a clay tablet, only to be shattered accidentally by its messenger. The Bohemia set, by contrast, is a gimmicky agglomeration of wool-tufts and boring 3-D projections amid which the inefficacy of the clowning comes as no surprise.

The one wholly satisfying production for me was a new play by Tankred Dorst called *Korbes* (also the title of a Grimms' tale), directed by Harald Clemen at the Komödie Theater in Basel. Written in Dorst's Upper Frankish dialect and punctuated with verse and music from Handel's "Brockes Passion," this was apparently an attempt to write a modern mystery play. A hard-drinking, provincial lout who abuses everyone around him wakes up blind one day for no apparent reason, but instead of seeking Good like his medieval precursors, he sits around waiting for his pouty daughter to come help him. As one character complains: "You're exactly as bad as before . . . When you're blind, you have to become another person. Otherwise it doesn't make any sense!" Siegfried Mayer's stage-as-world is a giant, sloping lozenge that keeps everyone off balance the entire time and contributes

*Norbert Schwientek in the title role of Tankred Dorst's **Korbes**, directed by Harald Clemen, Komödie Theater, Basel, Switzerland, 1990.*

CLAUDE GIGER

superbly to the play's unforgettably Beckettian final image: as a square of morning lights sweeps slowly across the stage, the daughter methodically jerks Korbes' chair away from it.

Botho Strauss was probably under the impression that his most recent play *Final Chorus* (*Schlusschor*), directed by Dieter Dorn at the Münchner Kammerspiele, had all the persuasive weight of these fables. In fact, his assemblage of three long scenes loosely connected by the theme of German "finales" (no more Beethovens, no more tenable *Volk*-myths, no more GDR!) is so transparently opportunistic it's hard to see what the jury could possibly have liked about it other than its Martian-cool, blinding-white settings. Jauntily offering a series of would-be profound, superficially political conundrums, *Final Chorus* may be, in the end, something of a rarity: seldom has a playwright of serious literary reputation done a more convincing impression of a boulevard hack hired to capitalize on a faddish topic.

In Berlin, it made its guest appearance at the Deutsches Theater, jewel of the former GDR, and the audience booed during a scene, taking place on November 9, 1989, that presented a pair of *Ossies* as laughable stereotypes, replete with wide eyes, cheap clothing, and provincial accents. Strauss and Dorn clearly thought the image acceptable, since its point was to reveal the Western characters' insensitivities, and when the boos returned at the curtain call, Dorn booed back. The real finale there had to do with the disappearance of fraternal sympathy. Heiner Müller couldn't have put it more eloquently.

German Theater
After the Wende

When I arrived in Germany for a month-long theater trip in May, 1990, I was reminded once again how impossible it is for the theater, even the German theater, to respond quickly to social and political change. I say "even" the German theater because, historically, the enormous governmental subsidy for theater in Germany has allowed the medium to change faster there than in other places.

As anyone who's been to a major production at a West German Staatstheater during the past twenty years can testify, these institutions are, among other things, fantastic aesthetic and intellectual playgrounds. Set designers work blithely with photorealism, neoexpressionism, appropriationism, post-appropriationism and other styles and ideas that date only from the past decade or two. Directors treat techniques and ideas from performance art, such as the use of holograms, video monitors, and other high-tech machinery and materials, as if they arose with the box set. And until the late 1980s cost—while discussed constantly behind closed doors—was discussed openly, as a pressing public issue, only at that time of year when the *Intendanten* (Artistic Directors with political positions and clout) went to the government to plead, usually successfully, for more money. Of course, as in any art form, much of the experimentation ends in failure; the truly new is no more common in the German theater than elsewhere. The superficialities, however, are always *au courant*, and that is the strange point for a theater person from another culture: the atmosphere of currency, or contemporaneity, makes it *seem* as if the truly new is just beyond the horizon at every moment.

So perhaps what I should have said before is, "especially" the German theater. It may be especially difficult for the German theater to respond quickly to social and political change, precisely because it has become such a huge bureaucratic behemoth, as encumbered as it is refreshed by its fascination with the latest technical marvels.[1] This is desultory speculation, and in any case I have no interest in making self-righteous comparisons. My point in mentioning it is only to contextualize the fact that, during my annual theatergoing sojourns to Germany since 1989, the question of how the *Wende* is affecting the theater has defined itself to a large degree as a question of money. Only in the course of discussing problems relating to subsidy, it seems, can people even begin to think about what is obviously the deeper issue: the search for a new identity and function for theater in general now that the GDR, along with *its* identity and function, has been swallowed whole by the Federal Republic.

For various reasons, the theaters in the former GDR have been bearing the brunt of the so-called "crisis" since the *Wende*. Operating costs increased sharply after the currency union, without corresponding increases in subsidy, which exerted enormous financial pressure on all theaters in the "five new States," most acutely on small- and medium-sized houses. Also, intensifying a trend that had been apparent for several years and periodically before that—theater people could be heard bemoaning the *Aderlass* (bloodletting) since the Wolf Biermann affair in the mid-1970s—many actors, directors, designers and dramaturgs "fled" westward in 1989 in search of higher pay, or in an effort to take the bull by the horns and find new, secure positions before their old ones were eliminated in the budget crunch.

Most important, however, has been an utterly unexpected shortage of spectators, a strange phenomenon indeed in a country where capacity crowds had long been the norm.[2] In 1989-90, attendance at GDR theaters dropped by five million, box office receipts by fifty percent, below the previous season, contrasting starkly with statistics in West Germany, which *Theater heute* called the "best" in twenty years: a box office increase of fifty million Marks, or two percent over the season before.[3] Some, such as playwright Peter Brasch, have blamed this public desertion on the theater itself, arguing that the GDR stage became a "substitute for political journalism," constantly slipping into "elitist aestheticism on the one hand and clumsy agitprop-quickfix theater on the other."[4] Equally likely is that the East Germans have had other things than theater on their minds as the enormity of the social and economic changes they have wrought sinks in; in the words of one actor, they are busy learning entirely new "game-rules" that "fill several volumes." (135)

Moreover, spectators aren't the only ones whose minds are elsewhere. Another, related problem is that the repertory schedules of plays—almost all of which, in 1990, had been planned before the *Wende*—have had to be overhauled at a time when the best known contemporary GDR playwrights (e.g. Christoph Hein, Heiner Müller, Volker Braun) are far more interested in social and political realities than in creating stage fictions. Good new plays relating to the *Wende* have been as scarce so far as good old plays from bottom desk drawers in the GDR—which everyone, East and West, hoped would appear by the dozen after the Berlin Wall was breached. Those plays, it seems, just did not exist, and the playwrights and auteurs who are active in the theater have not yet had time to ruminate on the current changes sufficiently to spew them out as effective theater. This last point was particularly evident at several painfully sincere premieres in 1990: Johann Kresnik's textless and irresponsibly simplistic dance-theater work *Ulrike Meinhof*

(Bremer Theater), created as a direct response to the *Wende*; and Sewan Latchinian's *Berlin* (Deutsches Theater) and Jörg Michael Koerbl's *Gorbatschow-Fragment* (Volksbühne), both allegories about life under totalitarianism, written before the *Wende* and downright risky then, that seemed a hundred years old at their openings despite competent direction.[5]

"Enduring new texts on the present situation will first appear at the turn of the millenium," said Dresden-based director Wolfgang Engel in an interview. (51) His opinion was echoed by Heiner Müller at Experimenta 6, the enormous 1990 festival in Frankfurt dedicated solely to his work, also planned several years earlier. I asked Müller informally then whether he intended to write anything about the current changes, and he answered: "No. I've said everything I have to say about it already. It's just 1945 all over again." His comment suggests a touchy point of comparison: between current, foundered attempts to write *Wendestücke* and the largely forgotten efforts by Friedrich Wolf, Gustav von Wangenheim, and others to write *Aufbaustücke* (reconstruction plays) immediately after the founding of the GDR.

What's a theater practitioner to do under these "crisis" circumstances? Just after the opening of the Berlin Wall, Müller suggested publically that one third of the theaters in the GDR be summarily closed, which sounded at the time like an unnecessarily dire and mordant statement but turned out to be exactly what was occurring, anyway. What is remarkable about the com-

Ulrike Meinhof, directed and choreographed by Johann Kresnik, Theater der Freien Hansestadt, Bremen, Germany, 1990.

JÖRG LANDSBERG

ment, however, is its spirit: tough-minded pragmatism mixed with a touch of extremely atypical defeatism. Peter Stein, in his first published interview since 1976, offered a West German version of the same sentiment, half in jest: "When someone asks me, 'What's your concept for the overall Berlin theater?' I say, 'Close it!' "[6] That wise-crack, too, was remarkable mostly for the conflicting feelings it betrayed—frustration with the flood of new open-palms in the theater world mixed with lingering anger at the GDR for professional slights over the years (see his other remarks in the interview). It is still far too early for clear answers about the shape of the German theater's future, but the part of the story that can be told at this point—about the hopes and anxieties of specific players in a game whose rules changed overnight—is fascinating in its own right.

My own comprehensive understanding of that story dates from a colloquium held as part of the Theatertreffen festival on May 20, 1990 entitled "Opportunities and Hazards for the Theater in the GDR," in which a large, diverse panel of artists and critics discussed the tensions and issues defining the "crisis" for two and a half hours, in diatribes, dialogues, and mutual recriminations that frequently seemed to me more dramatic than the productions in the festival. The following is a narrative of those proceedings, which I recorded as well as possible, given the terrible acoustics in the auditorium where it was held.

The panel is moderated by Dieter Kranz, long-time editor and critic for many different publications, chiefly and most regularly *Theater der Zeit*, the main East German theater magazine. Thus, Kranz, although a broadly literate man, comes to such a colloquium having alienated many of the panelists for years, if only by writing for a publication that was acceptable (most of the time) to the Honecker government.[7] Kranz begins by briefly describing some of the relevant issues—mentioning specifically the question of whether the government in a unified Germany will want to continue financing, for example, eight state theaters and three opera houses in Berlin alone—and then immediately turns to Michael Merschmeier, editor of *Theater heute*, the main *West* German theater magazine, asking if he'd mind giving an opinion "from outside" on the provocative question, "what is worth preserving [*bewahrungswert*] in the GDR theater?"

Merschmeier cleverly avoids the issue, or, more accurately, he avoids the trap of accepting the question at face value and instead makes some general comments about how ironic it is that "we in the West" are now the observers "from outside" instead of the other way round, as was true for so long. Then he turns to the audience and says bluntly that the real problem at hand has to do with the GDR theater's "necessity." The public has to come to believe, once again, "that the survival of the theater is as necessary as that of the public itself." Theater in the GDR always enjoyed a sort of holy status, since it was able to serve again and again as a release valve, a place where things could often be said that were too dangerous to say in print, television, or other media. Even in times when the censor was extremely restrictive, actors often managed to comment through their performances on the officially sanctioned texts they spoke. Now, says Merschmeier, artists are forced to consider other basic questions, such as, "What *is* the need for a *Theaterkultur* in this place," under these new circumstances?

Kranz lets this question hang in the air and turns to Gero Hammer, Intendant of the Hans-Otto-Theater in Potsdam, asking him a specific question about finances. Hammer then answers by saying that he doesn't think that's the proper subject for discussion either. "The guaranteeing of pensions and so on. . . that's the government's subject," he says. "Our subject is to prove, with our work, the necessity of our existence." Gerhard Wolfram agrees with him. Wolfram (who died in 1992) is Intendant of the Staatsschauspiel in Dresden, one of the last institutions likely to be eliminated in any budget cutting after unification, being the major stage in a city that is, as he points out, famous for its *Kulturfreundlichkeit*. Wolfram says: "Our question isn't, 'Oh my God, what are we supposed to do now?' Rather, our question now has to do with self-regard [*Selbstbeachtung*. Or was it *Selbstverachtung* (self-contempt)? Problem of acoustics.] What's going to become of the theater that we've accomplished up till now in our country?" "I'm concerned about the caution," he says, "the inspection [*Vernehmung*] that's going on in the ensembles. Artistically, no awakening has grown out of the upheaval," which is a problem to be dealt with soberly. It's a problem, moreover, that he calls "quasi-financial."

Kranz turns now to the only man on the panel wearing black formal attire. This man was a last-minute surprise addition to the group, his name is not on the program, and he is introduced as a "*Theaterreferent* [theater official]" named Boettcher from the Ministry of Culture. He is here to represent the soon-to-be-defunct government's point of view. Kranz asks him whether there's really any chance of the government freezing theater ticket prices, as had been rumored around Berlin at that time, and the man answers that a proposal to that effect is on the table but hasn't been decided yet, adding that all such proposals have become complicated because of the monetary union. He goes on to make some eloquent, reassuring comments about the future, focusing on the government's firm commitment to keeping open as many theaters as possible: "When you close a theater, you don't just disturb communication between stage and audience. You disturb the whole cultural-spiritual climate." When he finishes, there is general uneasiness in the room, a distinct air of impatience at the pace of the discussion.

Kranz now asks Peter Sodann, artistic director of Das Neue Theater/ Schauspiel in Halle, for his thoughts. Sodann, a no-nonsense, avuncular fellow, is in what might be called the opposite position to Wolfram's, since he comes from a provincial theater whose existence is indeed threatened by the coming unification. (It was subsequently closed.) Sodann proceeds to offer his highly emotional reactions for some fifteen minutes, almost without pausing for breath. It would be pointless to try to duplicate his remarkable flow of words, which transformed the atmosphere of the panel, but the gist was as follows.

"I can't sketch out Das Neue Theater. I feel ill at ease here, anyway, and actually I only came so that you would know that a theater still exists in Halle. [applause] I feel ill at ease because it's speculation being dealt with here." It's "obvious," he says, that some theaters will be closed, but the problem has nothing to do with the public or with any sort of crisis in the "need" for theater. The problem is only that the East German ensembles were never held accountable for financial efficiency. "Obviously the residents of [Halle] would like to have an immediate [*augenblickliches*] theater, but it isn't efficient, and an inefficient theater. . . well, I don't know." "I believe our theater had the cheapest admission tickets in Europe," says Sodann. "The top ticket price was five Marks—more wasn't permitted by the state—students paid two-fifty, the average was three-sixty [about thirty-three cents by 1989 exchange rates]. No theater can live from that. We all know this. But I don't have the anxiety that a city like Halle doesn't want a Neues Theater anymore." He ends by saying: "You know, I recently received a letter from a director in which he wrote: 'In these complicated times we live in, do you still want to do this work?'. . . I simply wrote back to him: 'Before the times were very complicated for me. Today they're to a large degree complicated. So for me everything stands as it was.' . . . I am not looking for a sponsor."

To this long oratorio, which is greeted with warm applause, is added a rejoinder from an unexpected quarter. The powerful Günther Rühle, well-known critic and Intendant of the Schauspiel in Frankfurt, says, with almost palpable condescension, that this is indeed a time to try to understand "*die Ängste unserer Kollegen aus der DDR* [the fears of our colleagues from the GDR]." We cannot take the situation lightly and just say that what's gone is gone. We have to recognize "that the West German theater has gotten an awful lot from the GDR theater, not only directors and actors"—he does not say *defecting* directors and actors—"but also ideas and aesthetics"—which he leaves in general terms, rather than spelling out, say, the time-honored West German aesthetic tradition of using the very idea of the GDR as a political whipping horse. "The German theater has always functioned in this way, as a place of unity," he says, going on to quote a comment by Willy Brandt to the effect that *Kultur* shouldn't be seen primarily in economic terms, since it's one key to a common understanding between the two countries. "Financial possibilities should now be sought together for all of Germany."

The expressions on the faces of the other panelists are priceless after these comments: it's all very well for the Intendant of the Frankfurt Schauspiel to say this, they imply, if only we too had the bird in the hand. The actor Ulrich Mühe, ensemble member at the Deutsches Theater in East Berlin, speaks up. "I think that one of the greatest dangers really is the loss of valuable people—actors, directors," he says, not only because they know they can earn more money in the West but also because of decades of built-up curiosity. "Naturally, you want to see for once how theater's done in Munich, or in Hamburg." To survive, he says, the theater must not only solve this problem of losing talent but must also "repoliticize" itself.

Ursula Karusseit, an actress who has worked in Cologne since her defection from the GDR in 1987, answers Mühe: "I don't see such great dangers," she says. "These dangers actually existed all along in the Federal Republic. I also don't understand so easily why people have such fears. I've experienced that too. Recently, after three year's employment in Cologne, I was, for the first time in my life, given notice." Going on to explain that this happened because a new Intendant came into the theater along with a house full of people with whom he was used to working, she says valiantly that it's just part of the profession to have to deal with such changes. Then she mentions the example of a colleague who decided to leave Cologne in order to work at the Maxim Gorki Theater in East Berlin, for a much lower salary—exactly the opposite of the feared scenario. The real danger, she says, "is that the theater *doesn't* find its political function again. . . . The danger is in its becoming arbitrary [*beliebig*]."

Frank Castorf, until this year a freelance director and *enfant terrible* of the East German theater, now a house director at the Deutsches Theater and soon to be Intendant of the long moribund Volksbühne, gives yet another view. As might be expected of someone who recently began earning a regular theater salary for only the second time, Castorf is in favor of the idea of firm contracts, at least for the time being. He doesn't want to collaborate with people who are always being let go, he says: "You can't make good theater for one moment under those conditions." Furthermore, he wants to be in a position both "to defend the GDR" in the theater and "to give work to people who found it hard to get work before." Sodann, the man from Halle, agrees, again pleading for a "*Deutsche Ensemblekunst.*" What the actor needs, he says, is a "home." "He needs a climate where there's a little warmth. That's what we have to watch out for in the German theater, that the ensembles don't completely fall apart."

Kranz ultimately returns to Merschmeier and asks whether he thinks it's even possible to build a "free enterprise operation" for the theater in the (former) GDR. Merschmeier snaps back: "A free enterprise theater! We haven't got a free enterprise theater here in the West. About eighty percent of it is paid for with state money." The only significant difference "is that the GDR has a centralized system and the Federal Republic has a decentralized one." And in any case, he says, again repeating himself, we shouldn't be thinking about how the money's going to be distributed. We should be thinking about what the theater's "function" will be, should be, in a unified Germany. "The loss of the utopia is mutual. . . . So now that we find ourselves in this situation, let's put our heads together and figure out what we're going to do. The main thing is that the people who've been making good theater in the GDR continue to make it, and make it well."

When this colloquium was over I sat back and tried to collect my thoughts, figure out why I was feeling such sympathy for the likes of Sodann and

Castorf, and such resistance to the obvious truth of what the likes of Karus-seit and Merschmeier were saying. Clearly, my bias had much to do with the profound envy we Americans have traditionally carried with us when visiting the German theater, East or West. As is well-known, the GDR theater was never poor. It was, in fact, almost embarrassingly rich, measured against the average GDR citizen's standard of living, which made the fact that it functioned as a release valve all the more bizarre.

Hence, to visit meant necessarily to be reminded of certain stark facts: for instance, that no more than a handful of American actors living today could ever have experienced first-hand what Peter Sodann meant when he talked about the "warmth" of a place where a theater ensemble feels "at home." The harsh realities of the marketplace—manifested in the high salaries offered in television and film contracts—have enervated or foiled every serious attempt to create a real repertory ensemble company in the United States since World War II. Thus, I left this colloquium reminded, more than anything else, of the enormity of what was lost in the thoroughly understandable rush to bury the GDR's dictatorship. The bathwater stank so badly, it seems, it overwhelmed people's senses and made them forget that there might be babies in it.

Of course, decency obligates anyone in my position to concede that I did not suffer personally under the GDR system, nor did my work in the theater. Perverse indeed is the argument that ignores or seeks to minimize the disgusting and dehumanizing aspects of that country's arts administration policies. Control of publication and performance rights, censorship and access to foreign material by bureaucratic philistines; extinguishing of political resistance among artists through the granting of privileges; the pervasive atmosphere of terror that ultimately affected even the simplest of creative acts: all of that, and more, was indefensible. Nor was parasitic art any less characteristic of theater than of other arts in the GDR; many heavily subsidized houses existed for no purpose other than to purvey state propaganda. To imply, however, as does Rolf Schneider, that all creative endeavor was contaminated—he writes that, because of the scope of public subsidy, "artists must see themselves as partly responsible for the total economic collapse of the country"—is to to blur an already complicated picture with vindictive anger. (138)

The foregoing concessions understood, surely that picture ought to include recognition that some of what was truly new in the German theater over the past several decades was born and cultivated in the GDR. Newness in this context, of course, has nothing to do with spectacle, nothing to do with the technical can-you-top-this? contest that raged back and forth in Berlin since the 1960s as if the Wall didn't exist. It refers rather to philosophical matters, such as Müller's impassioned defense of Brecht (whom he claims was betrayed by the Berliner Ensemble) and of the notion that the proper function of literature and theater is "to look history in the whites of the eyes." And it refers to operational matters that reflected a different working dynamic, a different impetus for artmaking in the GDR. For instance, despite the problems of life tenure, finances within the ensembles were much more egalitarian, and hence conducive to cooperation and stability, than in West Germany, the difference between the highest and lowest actors' salaries being many degrees of magnitude smaller. Actors attitudes, too, were distinct, as repeatedly witnessed by directors with experience in both Germanys.[8] "We can argue over whether there was ever a GDR *Kultur*," wrote director-author Werner Buhss; "there was GDR art." (130)

More than likely, a few GDR plays now gathering dust—plays bravely written before the *Wende* about frustration with the aging, calcified leadership, such as Christoph Hein's *Ritter der Tafelrunde* (*Knights of the Round Table*), Volker Braun's *Übergangsgesellschaft* (*Transitional Society*) or Müller's *Wolokolamsker Chaussee* (*Volokolamsk Highway*)—will some day seem frighteningly timely to us again. Perhaps then, if we are free to read and play them, will it be clear what was truly *bewahrungswert* in the GDR theater.

2 Stücke/2 Gegenstücke

Heiner Müller's reputation rests on nothing if not slipperiness, a quality hardly unique to him but nevertheless remarkable because it is so thorough-going and because it finds its source in his writerly standpoint, the peculiar place he writes from. While German critics have argued incessantly for years about the proper political context of his work, he has always begun writing with analysis of self, of his "self's" position in history and society, confronting that surrogate persona with tough questions about complicity and bias. During several months of immersing myself in his works during 1989 in Berlin, this question began to weigh on me more and more: should the critic, the person responding to his response, do any less?

Müller's work, like Beckett's, is full of traps—not least of which is the temptation to "catch" him and thus undervalue the significance of his slip-periness—but the difference is that Müller's traps are invitations to engage in polemics. To me, all his works are polemical, even when they're highly personal, and even when they appear willfully discontinuous and elliptical. I often imagine him smiling in the wings, or behind the book covers, at those who see him as a passive victim of history or, an even greater temptation, an advocate of this or that ideology. His ideology is in fact the same as Tristan Tzara's—he has none—yet he has idiosyncratic biases and illusions (concerning Marxism and women, for instance), which he'd readily confess to, and which are also ultimately traps for those prone to detached and paternalistic commentary. On one level, the following *Gegenstücke* could be seen as attempts at elusion, premeditated "misreadings" designed to reveal Müller's biases through rearrangement of the textual elements he himself used. More fundamentally, though, they began as responses while reading that were so intense they made me want to address him directly, as if engaging him in a sort of pure dialogue literally in his own terms.

Because I saw *Nachtstück* as a blatant provocation, for instance, *Tagstück* was polemical from its inception. Müller takes a Beckettian situation of stasis, worsens it to the point of Artaudian horror (the lice image is a variation on the ending of *The Jet of Blood*), and finishes with a Brechtian implication that the newly born mouth will allow the character to complain, albeit inarticulately—a first step toward demanding his rights as a possibly human "self." The progression implied runs Beckett-Artaud-Brecht. (*Nachtstück* is itself a *Gegenstück*, a variation on the gruesome clown episode in the third scene of Brecht's *Badener Lehrstück*.) Since I don't see Beckett as subsumed in the notion of stasis, of course, my impulse was to rearrange things "properly." In the beginning, my potentially human character finds himself in a didactic parable, victimized because he doesn't understand the rules, is then victimized again by the morbidity of others despite, in fact because of, his ability to scream (Dr. Pale and Isabella are from Artaud's *The Philosopher's Stone*), and is finally born into "selfness" through the acquisition of language. For me, the progression runs Brecht-Artaud-Beckett, which is not to argue one way or another about particular events in theater history but rather to describe a bias, a condition resulting from the way history has worked on me.

Somewhere between Walter Benjamin's ideal of a criticism of quotations without accompanying text and the kind of ruinous explanatory criticism he called "excavation" may be a criticism of imitation, specially suited to the present cultural moment—self-revelatory, opportunistically confessional in the sense that it includes within its form both a critique of bias and context and a certain admission of failure. Failure of conventional exegesis. To build on Benjamin's metaphor, the diver who emerges uncertain whether his catch has yet crystallized into a pearl comes, rightly or wrongly, to view his act of diving as a treasure.

SELF-PORTRAIT TWO O'CLOCK IN THE MORNING
On August 20,1959

Sitting at the typewriter. Skimming
In a detective novel. Toward the end
Knowing what you now already know:
The soft-faced secretary with the heavy beard
Is the murderer of the senator
And the love of the young sergeant from the murder commission
For the daughter of the admiral will be reciprocated.
But you won't omit a page.
Sometimes while turning over a leaf a quick glance
At the empty sheet in the typewriter.
So we'll be spared that. At least something.
In the newspaper: somewhere a village has been
Razed to the ground with bombs.
Too bad but what's it to do with you.
The sergeant's just about to prevent the second murder
Although the admiral's daughter offers (for the first time!)
Her lips to him, duty is duty.
You don't know how many are dead, the newspaper's gone.
Next-door your wife dreams of her first love.
Yesterday she tried to hang herself. Tomorrow
She'll slit her wrists open or whatdoIknow.
At least she has a goal in mind
That she'll reach, one way or another.
And the heart is a spacious graveyard.
The story of Fatima in *Neues Deutschland*
Was so badly written that you laughed at it.
Torture is easier to learn than the description of torture.
The murderer has fallen into the trap
The sergeant clasps his prize in his arms,
Now you can sleep. Tomorrow's another day.

——HEINER MÜLLER
translated by Jonathan Kalb

SELF-PORTRAIT IN BERLIN FIVE O'CLOCK IN THE AFTERNOON
On April 20, 1989

Sitting at the computer. Skimming
In a Heiner Müller Rotbuch volume.
Toward the end knowing what you already know:
The stories of Horace and Homer and Ulysses
Ur-chameleons in proto-colonial landscapes
Are of Müller-Deutschland
Not of you.
But you can't omit a page.
Sometimes while leafing a quick glance
At the empty screen on the computer.
We'll be spared that. At least that.
Today on the news: *Feiern* for the *Führer*'s 100th
In every West German state.
Too bad but what's it to do with you.
Homer's just saddling his student with the riddle
That the truth clothed in lies remains truth
Although once upon a time it seems to you
You read the opposite, maybe in *Mauser*
Or some other *rot* book not to do with you.
Outside your window in Neukölln the roar of *"Schutz-Truppen"*
American planes landing at Tempelhof
Mostly Turkish crowds of teenage vigilantes hunting Skinheads
Drowns out the news.
Yesterday was the first night of Passover.
Your wife, who is not Jewish, searched the city for matzoh
Found it in an obscure store without a sign.
Tomorrow the store will have markings
Of one kind or another and so will your wife.
At least time lends the look of having suffered through history.
Seen from Berlin, privilege is only the coincidence
Of living between catastrophes.
And who needs that view?

The editorial about Salman Rushdie in the *Herald Tribune*
Was so beautifully written you had to cry.
Indifference is so much easier to learn than the description of indifference.
Ulysses in the Hell of the Curious has been seen by Dante
And the Müller-Double has recognized himself in the mirror
Before slaughtering his father, again.
You can quit for the day now.
Tomorrow begins a new century
Judging from the half-heard news
And there is no seder dinner to get in the oven.

——JONATHAN KALB

NACHTSTÜCK
(NIGHT PLAY)

On the stage stands a man. He is larger than life, maybe a puppet. He is dressed in placards. His face is without a mouth. He looks at his hands, moves his arms, tries out his legs. A bicycle, whose handle-bars, pedals or both, or whose handle-bars pedals and seat have been removed, goes quickly from right to left across the stage. The man, who may be a puppet, runs after the bicycle. A threshold rises out of the stage floor. He stumbles over it and falls. Lying on his belly, he sees the bicycle disappear. The threshold disappears, unseen by him. When he stands up and looks around for the cause of his plunge, the stage floor is smooth again. His suspicion falls on his legs. He tries to rip them out while sitting, while in the supine position, while standing. Heel against buttocks, grasping the foot with both hands, he rips out his left leg and then, falling on his face into the prone position, his right one. He is still lying on his belly when the bicycle goes slowly by him from left to right across the stage. He notices it too late and, crawling, can't catch up with it. Drawing himself up and supporting his unsteady torso with his hands, he makes the discovery that he can use his arms for locomotion when he gets his torso going, hurls it forward, grabs after with his hands, etc. He practices the new walk. He waits for the bicycle, first at the right doorway, then at the left. The bicycle doesn't come. The man, who may be a puppet, tears out his right hand with his left hand, and his left with his right, and at the same time both arms. Behind him the threshold rises to head-height out of the stage floor, this time so that he doesn't fall. The bicycle comes from the grid and remains standing in front of him. Leaning against the head-high threshold, the man, who may be a puppet, observes his legs and arms, which lie strewn all over the stage, and the bicycle, which he can no longer use. He cries one tear with each eye. Two Beckett-goads enter at eye-level from right and left. They hold onto the face of the man, who may be a puppet. He need only turn his head, once to the right, once to the left; the goad takes care of the rest. The goads exit, an eye on the point of each one. Out of the empty eye-sockets of the man, who may be a puppet, lice crawl and spread, black, over his face. He screams. The mouth comes into being with the scream.

From *GERMANIA TOD IN BERLIN* (1956/71)

——HEINER MÜLLER
translated by Jonathan Kalb

TAGSTÜCK
(DAY PLAY)

On the stage stands a puppet, life size, maybe human, it is dressed in plain
street clothes. Its face is without a mouth. Around it a group of people walk
on their hands in a circle shouting slogans and brandishing placards,
strapped to their legs, that exhort sundry forms of activism. The puppet,
which may be human, listens, reads, considers, then joins the circle, walking
on its feet. When the others notice this, they pause and, without anger, tear
off its legs. At first it is dismayed but then gradually accepts the measures
taken. Discovering that it can move about by propping itself up with its
hands and swinging its torso forward, it rejoins the group, now able to walk
on the proper appendages. After a few minutes, the group grows bored and
exits. The puppet, which may be human, keels over and screams out of its
wounds. After its screaming stops, a platform rising out of the stage floor lifts
it to table height. Dr. Pale enters with a tape recorder and a large saw and
declares his intention to extract the Philosopher's Stone from the torso, with
the assistance of his wife Isabella. Isabella distracts him by making love to
him, after which he falls asleep. The love-making excites the puppet, which
may be human, and it flirts with Isabella until she mounts it. This activity
awakens the doctor, who becomes angry. At the moment of simultaneous
orgasm, Isabella amputates her partner's arms with the saw, another scream
emerges from the wounds, and the doctor is happily satisfied. He switches the
tape recorder off and he and Isabella exit coddling it like a baby. The stage
rises into a raked position; it now represents a stage. A black-caped kuroko
from Kabuki Theater enters, reattaches one of the torso's arms and arranges
the other arm and both legs on the floor, just out of reach. The puppet, which
may be human, tests its one limb, then lies still, goes to sleep. A goad with
a pointed index finger on the tip emerges from the wings, pokes the sleeping
figure until it awakens, then points to the severed arm. Exit goad. Pathetic
attempts to reach the second arm by various flopping activities, all in vain.
The kuroko moves the arm closer, within reach. The puppet, which may be
human, reattaches the arm to itself, tests it, then lies still, goes to sleep. The
goad enters again but from the opposite wing, pokes the figure until it
awakens, then points to the severed legs. Exit goad. Pathetic attempts to
maneuver along the floor in a sliding motion give way to gradual rediscovery
of the swinging-torso motion used earlier. After making several circuits of the

stage, savoring the blessings of mobility, the puppet, which may be human, comes to rest besides its legs, contemplates them. Stillness. The goad enters and pokes. No response. Exit goad. The kuroko moves the legs closer, within arms' reach. Long stillness. The kuroko starts to take the legs away. It is abruptly stopped when the puppet, which may be human, blurts out: "MINE!!" The mouth comes into being with the word.

——JONATHAN KALB

HEAD SHOTS

A Conversation with Beckett

I don't know why Samuel Beckett agreed to meet me in November, 1986.[1] I would like to think it was because he liked the idea of the book I was writing then about the problems of acting and directing his work. But I have heard many stories about requests for his time, both successful and unsuccessful, and have never been able to recognize a pattern. One of my favorites came from a man who wrote asking to be hired as Beckett's gardener and had the offer declined personally over tea at his apartment. To be sure, my case was helped by the actor David Warrilow, a friend of Beckett's, who did me the incomparable honor of sending a letter of introduction. But I will never know for certain, and that delights me.

I do know that the idea of meeting the eighty-year-old master was one of the most difficult I have ever tried to impose on my imagination. At the beginning there was no sense of rare privilege, as I expected, but rather an utter terror attributable somewhat to my schoolish awareness of his place in literary history, but probably more to my passion for his works. For I have never been able to escape this man's writing, in fact have had to put aside my own literary efforts for years while reconciling myself to his achievement. By the time I received his first letter, his legend had crystallized so solidly in my consciousness that I had lost any image of a man and thus could not picture anyone sitting across from me, save as some abstraction of self-evident genius, or at best an engraved classical portrait like those of Homer, Shakespeare, and Dante.

Indeed, what does one, what can one, possibly say to Samuel Beckett? How can one as much as speak, without sounding superfluous, to a man whose eloquent brevity has made the greatest phrasemakers seem wordy, and whose talent has matured in a search for language as beautiful as silence? What will I say when there is everything to say? Perhaps I will sit tongue-tied like a shy child, unable to choose among the everything.

I was almost late for our appointment due to passing the hotel coffee shop, where we were to meet, in a fit of sheer abstraction. I had been a skein of anxiety for three weeks, since receiving his note specifying the time, which forced me out of the protective torpor my mind had developed to convince me that none of it was real, and I counted myself lucky just to have made my way to France without accident. I had read somewhere that he liked Irish whiskey and had spent an entire afternoon finding a bottle in Berlin, forgot to pack it, and embarked on another nervous search for the stuff on a Saturday morning in Paris, with eleventh hour success. I eventually forgot to give him that bottle, too.

Out of breath from running back up the street, I caught sight through the glass front of the building of a tall becapped man, huddled close inside his raincoat, walking slowly, punctual to the minute. And I did not so much forget my fear as become suddenly confused about its cause. If you make the mistake of conflating Beckett with his narrators, as so many have done, you may share my impression of someone who was always tactically old, even in his youth, because that was the viewpoint necessary for his personas to joke and speak poetry about time's passage and flesh's decay. But that Beckett should be physically frail, that the man himself should actually grow old, would actually die, shocked me. It seemed tasteless and redundant, like a bit of story he would reject in composition, and it removed some mythicism from the encounter.

He caught my glance immediately and extended his arm in a bizarre side motion, lifting it from the shoulder like a wing that remained bent at the elbow—a gesture as much of enfolding as lineally connecting. The arm was so long and lanky it had no trouble reaching me even bent, nor would his fingers straighten out completely when I grasped them. It was an extraordinarily crooked hand, not at all repulsive because it wasn't especially thin and thus looked overused rather than decayed, and I was fixed on it when he spoke my name in an unexpectedly high voice. An Irish accent—still there, after half a century in France! With a wave he made clear he was uninterested in hearing how pleased I was to meet him, and led us to a table where for some moments we did nothing but exchange smiles.

Among the many surprises in the ensuing hour-and-a-half conversation, none stunned me more than his willingness to answer questions. Beckett had always been notoriously reticent about his work, and my first thought was to suppress the dozens of specific queries I had formulated in the course of writing *Beckett in Performance*, to say nothing of the hundreds of general questions I had formulated in the course of living my life. To my astonishment, though, he turned out to be more generous, helpful, and open than many others of lesser talent and fame whom I approached during my research. I dodged about for a neutral topic for minutes, and then realized I was devising my own obstacles; for the kind of exegesis that always put him out of patience had little to do with my work, which concerned rather concrete issues of theatrical production. He was actually interested in hearing about some of the sixty-odd Beckett performances I had seen in the preceding four years, many done by his close friends. And thus in the end he made me feel able to offer him something, too, which I recognize in retrospect as his gift.

"I've just come from seeing Ekkehard Schall in *Das Letzte Band*," I say, speaking of the famous Brecht actor from the Berliner Ensemble, who had recently played in the East German premiere of *Krapp's Last Tape*, twenty-eight years after its 1958 world premiere in London.

"Oh yes. We've finally broken through the iron curtain. They wanted me to go," says Beckett, his blue-grey eyes twinkling with irony. Without his knowledge, the theater had printed in the program his polite note declining their invitation. "Did you see it?"

"Yes." I don't elaborate because I think the production very weak and am not yet sure how free I should feel to make criticisms. "This isn't the first time your work has been performed in a Communist Bloc country, is it?"

"No, the first time in East Germany, though. It's done sometimes in Yugoslavia and some of the other countries, but never in the Soviet Union, of course. Never been done there. But that actor, Schall, he's very good. I saw him years ago in *Galileo*. He did a wonderful job."

"Did you know he's married to Brecht's daughter?"

"No, I didn't know that. But before he died, you know, Brecht wanted to do a parody of *Waiting for Godot*, well, not really a parody but . . . he never finished it." And here his lips betray an unmistakable half-smile; he seems actually flattered by Brecht's infamous plan of adaptation, despite the fact that the German author's un-Beckettian intentions involved eliminating the play's delicate ambiguities of time and place and locating the action in a specific social history. "This *Krapp* must have had something to do with that," he continues. "They got an English fellow to direct it, I heard. What did you think?"

I have no choice now but to report the circumstances and quality of the production, explaining how it was paired with a musical version of Brecht's *Die Erziehung der Hirse* (*The Education of Millet*), a long, allegorical poem celebrating Soviet strength. The audience received lengthy program notes about "bourgeois decadence" and Beckett's unconcern with improving Man's social condition; and Schall portrayed Krapp as a filthy, decrepit wretch who literally indicates his death through repetitions of bad clown bits, rather than subtly suggesting it through a relationship with his treasured tape recorder.

Beckett listens to my tale with obvious disgust, but something I say changes his demeanor and he interrupts: "But the repetition, that's right. That's as it should be. You do it the same way every time, but not in an ordinary way. If you do it strangely the first time, and the same way thereafter, then it works . . . ." He is suddenly silent. And what I see now chills me, perhaps partly because I have read countless descriptions of it before. His head sinks low, his hand covers it near the neck, and I wait a long moment for it to rise. "It's very difficult for me to talk about my work," he says gravelly.

So there it is! The famous gesture, the famous sentence, spoken in almost exactly the same words to nearly all those who have journeyed to meet him over four decades. I feel simultaneously privileged to receive it personally and nervous about having overstepped the bounds of acceptable conversation. Moreover, I can see that Beckett is not feigning anything; he seems genuinely to want to help me, but also to experience real pain at the very thought of exegesis. I recall a statement he made years ago to the effect that he would feel superior to his works if he presumed to explain them, and resolve to change the subject. "I wouldn't think you'd feel much affinity with Brecht. What do you think of his work?"

"Well, I can't say I know it well enough to say," he answers, and already I can tell that this is also not an ideal topic. "You know, there's a Brecht on here now. The early one, I forget the name, the one with music. It's making quite a noise here at the moment . . . I like *Galileo*. But the socialist moralizing does get to be a bit much for me. He wrote some good poetry, some fine poetry."

And as his head drops again I remind him: "You know, it's not known whether Brecht gave up the idea of adapting *Godot* because of ill health or because he eventually came to realize its significance as written and no longer wanted to change it."

"Yes, perhaps it had a powerful impact on him."

I explain my conviction that since Brecht believed a certain kind of writing was obsolete, he may not have been prepared at first to see value in Beckett's efforts. "I'd like to believe he was flustered at the idea that anyone could write that well . . . in the old style," I say.

And here again I am totally unprepared for his reaction, which is so idiosyncratic, so touching, that even as it happens I can feel it sticking fast in memory. His head sinks almost to the table, into his hands, and he intones with deep emotion, under his breath, "Ah, the sweet old style."

It seems to be an opening. It is, in any case, more intimate a statement than I ever expected, and since I am near to bursting with intimate feelings about his old style, my heart cannot help but leak a little. "Mr. Beckett, I must tell you that your books . . . I've never experienced anything quite like them. And I hope it won't embarrass you if I say that, far more than any others, they have helped me to see better. You know, I keep your novels by my desk and read passages from them when I'm stuck."

"Why?" he asks, genuinely curious.

"I don't know. They make me feel better, about being stuck, when my mind won't go on." And this, I realize, is perhaps where I ought to have started, speaking of who I am and why I am here taking up his time, for he responds candidly and with unexpected warmth.

"Those novels. I don't even know how they happened. You know, when I think back on that period after the war, how much I wrote, how much I produced—stories, plays, novels, all in a couple of years—I don't know how it happened. I don't know that youngish man. I don't know him anymore. He's like another person."

"I wish you could have the experience of being seventeen or eighteen years old, and reading or seeing *Waiting for Godot* for the first time. Someone ought to tell you what an astonishing experience that is. It's not like any other I've had. The primary feeling is one of courage, especially if you have any familiarity with theater and the way plays are usually written. It seems like an unprecedented act of bravery, for how can anyone just dispense with all the traditional modes of dramatic communication and expect anyone else to listen?"

"You know, I have no more manuscripts," he rejoins quickly. "I've given them all away, except for *Godot*, which is in my French publisher's safe. And if you look at it you can see it has almost no corrections. It came out all at once, just like that. I wrote it in three months, in 1948 I think."

"In other words, you never saw it any other way, from the first."

"No, I never saw it any other way. And that wasn't my first play, you know. There was one before that, never published, terrible business, all scattered, hopeless."

"You mean *Eleutheria*?"

"Yes."

"I read recently that you'd finally decided to adapt it for publication."

"Yes, I said that. But when I went back to work on it I saw it was hopeless. Nothing to be done. I couldn't face publication." Lightly, he drops the familiar first line of *Godot* into conversation, off-handedly, like a habitual phrase.

His reference to a disliked early play puts me in mind of my own efforts, both aborted and ill-advisedly finished, baldly incomparable to his, and I describe confessionally how I left America for Germany to find time to write. His openness has released something in my brain, which now allows those legion questions to come tumbling into consciousness, where they gather in an inarticulate mush and urge me to try to shove all of life into a single inquiry. "How did you do it?" finally burps out. But I am quick to clarify, "How do you do it? I mean, how do you get the world just to leave you alone so you can sit at your desk and do your work?"

"Well, that's not hard early on," he says curtly. "The really difficult thing is . . . afterwards—all the meetings and so on. I haven't written anything in three years, since *Worstward Ho*. But that's not the only reason. I've lost interest. The heart's not in it anymore."

"What do you do?"

"I deal with the mail. Lots of correspondence. And I sit, listen to the voices." He tempers the last phrase with a flat grin, inscrutable, ambiguous, unanswerable, leaving me to speculate on its veracity, coming as it does from the author of numerous books that tell of voices imagined to keep the narrators company.

The talk turns to specific productions. He tells me that he never goes to the theater anymore, and I ask him if he knew about a Brussels production of *Fin de partie* two years ago that was staged in waist-deep water instead of the bare, grey room the script specifies. His answer is vehement, almost angry.

"I detest this modern school of directing. To these directors, the text is just a pretext for their own ingenuity. No, I didn't hear about that one, but I did hear about that awful one in Boston, set underground. Ach, how can you do that?" He raises a subject I probably would not have broached, JoAnne Akalaitis' 1984 *Endgame* at the American Repertory Theatre, the setting for which was a burned-out subway tunnel. A minor scandal had occurred when Grove Press, Beckett's American publisher, tried to stop performances.

Beckett's opinion about "director's theater" is well-known, and his various publishers have made heroic efforts over several decades to enforce his wishes that his plays be performed exactly as written, stage directions and all. But publishers cannot effectively police all theaterₛ nor (I imagine) do they necessarily like that role, and scores of concept productions continue to be mounted throughout Europe and America. So many have occurred, in fact, that it was difficult to understand at the time why Beckett chose to single out Akalaitis and ART. I ask him directly.

"Because I heard about it," he says. "And it was a reputable theater, with a very famous director. I don't understand. How did she get such a reputation when she does such things? It's terrible. And also, they had dedicated the production to Alan Schneider, which was just . . ." He gestures in disgust, obviously saddened at the memory of his director and friend who was killed in an accident in 1984; Schneider was famous for his fidelity to Beckett's texts. He adds, "I heard she said somewhere that she prefers to work with dead authors. But I'm not dead yet. Not quite. I'm a dying author, certainly."

"Why is it less important to respect an author's text after he's dead?"

"Well, just because then you can't hurt his feelings."

I let a moment pass, and then venture, "Perhaps it wasn't wholly unconstructive in the end, though, that Boston experience."

"Yes, it did open up certain questions about text and authority, and that was good."

Despite this comment, I feel obliged to apologize for giving serious attention in my book to productions that clearly run counter to his wishes. "No, no, that's all right," he answers calmly and temperately. "Look, you have to visualize the play on your mental stage while you're writing. That is the important thing. It's not that I deny that people can make improvements; if the plays can be made better, fine. But I don't see how they can work with any other stage directions. If someone can explain to me how it's better another way, okay, but I can't imagine it. That's by the way why I prefer *Endgame* to *Godot*. Because it was better visualized on my mental stage, it's a more complete and coherent movement."

I say little in response to this, although I mark the anomalous humility with which he phrases it, for it is clear that something has shifted and he is now prepared to speak a bit about his work. I ask what qualities he thinks one needs in order to be a great Beckett actor, and he seems to like that question. He answered in some detail.

"First of all you need a certain vocal ability. And then you must be able to do the physical activity in an interesting way. I'll give you an example: Clov in his opening movement. He's been doing these same movements for God knows how long, always the same, and it's the same today except that he notices something is different. We don't know what it is. But if you say to the actor something like this: 'It's the last grain. With the falling of the last grain, suddenly there's a heap' then sometimes you can get the right quality." You have to have actors who can learn from statements like that and translate them into coherent performances.

"Repetition is the most important thing. But not just any repetition. For instance, there's a phrase that keeps repeating in *Endgame*; it comes up about ten times: 'there are no more.' And if you say it like this, it doesn't work." He speaks the phrase matter-of-factly, as a store clerk might speak of inventory. "But if you say it like this, it's effective." He says it again with equal volume on all the words, elongating the "more" in a deep tone, his eyes staring fixedly off to the side. "So you say it in a strange way the first time, and then the same way thereafter. Then they remember."

"You mean the audience."

"Yes."

He makes an effort to think of another example, but I know it will not emerge. The encounter is reaching a natural closure, he has told me much already, and I am more than grateful. That he has shared these things with me at all implies a degree of trust, or at least I choose to see it that way, and I want him to know it is not misplaced. He knows in any case that I have not come bearing yet another theory about what his plays *really* mean, am not out to reduce them to precious collections of hidden allegories, symbols, signs, as so many others have done.

"Yes, they're *Gegenstände*," he says, the German word apparently significant to him. "Theatrical artifacts is what they are. Like objects."

He takes up the check before I even see it and pays with a badly crumpled fifty-franc note he is several moments locating in his numerous pockets. Another curious, angular handshake. And he waves goodbye, his thoughts already on Berlin and the sprawling, wooded park near his old haunt, the Schiller Theater. "My love to the Tiergarten!" I hear at the last.

After leaving Beckett, I walked around Paris for hours, and I could not tell you, even later that day, where I went, for I never saw the places. My mind kept flashing pieces of the meeting at me, like replays of sporting feats, only every moment counted as a feat. I had nearly no sense of present time until these flashes began to slow down and I recognized at once the first losses of memory. It was strange; I had never before perceived so acutely the mechanism of experience slipping away. It was as if each passing second physically destroyed several specific flashes, and an hour or two would mean the irretrievable loss of half the event. I searched out a pencil and the nearest quiet place, and commenced to write down everything I could call back.

Some of my strongest recollections, the ones that still occasionally flash by months later, are of his movements. He had a kind of chink in his gait like the limp of someone with a false leg, only he didn't favor one side, so the end result was a slight side to side hobble. It would have been embarrassingly awkward on someone else, this walk, but something in Beckett's slow gait, in the way he held himself bolt upright and peered seriously about the street, gave it an uncanny gracefulness. Even his little movements were tantalizing. I remember in detail, for instance, the gentle way he smoked, holding the long, brown cigarillos so lightly between his fingers that I was sure it was magic kept them from falling. Most of all, though, I remember his stare. Those eyes, no longer wholly clear but obviously seeing, set deep inside the huge head. They looked straight at you from an exquisitely lean face, which still managed somehow to appear chiseled despite its sea of wrinkles. You could not ignore them were you a thick-skinned, oblivious stranger. And if acquainted with him, you became thralled in their energy and in the persistence of your own anxious wondering, what did they see?

Oh I know I too shall cease and be as when I was not yet, only all over instead of in store, that makes me happy, often now my murmur falters and dies and I weep for happiness as I go along and for love of this old earth that has carried me so long and whose uncomplainingness will soon be mine.

—"From an Abandoned Work"

In Search of
Heiner Müller

It was at a crowded colloquium in West Berlin in 1987 that I first met Heiner Müller. Elbowing my way through dozens of journalists, photographers and autograph-seekers surrounding him, I introduced myself brazenly and asked if he'd like to have coffee some time. He nodded and gave me his phone number, and I felt honored despite the certainty that he hadn't given it because of my scintillating personality, or anything else about me in particular. We didn't manage to get together then, but two years later, upon returning to Berlin, I had more time to arrange an appointment and decided to try again.

In the meantime Müller's fame had exploded. No longer merely a darling of the intelligentsia, he was now material for the popular press, the most frequently produced playwright in both Germanys and an alternate for the 1988 Nobel Prize. A Western journalist had nicknamed him "Müller-Deutschland," as if to say that the twofold context of his work—the cultural politics of his native German Democratic Republic and the continuing Western tradition of the historical avant-garde—had made him into a living symbol of the divided German nation. Even his government had been forced to recognize his stature—from 1961 to 1973 he'd endured a production ban (and from 1965 to 1973 a publication ban) in the GDR—and on January 9, his 60th birthday, an official party for him was planned at the Deutsches Theater in East Berlin.

I bought a ticket for the performance of his play *The Scab* that evening, hoping to finagle an invitation to the party afterward, but that proved unnecessary. He greeted me on the sidewalk outside the theater and said, "Call me—I'm in the phone book," his quizzical expression implying that the trouble I'd taken was ridiculous.

Now, the dizzying political events over the past several months [Fall 1989] have permanently changed the character of the GDR, and future visitors may find it difficult to understand the sort of obstacles that once stood, and to a large extent still stand, in the way of communication there. Only someone who's actually done it can ever truly comprehend what it means to call East Berlin from West Berlin. The GDR cut all phone lines connecting the two halves of the city when it built the Berlin Wall in 1961, and only a limited number have been replaced (presumably as many as could be monitored with tape recorders, though this situation may now change), so a busy signal is almost certain. Moreover, touch-tone phones are rare and the switching mechanisms in the East are old, so even if you do get a line, you'll reach a wrong number unless you've dialed all eleven digits with meticulous, mind-deadening slowness. Only after two months of trying unsuccessfully nearly every day to call did it occur to me that Müller, who has been free to travel since the mid-70s, is not only aware of these difficulties but in fact welcomes them as a means of protecting himself from all but the most indefatigable pursuers—another condition that may now have to change.

But so what? I asked myself. What do any of us know about how we'd respond to the pressures of world fame? And besides, who was I that Müller should accommodate me? It was with this kind of humility that I went out one snowy evening in March, intending to intercept him at another perform-ance I was told he'd attend. Again outside, he took my hand warmly and invited me to his apartment the following week—in retrospect, the gesture I value most out of all those he made toward me. For that week was the last time until I left Germany in mid-August when I wasn't completely and obsessively preoccupied with contacting him.

The crow's journey from my apartment in Neukölln to Müller's in Fried-richsfelde was about two miles; since human beings had to use the official border crossings downtown, though, the trip was actually seven times that and, when you're searched down to the socks as I was that day, took nearly two hours. (For Westerners, this situation did not change when the Wall was breached on November 9, 1989; certain relaxations were implemented only later.) I made my way to his building—which had a charm of its own as the least assuming unit in an enormous complex of unassuming housing units, all cheaply constructed of concrete and glass—and he greeted me at the door, wearing torn jeans and a threadbare T-shirt. The disorder in the living room was laughable and, after a moment, started to seem like an expressionist exaggeration of itself: books, papers, dishes, ashtrays, cassettes everywhere, a long, discolored rip in the ceiling out of which grey dust occasionally fell, several dying plants in front of the smudged plate-glass windows.

I felt welcome and immediately comfortable—that is, as much as one can, sitting on two volumes of Gottfried Benn—as Müller's pasty, unshaven cheeks puffed calmly on cigar after cigar, his eyes inquisitive and friendly behind those aggressively unstyled, black glasses. You wouldn't call him chatty, yet our conversation ranged over a dozen topics, and he responded to every question in a quiet, straightforward tone that left an impression of complete ingenuousness, even when, as often happened, his answers were utterly elliptical. I didn't tell him that day what had originally drawn me to his works: the idea the he had redeemed Brecht's notion of theater as a forum for examining history, had actually become the playwright Brecht only claimed to be, inventing new dramatic structures to accommodate complex historical forces instead of insulting his audience's intelligence with simplified parables. I'd never hesitate to say such a thing now, but Brecht had always been a holy cow in the GDR, and I didn't yet know how "religious" Müller was.

I also neglected to mention why I'd become so eager to interview him. Despite my deep respect for his plays, many of his public comments over the years had made me not only uncomfortable but downright angry. Reading through *Gesammelte Irrtümer* (*Collected Errors*), his published collection of interviews laced with flagrant contradictions and provocative statements whose implications often embarrassed the interviewers, or should have, I felt more and more a desire to challenge him on questions extending far beyond theater into history and politics. I recognized from the beginning how shrewd he was, how expert at turning interviews to his purposes, and no doubt I deserved everything I subsequently got in entering the fray. That day, however, I was loath to start debating without a tape recorder.

He seemed genuinely glad to have met me and agreed to the interview, saying we could do it in English to save me the trouble of translating and suggesting we meet in West Berlin in order to avoid "these difficulties at the border." Two months later, for our fourth scheduled appointment—two afternoons in April spent waiting in vain, on the third a call to cancel—he showed up, ninety minutes late, and installed himself on my sofa as reposefully as a cat. Though I'd stocked up, each of the four times, on mineral water, coffee, beer, and other favorite German beverages, he poured himself a glass of vodka with milk and mentioned another appointment in an hour. It was unimportant that we do the interview that day, he said. "We can meet again—five, six times if you want, don't worry." I coughed, pressed the "record" button, and did my best to interest him in the reception of his work in the United States.

A thin volume of your writing has been available in English translation since 1984. Now two new volumes, containing many more plays, are about to appear with PAJ Publications. When we last met, I mentioned that I thought it likely these books would make you much more famous in America, and you responded by wrinkling your brow and looking at the ceiling. Could you possibly translate that expression into words?
I don't know. Maybe the idea was that I'm afraid that the more they know of my texts, the more they will be disinterested in them, because now it's just a legend or a myth or whatever. Since they don't know the background and the context, they pick out what they need, or what they think they can use. If they get more context and background, maybe then it'll be stranger or more exotic for an American audience.

Would you rather remain a myth?
No, no, it's not my problem. I never think about that. I can exist with any situation.

What are your hopes for the future of your plays in America. Do you see them being done widely in the regional theaters?

I don't care. Really, my only problem is to find time to write the next plays, and that's a problem because now I've got this marriage with the theater, which costs a lot of time. I have to get a free space next year to write again, to write four or five or six more plays. That's what matters. I'm really not interested in the future of my plays. They just exist . . . From time to time I may be interested in directing one of them. Then I'm interested again, but otherwise it's over, and I'm interested in the next one.

What about when the plays are produced by others? Are you interested in their effect?

Mostly not, because in most cases it's disappointing. The production is disappointing. But that's normal. You know, there are two time levels—one is the time of drama, the time of the text; and the other is the time of theater. And in drama you can be innovative much more easily than in theater, because you just need a typewriter or a computer or whatever, and you write it. There are no restrictions, no obstacles. But theater is an industry, small or big, and there are so many material conditions, so theater needs more time to find a way to produce new drama . . .

Heiner Müller's **Quartet**, *directed by Robert Wilson, American Repertory Theatre, Cambridge, MA, 1988. Jennifer Rohn as the Young Woman and Bill Moor as Valmont.*

In a country like the United States, or even the Federal Republic of Germany, there is a link, a very close relationship between business and literature, or business and theater. And for me that doesn't matter, because in the Eastern societies there isn't this link. I don't have to have a best-seller, or a best-selling play.

But is it really all the same to you what people think of your work in the West? Maybe it's not only in the West. I write it and then one or two years later I know what it is, and then it doesn't matter what people think about it. Maybe it would be interesting to ask people fifty years from now. I'm much more interested in what young people think about it than old people, and I would be more interested to know what people in fifty or a hundred years thought. But I won't know, so it's okay.

Maybe I can put the question another way and ask what you think one can reasonably expect from American audiences attending a Heiner Müller play. How do you talk to a public with all but no historical consciousness about issues like remembrance and historical conscience? This is also a problem for American playwrights.
I think you overestimate the difference between an American and a European audience. The sense or consciousness of history gets wiped out more and more here too, so there is no real difference between American and European audiences, even East European ones. In producing these plays, the main question is not a sense or knowledge of history. The main problem is attitude to theater. What does it mean? What does it mean to act, to be an actor, to tell a story? Nobody in the world knows enough about the history of the War of the Roses, and yet any audience can enjoy Shakespeare's histories if they're done well. It's not a problem of knowledge. That doesn't matter.

I found very interesting something Bonnie Marranca told me once when she was in San Diego. She had a seminar, I think on *Hamletmachine*, and these students were mostly surfing—I think they were surfing much more than reading, which is quite understandable in California. She talked about the play, and they read it, and then they decided that it was "surf-dramaturgy," so they began to like it. And they began to try to understand it, because there was something that had to do with their lives and their context. So they could find a way into this strange European thing. Another experience was in New York, at New York University—this performance of *Hamletmachine* that Robert Wilson did with the students. The performances were quite late at night. And this has something to do with what I feel about the Elizabethan theater situation. These people came, well, mostly by car, but some of them by subway, and they came out of danger and went back into the dangerous subway. And that was a great precondition for accepting this play.*

Why?
There is a description by Giordano Bruno of the way to the Globe Theater, Shakespeare's theater, and it's like going though the Lower East Side of New York. You get robbed, you get raped, you fall into a construction pit, or

whatever. It was a dangerous way to the theater and a dangerous way back home. And this is a good condition for watching my plays, so I am quite hopeful about the American reception. Life is not dangerous in East Berlin. It's not as dangerous in West Berlin. But New York is a dangerous city at night. The audience has another sensibility, and then it doesn't matter if they know about Hungary, or whatever. They understand the structure of conflicts; they don't have to know the contents.

•

Strangely, the man who may well be this century's most highbrow dramatist takes a position on elitism and inaccessibility that amounts to this: denial that an author's ideas have any importance *per se*. Nevertheless, knowing of his habit of playing devil's advocate, I suspect that he may be exaggerating his laissez-faire attitude, possibly due to a desire to dissociate himself from the tacit criticism of America implied in my last question. I decide to drop the topic of America completely and ask him more specifically about ideas, but he raises it again himself and proves my suspicion wrong.

There's a little paperback on Hamletmachine *available here in Germany, edited by Theo Girshausen, that begins with an extremely erudite discussion among three dramaturgs, recorded as part of the preparations for a production of the play in Cologne. What do you think of that discussion, and to what degree are you trying to encourage that kind of hard, analytical response to your work?*
I'm not interested in that. What I like most is this primitive American attitude of learning by doing. That's what European actors need. They want to learn before they do, know before they do, and in this aspect I really prefer the American attitude. You do something, and then maybe after or during the process, you learn what you're doing. Then you go on and forget what you learned. You just do things that you can't analyze, you don't know what you're doing, and then it's theater.

What's the goal?
I don't know. I think it depends on the situation. There is always another city, another audience, other actors, and it's always another context. The play is just a catalyst for vision, streams of power, situations of energy, or whatever. That's the function of these texts, I think, just to be there as a catalyst, not to correct things.

But this is all so open, the way you describe it. Like any author, you have intentions when you write, you put thoughts into a text . . .
Yes, but my intentions and my thoughts are as important as yours when you read it, not more. I don't know what I'm writing.

The notion of communicating a thought clearly to me as a reader isn't important to you?
No. I write something—I don't know what. You read something—I don't know what. Maybe if you tell me what you read I can learn something about

what I wrote, but another reader will read something else and I will hear something else from him. The text is a fact, and you can't discuss facts, can't analyze them. You can just handle them and play with them.

But the nature of facts is that they can be seen clearly or blurrily or not at all. There is something to see. Or are you taking a position like Tristan Tzara's, that it's just up to chance, what falls out?
I'm afraid it is, yeah. Because you as an intellectual, you read the text of a play and you know about the ideas, you know about the history of them, but the ideas are just material—like words or emotions or stage design. The ideas aren't *more* important. And it's not my problem to tell people what to do with them. I have no ideology when I write. I can have one when we talk things over, but when I write . . . maybe I begin with some ideas and then they get burned up in the process of writing.

This is what you mean by "democracy" in theater?
Yes.

You don't come to the point where you have an affection for certain images or ideas to which you've, so to speak, given birth?
No, I don't think so. I'm on one side, I'm on the other side, I'm playing, I'm acting when I write. When you write a text for theater you act the parts. You feel that this person's quite right, and then the other person says something to the contrary, and he's quite right too. When I wrote *Philoctetes*, I remember when the reactions from the West came: "Oh, a great play about Stalinism!" I didn't even know it. I wasn't interested, frankly. Maybe I wrote that, but it's only one aspect, and a small one. The main problem in most productions is that they try to find an idea and then subsume the whole material under it. That's why it's a flop. The theater has nothing to do with ideas.

Never?
No, it has to do with ideas, but ideas are just a material to play around with. Because if you insist on one idea, you exclude some others. It should stay flexible and open for the ideas of the audience. But people close it with allegory, understand it, pray at it, and then applaud or not.

If you weren't thinking about Stalinism in Philoctetes, *what were you thinking about?*
About myself. (Laughs) I'm always thinking about myself when I write. And maybe part of me was Stalin, and maybe part of me was Hitler, but I didn't write a play about Stalin. That's stupid. I can use Stalin as a character in a play, but it won't be the point.

•

Müller is thoroughly convincing when he insists that he doesn't care about the fate onstage of the author's ideas, his or anyone else's, but the truth is, on other occasions he has taken precisely the opposite position. In March, a small Berlin group had mounted his play *Der Auftrag* (*The Task*) without procuring the rights, angering his publisher, and then invited him to see a performance on the assumption that he'd grant them the rights if he liked it. He accepted the deal but walked out in disgust at intermission. Later in the year, when asked what he thought of the late French playwright Bernard-Marie Koltès' fierce objection to the German premiere of his play *Return to the Desert*, Müller responded, "That was absolutely right, because it was a reaction to the arrogance of a director who was only interested in displaying his own stylizations."

All right, let's take a specific example, the recent Schaubühne production of Philoctetes, *directed by Herbert König. König cut, among other things, the beautiful final image in the play where Odysseus literally unburdens himself onto Neoptolemus by dumping the dead body of Philoctetes onto him. Now, regardless of any controversial concepts like "textual fidelity," don't you sense any sort of loss there? It doesn't strike you as an inferior version?*
Yes, it was a stupid production. Quite clear. No question about that. But there's only one possibility—you can forbid it, and you don't get away with that. Beckett tried it in the past, to forbid productions. I understand it quite well, but he didn't get away with it.

You would try it if you thought you could get away with it?
It's not my job to fight stupidity in the world, stupidity of directors or theaters. Just forget it. The next one will do it better.

But Beckett doesn't demand authority in productions because he likes to control people. It's that he doesn't see himself as writing only literature. He sees his texts as blueprints for stage action. He thinks his vision is more interesting than most directors' visions, and he wants the director to be a functionary.
I think that's because Beckett doesn't write drama. I remember what Gertrude Stein said about writing drama, or texts for theater. She said that everything is part of the writing process, what happens to the writing in time, to the form, to the people who work on it, and so on. That's drama. The main need of drama is chance, accident, and Beckett wants to exclude chance and accident. It's a theater of dead, theater after death. You know, this situation of Feydeau seen from the grave, that's Beckett, and it's not my vision of drama.

Other writers have taken the viewpoint that the director somehow "completes" the work. But your texts as they're published appear already very complete to me. How do you know when a text is complete?
No, I never said it's completed by the director. I would never say that. It's completed when I'm finished with it. And I wouldn't change a line afterward. It doesn't make sense to change a line. But the director doesn't complete it. No director can complete Shakespeare. He can just show one aspect of a Shakespeare text, or maybe two, but not much more; it's never the whole play. That's what I mean by drama. Drama is much more than theater. It

lasts longer than theater. It's not that theater is the completing of drama; it's that theater is trying to get close to the drama. That's its function.

When you say you wouldn't change a line, I think of the time when students in Hamburg produced your piece Der Horatier (The Horatian). *They suggested numerous changes to the text and you didn't make a single objection.*
It was a different situation in Hamburg. These were young people, amateurs, and they had some very naive ideas about socialism, so I thought I had no right to tell them they should stick to the text. It was interesting for me, what they changed. It was stupid, but that's okay, it was interesting.

Would you have made a stronger objection to a more professional company asking you the same questions?
Yes. Professionals have to do the text. That's for sure.

·

Here is Müller in his classic role, the Great Self-Contradictor; for his statement controverts the most cherished received ideas about his attitude toward directorial freedom. Again and again, not only in Germany but also in America, directors and dramaturgs have quoted in their program notes one particular comment of his from a 1979 discussion on postmodernism in New York: "The great texts of the century work toward the liquidation of their autonomy . . . the disappearance of the Author"—the subtext of those notes being, "At least Müller knows the Author's dead, or should be." In person, though, he sounds suspiciously alive and thoroughly uninterested in functioning as an apologist for willful disrepecters of text.

This topic is, of course, a monstrous can of worms, but no sooner do I pry it open than I have to let Müller go. Already an hour late for a colloquium at the *Akademie der Künste* that seemed of little interest to him, he went away. And as he left, saying we could finish up the following week, I had the distinct impression that seeing him again wouldn't be all that easy. In fact, we didn't meet the following week, or the following, or indeed at any point during the next three months, despite numerous firm appointments, and when I think back on my constant pursuit of him in that interval, I'm at a loss to offer satisfying explanations for my persistence. After a while, it was obvious to both of us that the point had become the chase itself, a sort of fox hunt where the fox had a foolproof refuge and could thus enjoy himself as much as the dog.

Around this time I became friendly with Renate Ziemer, Müller's personal secretary, a patient and sympathetic soul who frequently had no more idea than I did about her employer's whereabouts but who ultimately provided a key bit of information: nights after 10 p.m. or so, Müller could often be found at the Paris Bar on Kantstrasse. If I wanted, I could talk to him there—which I did on several occasions, sliding in among the half-dozen young women surrounding him, each time receiving a warm welcome and a firm commitment to another appointment, which was never kept. I always had the feeling that Müller would gladly have chatted over drinks until dawn, about anything and everything, but the prospect of another quasi-official session with tape recorder was more than he could bear. So much time had already been invested in preparing the interview, though, that not finishing it meant a waste that *I* couldn't bear, so there we stood, more or less at loggerheads.

Not until the evening of my very last day in Germany, when I'd all but given up on him, did we finally find a common ground. Our latest appointment—and by this time they'd taken on a pungent *Godot*-like flavor—was at 7 p.m. and, finding myself with a half-hour to kill, I went into a bookstore where I found (yes, contrived as it may seem) the man himself, browsing through contemporary fiction. He looked gray, and, frankly, not very happy to see me. In fact, I'm still not sure that I didn't spoil his plans for that evening, that he wasn't hiding in that bookstore as a conscious attempt to avoid me, again. I suggested we drive together to the place we'd arranged to talk, but the walk to my car happened to lead right by the Paris Bar. As we passed the entrance way, he ventured, *"Trinken wir schnell eins?"*—"Shall we have a quickie?"—and I felt myself swept inside before I could even answer.

You might call the Paris Bar the Sardi's of West Berlin, except that its clientele extends far beyond the theater world. This is the place in the city where you go to see and be seen, the overpriced celebrity hangout, its walls covered with original artworks and candid photos of famous patrons: Jean-Luc Godard, Marcel Marceau, Konrad Adenauer, Joseph Beuys, Günther Grass, Wim Wenders. As Müller slipped into his customary booth with an air of comfort I hadn't seen even at his home, my mind flashed to a German critic's famous observation about Brecht, that he "wore his worker's clothes like a tuxedo." Müller, tireless reviler of capitalist excesses, also apparently thrived on celebrity, publishing his listed (but unreachable) phone number like an advertisement, cultivating a public image of the ultra-accessible people's poet while actually behaving like a Hollywood star.

He ordered a second scotch, then a third, and for a while I tried to match him drink for drink, noticing that the more we drank together the more his taciturnity waned. It wasn't only the lubricating qualities of the liquor but also the drinking camaraderie that he appeared to enjoy. I couldn't keep it up for long, though, so I ordered a pack of cigarettes—I don't smoke— thinking smoking together might have the same effect. He ordered a meal, was engaged in conversation every few minutes by some other famous person—authors Peter Schneider and Daryl Pinckney, diplomat-author Gunter Gauss—and finally I said flatly that we really ought to be going to finish the interview.

"But why?" he asked impatiently. "Look, why don't you just write an article about talking to me? Write about all this—the atmosphere at the Paris Bar, the difficulty of coming to conversation, and so on. What we're saying to each other here is much more interesting for the people than an interview."

"But that's just gossip," I objected. "Gossip is all they read, anyway, and ultimately it's all that's true as well," he said. "May I switch the tape recorder on, then?" I asked, wondering fleetingly how I would ever transcribe a conversation, entirely in German, taped in this noisy, crowded bar. "Sure," he answered and sat back, visibly relieved at not having to budge.

You once said that you believed in a third and a fourth world war. Is that still true?
At the moment no, but it's not out of the question.

What did you mean by that?
That was a joke. There was, then, this cliché about historical pessimism, and I made this joke on it. I believe not only in a third but also in a fourth world war. That's the proof that I'm an optimist.

But you've written a lot about a time after "the catastrophe." In one text, Landschaft mit Argonauten (Landscape with Argonauts), *you say the action "presumes the catastrophe." And then there's this stage direction at the beginning of* Quartet *that sets the action both in a "salon before the French revolution" and in a "bunker after World War III."*
All of Beckett touches on that, actually. It's the literature after the catastrophe.

Heiner Müller's **Quartet**, *directed by Hans Peter Cloos, Schlosspark Theater, Berlin, Germany, 1988. Joachim Bliese (Valmont) and Sabine Sinjen (Merteuil).*

And that's a form of optimism?
Well, what does "optimism" mean? The function of literature is the handing down of experience, whether it's for human beings or for extraterrestrials. It doesn't matter. It's information, experience that's handed down. That's its function, independent of whether this planet is destroyed or not.

A literature for extraterrestrials is worthless for me.
No, no, it isn't worthless. The conservation or handing down through writing or printing is essential. The state has a bunker, a nuclear-secure bunker, where the most important artworks are stored in diskette form. It's certain that they'll withstand destruction. This bunker exists in the Federal Republic near Bonn. I don't know about the USA, but in it are stored, for example, the texts of the winners of the Georg Büchner prize . . .

So you're there.
Yes, or course. And then when everything else is dead and gone, any Martians who land here can find this and learn something from it about the conditions here.

That's a frightening and disgusting notion.
Why?

Because it "presumes" the catastrophe.
You can only contribute something to the prevention of the catastrophe when you look upon it as possible. Everything else is blind. That's obvious. A catastrophe can occur any day, but not without someone having planned it.

Yes, but isn't there an important, and hopefully strong, line between possible and probable?
Yes, but the whole tendency in most European art and literature is toward realism.

Isn't catastrophe a bit more probable when we've done something, as you just described, to protect our artworks? Haven't we then, in a way, already given up?
No, I find it unrealistic to work on the assumption that nothing can happen . . . And it's an altogether terrific question that American computer philosophy asks: what is more important, the information or the organic life? At the moment the organic life is still the carrier of the information, but maybe that doesn't have to be so. A machine could also be the carrier.

In spite of that, human beings will still be living.
Tolstoy always had an answer to that: the dinosaurs also died out.

Okay, but when one says, as you once did, that "the real pleasure in writing is the pleasure in the catastrophe," the more important word there is "pleasure," not "catastrophe." No?
Of course. But it's not so simple. In a novel by Grossmann called *Life and Fate*—a dumb title but it's a great book—the battle of Stalingrad is de-

scribed. He was in Stalingrad himself as an officer, and he stood safely over the Volga as a bombardment took place. The Volga burned, the water burned, his own country violated, and he looked down and thought about the beauty of the sight. You see, the pleasure in the catastrophe would be absurd without catastrophe. It belongs to the human condition. That's for sure, because every human being knows he's going to die and out of that comes pleasure in the catastrophe.

But to emphasize the catastrophe, that's madness.
Only for nondramatists. Drama has always been concerned with catastrophe. It needs catastrophe.

All right, I understand what you're saying. Maybe it's because we're sitting here drinking ourselves silly, but I still wonder why anyone would say it, why anyone would emphasize that. Maybe what I'm asking is why anyone becomes a dramatist, or wants to become one.
That's a good question. Maybe, in principle, there is no drama anymore, or there is but we don't know it. Computers don't need drama, for instance. The dramaturgy of the computer is unthinkable. That's a great sci-fi fantasy, for computers to take up drama. The only attempt to write a computer-drama was *Blade Runner*, which is a very interesting story. The drama arises from the fact that the computers want to become human beings. When everything works, though, there's no more drama. The drama needs catastrophe, needs things not to work.

•

At this point, a disheveled man selling used paperbacks walks up to our table, and Müller stops talking abruptly to look through what he has. A collection of letters from the political philosopher Carl Schmitt (1888-1985) to a scholar requesting an interview catches his eye. Schmitt, highly respected during the Weimar Republic, became a Nazi ideologue in 1933 and is now one of the most controversial figures of the century in his field. Müller spends several minutes perusing with serious mien, then laughs loudly and shows me a line: "Dear Mr. V——, Your friendly suggestion arrives a few years too late. I'm no longer capable of conversation." The man asks twelve marks for the book; Müller gives him fifteen.

I want to come back to this question of accessibility in your work. It still seems hard to believe that you don't see it as an issue at all. You know, some statements you've made are a bit hard for an American to swallow. For instance: "I am a Negro" [1985] and "I'm certain that I could come to an understanding sooner with a Puerto Rican in New York, even in he takes away my wallet, than with a white-collar worker in Bochum" [1983].
In that discussion on postmodernism that I attended in New York, there was a sentence something like this: "Talent is a privilege, privileges have to be paid for, and art is nothing as long as it's based on privileges." It was impossible to translate the negative meaning of the German word "*Privileg*"

into English. "Privilege" is something positive for Americans. You can't translate it negatively. For me, privilege is something negative; for the American that was unintelligible. That's the puritan tradition: privilege is something that you can own, that you're given, money or talent, and so on. And everything that is money is positive for the American. His money comes from God. That's the difference. So when I say, "I am a Negro" or "I'm closer to a Puerto Rican . . .," what I mean is wholly primitive: I mean the biographical experience of standing before shop windows and seeing things there that I can't buy, or that my parents can't buy. That's the experience of the Negro and the Puerto Rican, and that's what I mean.

I meant the question more in relation to language. For the author of a poem as full of obscure allusions as "The Wound Woyzeck" to say, as you have, that he'd like to count the illiterate among his public would seem, to the average American, like the delusion of an elitist.
That has to do with something else. You see this very often in discussions about productions of Brecht plays, and it's true. The worst audience is the half-educated audience—that is, the people who think they know something for certain but don't know enough. People who really know nothing about the material, and can see it naively, react more intelligently and can also speak more intelligently about it than those others, those who have a few thoughts, have inert habits of thought, but who don't take the opportunity to travel out of the country to develop their ability to make discriminations.

"A little learning is a dangerous thing."
Exactly. On the other hand, the great advantage of the American is his belief that everyone can do whatever he wants. If an American housewife suddenly decides she wants to do theater, then she does theater, and she doesn't need a diploma, or training, she does it. That's an advantage, this presumption of ability. Here you need a diploma to start out as an actor, or to direct, or anything. It has to be something lofty.

This difference is more pronounced due to the war. For the typical young person in Europe, all possibilities aren't, in fact, open.
Yes, the Americans are all dilettantes, all amateurs. That's beautiful. That's much more necessary, up to a certain point at any rate.

I have difficulty with a lot of what Robert Wilson does, partly because of its dilettantish nature. Is that part of your interest in working with him?
It's part of the interest, yes. Godard is another example. Godard is the inventor of the jump-cut. He was the first one to do that, and now they learn it in every film school. I don't know if this is still the case, but previously you learned in every film school what you weren't allowed to do. Thus, at some point a dilettante has to arrive who does something that the learned can't do because they've all learned not to. The quality of Wilson's abilities was such that it convinced others that he had a disturbed relationship to language, and out of that came his approach to language. In the beginning, when he began

doing theater, he could barely speak. That's why he has another attitude to the text.

What's your opinion regarding how Robert Wilson should treat a text by Heiner Müller?
However he thinks is right.

Haven't certain recent remarks of yours been critical of the way he uses texts? You said in the program for The Forest, *for instance, that you wished you could, just once, collaborate on a piece with him from the beginning instead of only providing a text afterward for a structure that was already developed and in place.*
Yes, that's probably out of the question. It doesn't have to be right for me, what he does; it has to be right for him. It can always be the wrong thing for me, but for him it's right.

But as I see it, text in a Wilson production, regardless of whether it's by Heiner Müller or someone else, is used as a sort of linguistic equivalent to movie background music.
Okay. He's really only done a text of mine once, with *Hamletmachine*, and I found what he did there at least interesting. With everything else he wasn't doing my texts; he rather made use of texts that weren't written for his purposes but were ready to hand.

In your opinion, he doesn't, in these cases, "direct" Heiner Müller?
No, no, he just "utilizes."

And that's all right with you?
Yes, what I give him he can use.

Do you continue to believe in his work, in its value?
Yes, I certainly believe, not necessarily in the result but at any rate in the work. We could argue about the result . . . Wilson comes out of a theater of images. That's very American. A country with many nationalities, many languages—that's the only universal language, and as long as you have a common language, then that language is still valuable. That's why there's no American drama. There's American theater but no drama. That'll take a while still. In Europe it's different; there the text is the body of the theater. But you can't expect that from Wilson.

Yes, but how can an author speak that way, especially a poet with as much mastery over language as you? How can you speak so much like a director, as though Wilson's stage images were exactly as important as your texts?
Because I know that nothing can happen to my texts that way.

•

He goes on to explain that he prefers Wilson's "utilization" to what usually occurs when directors try to interpret texts, which he refers to as *Verschleierung*, or "veiling." The conversation is now animated, and it grows even more so, extending into numerous other subjects, such as the nature of his contact with Brecht in the '50s, his experience of being banned, his opinions on Sartre, Barlach, Kaiser.

At some point after midnight, however, drunk and so hoarse from smoking I could barely talk, I glanced down at my tape recorder and noticed that the battery had died. Precisely when, I couldn't say. Mercifully, most of the talk turned out to be intelligible—that is, as long as I played it back with batteries that were neither new nor dead but rather *dying*. And three months later, as I hung up the phone for the last time, having finally received his corrections to the translated transcript, all I could think of was a comment Beckett once made in reference to a director who said she preferred to work with dead authors: "But I'm not dead yet. Not quite. I'm a dying author, certainly." At the Paris Bar, Müller and Pinckney had shared a long laugh over some graffiti one of them saw on a bathroom wall: "The author is dead. Heiner Müller is an author. Ergo, Heiner Müller is dead."

Out-Takes: Fragments From an Interview With Heiner Müller

The following bits of conversation with Heiner Müller are taken from an interview in West Berlin done in two parts on May 8 (in English) and June 28, 1989 (in German). Approximately half of the material I recorded on nearly six hours of tape is included in the previous interview-essay. Much of the rest appears here in a collection with a very different focus.

In a way, these fragments contain the richest material, because they include Müller's digressions. As will become clear, following his habit of steering interviews towards his own purposes, the author often veers off from theatrical issues to historical ones. His main focus as a playwright has always been on history, history-as-fiction, history as a form of psychological coercion, and, until recently, that focus constituted a blatant provocation in his native German Democratic Republic. (Müller says that the GDR has spent decades working "to stop history," and he has occasionally drawn a connection between that stuckness and his own search for new dramatic forms.) Thus, this author is in a peculiar position in relation to the recent revolutionary changes in Germany, and his comments about his country remain interesting despite the fact that they were made before the breaching of the Berlin Wall. Critics in the 1990s will invariably spill a great deal of ink over the question, "Whither Müller now?", and his opinions and formulations from 1989 and before (witness the book-length collections of interviews, *Zur Lage der Nation* and *Jenseits der Nation,* published in 1990 and 1991) will remain essential background for that discussion.

On Lehrstück Theory

In their (our) never-ending efforts to nail down your connection with Brecht, critics often ask you about your opinions on Lehrstück *theory, and in your public statements you've gone back and forth on it. The last I heard, you were endorsing it; in 1986 you said, "it's becoming current again." Can you say more about that?*

The first thing is, don't cling to this word *"Lehrstück."* It's very unhappy. Remember what Brecht said about it, for instance, that policemen shouldn't play the parts of policemen onstage. They should play the parts of criminals, and criminals should play the parts of policemen. Then they can learn something about each other. That's the problem. It's not this didactic thing. It's a theater of experience, which is a game very close to danger. I think the theater should have to do with dangerous games. Otherwise there's no chance for it, because what they do on Broadway they can do better on TV or in the movies. A policeman attempting to represent a criminal—that's very dangerous for his identity. And a criminal acting a policeman onstage—he will have some problems with himself. And that's the point. Theater should disturb people. It should take away their feeling of security regarding their identity. Theater should take identity away from the audience. That's its main function. You shouldn't know who you are when you leave.

Would you prefer a theater of non-professional actors to a theater of professional actors?

I wouldn't say that. But it's easier to establish what I just said with non-professional actors. It's much easier. But if you can get it with professional actors it's much more powerful

But a professional actor is by definition never a policeman. He's always an actor.

No, if he's a really good actor, you can get him over this threshold of routine. And that's what theater should try to do, so that he doesn't know it himself.

Is that what you meant when criticized the 1974 Schaubühne production of Der Lohndrücker, *when you said that the West German actors had tried too much to play away, to "cheat away" the difference between themselves and the East Berlin workers? You said they should have played that difference into the production?*

Yes.

This seems like a total rejection of naturalism.

Yes, but you shouldn't reject naturalism before using it to the extreme. Then you throw it away. There's no way for actors to find things without naturalistic means. But then you should forget it, and that's a problem. They should forget what they can, what they've learned, what they are. The precondition is a trained actor, but if he doesn't forget his training, he's nothing.

Forget his training and remember what? Or learn what?

It's not a problem of learning. He should learn that he doesn't know himself, that he's not sure of himself, that he's not sure of his profession, that he's sure of nothing.

And with this unsureness comes "theater"?

Then it's an experience for the audience. The aim of all theater is revealing this void, this nothingness, and then it's an experience and you can begin. And that's what I mean with *Lehrstück*, just to teach people that they have nothing to cling to, that nothing is sure or fixed.

How does that relate to this oft-quoted statement of yours from 1975: "I always have the need, when I write, to load the people up so much that they don't know what to carry first, and I believe that's also the only possibility."

I think it's just another way to say the same thing.

But it seemed to me that what you just described was a process of reducing. This is a process of overloading.

Yes, but what I described was a process of reducing the audience, or members of the audience and the actors, to bring them to their zero point. And that's the same.

On the Schism in His Career

People often speak of a crisis in your career around the time of Hamletma-chine. *It's not even "around" that time; it's in* Hamletmachine, *in the fourth scene, when the photograph of the author is torn up. That's supposed to represent a break, before which you were supposedly interested in plays about day-to-day life in the GDR and after which you became an avant-gardist. What do you think of this division? Is it true, or is it a construction imposed upon you by critics?*

I think it's a construction. You know, if you want, you could say that I'm always in crisis, I've always been in crisis. Or never. And you always write the same play, with different material. I wouldn't know what to write about the GDR now. I didn't know what to write about it when I wrote *Hamletma-chine*. The progress or development of the country is much slower than mine, because it will last longer than I will, so it's stupid to put the biography in congruence with the country or state. It never works. And parts of *Hamlet-machine* are quite old. Parts are from the '50s and have much to do with my first encounter with Western literature after the war, the surrealists and others. Then it was all covered over with Brecht, and then this Brecht-cover became thinner and thinner because I got closer and closer to the reality of this country, the GDR, which had nothing to do with the categories of Brecht. You couldn't use those categories to describe the situation of this country, and he could never know this country because of his biography. So the cover got thinner and thinner, and then the old things came up. There is never a chronology, a chronological order, in the work.

Do you find the classification "avant-garde" fully inappropriate?

You can't write with the intention to be avant-garde. That's stupid. Maybe you can in Western society, but I never thought about that when I wrote. I just used whatever I found to describe things, and I think it's not an attitude, it's just a problem of material, dealing with material. There are some things that you can't describe like Goethe when he wrote *Iphigenia*, and you can't write about the Hungarian uprising as Shakespeare wrote his histories. It's another material. There is no center, no center of the universe, and there is no subject. Subjects are categories. And maybe this is avant-garde, but I don't think about it.

Many people have said that the importance of Hamletmachine *lies in its challenge to the theater institutions which produce it. It forces them to change, which was always one of the main goals of the historical avant-garde. Do you deny that as being a central element in that work?*

No, it's true but it's not the intention. It was just impossible for me at that time to write a play in dialogue about this problem.

You mean the "Hamlet-complex"?

Yes. Beginning with *Mauser*, I think, my problem was that I had no idea how to do the texts onstage. I still have no idea. Maybe *Mauser* is a good example. It would be obscene to write a conventional play on this theme. That's just pornography. And so I took this form of telling a story, just a spirit present as the author who tells this story, independent of the character. But I never had an image of how to stage it. It's just a void. It's written for a theater which doesn't exist. And maybe that's the provocation in *Hamletmachine*. It's written for a theater which doesn't exist.

But that brings me back again to the difference between the earlier and later works. Isn't what you're describing a sort of épater le bourgeois, *which is not present in earlier plays such as* Der Bau (Construction) *and* Die Korrektur (The Correction)?

Maybe there is one aspect. When I wrote *Der Lohndrücker, Die Korrektur* and *Der Bau*, I felt that there was history in the GDR, and after a certain point there was no history anymore. It was just still, waiting for history, and that's the situation even now. The GDR tried to stop history, to stop the process. And from that point on I found no material for a play in the GDR. There's no material now for drama, so I have to find another avenue. It's just a professional thing. The only thing I can do is write drama, and if there's nothing there I have to take it from somewhere else.

Could you say a little more about what you mean when you say there's no history there?

It's quite simple. The GDR was planned by the Russians as something provisional. The concept was to have a united Germany, which was neutral, between the two blocs. That was the Russian concept, even Stalin's concept, and then it was cut by Adenauer and the Americans. From then on this was, in a way, a paradoxical situation. This eastern part of Germany became a Stalinist colony, colonized by Stalinism, and they had to stop history to hold it. The symbol of that is the Wall—just to stop it. And that's still the situation. Maybe it will change in the next years, I don't know.

On Gilmore and Manson

Why is a newspaper story about Gary Gilmore printed on the cover of the German edition of Germania Tod in Berlin?

That was a title page from the *New York Times* that was terribly cut. The clipping isn't good, I didn't do it, though I did choose the page. On the same page is the Gary Gilmore story, Gilmore-the-criminal, and a report about an American reception, I think—or the other way round—for Hirohito, the war-criminal Hirohito, who is honored. Hirohito was surely the worse criminal, but he's praised. Thus not only Gary Gilmore but rather this relationship was the idea.

What happened? Why doesn't Hirohito appear?

He doesn't have to. We know who he is. (Laughs)

That it's a comparison between the two concepts of "hero" is totally unclear without the Hirohito story. It seems like a sort of side-swipe at America.

No, no, it has to do with the relativizing of scales of value, or standards, or conventions. In San Francisco, I once met a journalist who had an exchange of letters with Charles Manson. He'd also visited him in San Quentin, and he had letters from him that were very impressive, very manic, in which Manson returned again and again to the point that he'd killed far fewer people than Nixon and McNamara, but he's a scapegoat. They needed a scapegoat, so they made him into it. That's an entirely realistic view of your nation. And back then I would have suggested, along with this journalist, "Manson for President." Unfortunately, it wasn't realizable.

I've seen a television interview with Manson, and he really is an evil guy. It's not ambiguous, whether he should remain in prison. He's not an interesting man or a genius or whatever. He's simply a murderer.

No, no, he's evil, clearly. This has to do with the fact that, when you look at statistics, individual violence, individual criminality, has produced far fewer corpses throughout history than state violence. There is a disproportion, which is basically Brecht's motif in *Dreigroschenoper*: "*Verfolgt das [kleine] Unrecht nicht zu sehr, in Bälde/Erfriert es schon von selbst, denn es ist kalt.*" ("Be careful how you punish [the little] wrong, for surely/Cold-hearted deeds will freeze and die away."—Michael Feingold's translation.) You need the small injustice, you always need murderers who distract the people from the greater crimes of the state. To that extent Manson is right when he says he's a scapegoat.

On Shame In Postwar Germany

Do you remember a panel discussion in 1987 about Elem Klimov's film Come and See *(much of which consisted of horrifyingly graphic depictions of German war atrocities in Poland)? You had some difficulties back then in response to your comment: "The film left me thoroughly cold."*

The point of controversy was, in fact, only that I thought you couldn't describe this phenomenon with the Hollywood aesthetic, with this emotionalizing, this moralizing. It then becomes a substitute or surrogate for analysis. That was the point of controversy. It's so emotionally set up you can't talk about it clearly anymore, and then it serves no purpose.

Yes, but Germans are frequently pointing out how important it is to see the annihilation of the Jews in, say, a 400- or 1000-year context, and somehow the specificity of the Holocaust drops out of the picture there. I understand why a person would do that, either to escape feelings of guilt or, if he or she is young enough for guilt not to be a question, to try to understand what happened. But the question remains: is it seemly to take the broad historical view at the cost of visceral sympathy with the victims?

There is still an overarching aspect there. Is it seemly to kill the Indians? I can also ask. The whole history of the European conquest of the American continent—north, south and in the middle—was a genocide.

Yes, but when the Americans or others make the same mistake, that doesn't mean . . .

No, I'm not saying that. It's just that one ought not to leave out that that was a point of rationalization for the German National Socialists: that something happened in Europe that was, for centuries, normal on every continent. The English treated the people in India as the Germans treated the Jews, the English treated the South Africans as the Germans did the Jews. The difference was only in the perfection; they didn't have the industry for it. It was also less abstract, perhaps. And it takes nothing away from the crimes, nothing away from the brutality, to notice that, during the entire war-crimes proceedings at Nuremberg, international law was legally very questionable. It was the first time that was done.

There were no precedent cases.

Yes. It was very questionable because in the meantime there should have been more. They were always private matters, never made public, but there the Tribunal had the united power of the Allies behind it. They could do that. The entire war was crime, though! But nothing could be done about that. What characterizes a "crime"? That makes it so difficult, to judge it only morally.

I still come back to the same idea, though, about the possibility of finding a new point of view on the issue. To combine the visceral feelings with the rationality about history—that would certainly be something new for Germany.

It hasn't had to do only with Germany for a long time. It has to do with the fact that American industry earned money on Auschwitz. Auschwitz was the consequence of bourgeois humanism as the etiology of capitalism, and the principle of selection is, before and after, the principle of politics. There is still no Hegelian pattern for Auschwitz. It's nonsense to make the Germans into the only monsters. No population of a capitalistically structured state would have behaved differently under those circumstances.

That's the appeal to Kafka: "What's possible is what happened."

Jörg-Michael Koerbl as Frederick in **Leben Gundlings Friedrich von Preussen Lessings Schlaf Traum Schrei (Gundling's Life Frederick of Prussia Lessing's Sleep Dream Scream)** *by Heiner Müller, directed by Helmut Strassburger and Ernstgeorg Hering, Volksbühne, Berlin, Germany, 1988.*

I mean, the first formulation for Auschwitz-selection is the puritanical maxim: "The only good Indian is a dead Indian." That's the first formulation for Auschwitz, the program, and it comes out of a particular tradition of thought, out of the connection between a certain kind of economics and social organization. The Germans suffered the consequence, and there it becomes critically visible. It's just as Brecht said back then: one is right in capitalism as long as he has his gloves on, but when he takes his gloves off . . .

Isn't it another question, though, how one reacts to all that? Now, you mentioned the Indians. If I say that I also think it isn't seemly that the Americans feel no shame over the Indians, can you see what I'm saying about Germany? There isn't really any true shame here. Do you think there should be any, or is that too much to expect?

No, you can't say that so generally. Those who participated aren't ashamed. Those who didn't are.

That's not true at all.

Yes it is. The young people are ashamed. The younger generation is ashamed of it.

I wish I'd noticed that. I've lived here for two years. I hoped I'd notice that.

They were at any rate, it could be that it's now being superimposed on them, but in '68 it was so. The protest started as a protest against the Vietnam War, but then it grew into a rebellion against the father-generation, against the parents who weren't ashamed for Hitler. The Vietnam War was just an occasion to rebel against the parental generation. And that's been absorbed again. The worst thing about the people of the Federal Republic is their innocence, that they feel, subjectively, innocent of everything. Every pedestrian zone in a West German small town is an "innocence zone." They sell there year in and year out all the products and trends in the third world, and the give-away is: they send them their atomic waste. Europe unloads its garbage in the third world and turns around and collects the products, but no one's ashamed. Everyone feels innocent. And the worst innocents are the Americans, I think, which I know from experiences with students in the United States around 1975-77. They're astonished that they're disliked as Americans when they travel anywhere. They really have the consciousness that they do everything for everyone. "We help the whole world, but people are ungrateful and only work against us." Monstrously uninformed, too, hm?

On Anti-Semitism and Jews

Andrzej Wirth told me a story about another colloquium in which someone asked you why you hadn't written more about Jews, and you reportedly an-

swered, impatiently, "Ach, I can't write about everything." At the risk of getting another impatient answer, I'd like to pose the same question: why haven't you?

I can only write about experiences I've had myself. My only experience with the Jewish problem was a childhood memory. My parents had a Jewish doctor. I visited him with a children's disease that was very painful, a middle-ear suppuration, which he knew how to deal with very well. The treatment was painful, but it had to be done, otherwise the hearing disappeared. So I had to go to him, I was four or five years old, and for every numeral that I could say, could repeat, could hear, I got a piece a candy. That was a very good method, and it was very humane and pleasant. Then a couple of years later, I heard from my mother that he'd been killed by the SS. There was a transport with a pregnant woman who gave birth during the trip. He helped her, which was of course forbidden, and then he was shot, the woman too, and the child too. And I have written about this story but in a very old text, one of the very first plays. It wasn't published. And it was my only personal contact with this problem. Everything else would be arrogance, and that would be obscene—if I wanted to write about the Jewish problem now.

Sartre wrote about anti-semitism, for example, and he wasn't a Jew.

Yes, Sartre was more a philosopher or a journalist than an author.

I didn't mean to make a comparison. I meant only . . . you know his book about anti-semitism?

Yes.

He speaks of anti-semitism as lying behind a certain kind of persecution of intellectuals; he implies that it's actually the main point and not a side issue. And you've written so much about the persecution of intellectuals, in Leben Gundlings Friedrich von Preussen Lessings Schlaf Traum Schrei *and other texts. Do you not agree that, as Sartre says, "anti-semitism is the elitism of the mediocre"? That it provides an easy way for the mediocre to feel elite?*

I don't believe that. I don't think it's right. Yes, sure, it's right, but despite that it's a superficial analysis, I think. Anti-semitism was always much stronger in Hungary and the eastern countries than in Germany, much stronger in Russia than in Germany, because the Jews were the agents of capital—exactly like today in Harlem—or at least that's how they were experienced by these populations. In Germany that wasn't so for the most part. So much the worse for this rationale about German anti-semitism and this identification of the Jew with the intellectual, with the intelligentsia. That's very much a result of Nazi propaganda. There was a hatred of intellectuals in Germany, a hatred of intellectuals in France, and then these two enemies were swept together with the Jews. But that was a result and not a cause.

Well, I think his argument is a little bit more complicated than that. You do allow that what happened to the Jews is an important event in German history.

Yes. There's another interpretation that I find more interesting for Germany, or for the phenomenon of anti-semitism in Germany—from Lyotard. In an old archive, texts were found about the missionizing of the Franks. The Franks were the main race of Teutons at the time the Teutons were missionized by priests from Rome. And the argument of the missionaries was: "You Franks, you are the chosen people in Germany. You're the chosen people, and that's why you must be foremost among your people." That's how the Teutons became Christians. Then suddenly in the middle ages, another chosen people emerged, the Jews, and there could be only one chosen people. That was the annihilation. And the whole Nazi mythology, and with it the terminology, came from a messianic Jewish terminology. It was exactly this point: there were two chosen peoples, and there can only be one. For that there's only annihilation. That was never the case for the Poles, also not for the Russians. Another story that touched me very much was a documentation about an Austrian village when the Nazis occupied Austria. One of the first steps taken by Hitler was to evacuate the people safely and then have this village obliterated by artillery. It became a site for target practice and is still used for target practice today. And the reason was: in the graveyard of this village lay buried a grandmother of Hitler, and this grandmother had had a relationship with a Jew. That's macabre, hm?

That was the proof that Hitler was partly Jewish.

Or the fear. That was his fear. He always had this suspicion about his own blood, that it was impure. Therefore the self-annihilation.

On Being Banned

How did you live during those years, 1961-73, when everything of yours was forbidden in the GDR?

I was given money by various friends. Well, not really friends, people with money.

That must have been difficult for you.

No, not really, it was all right. It was harder on my wife, I think.*

Was everything of hers forbidden that whole time, too?

No, only for two years around 1964-65. That's usually the way it goes in the GDR—a two-year ban, then you're allowed again for a time until you do something wrong again, and then you're punished for another two years. That's the way, two years on, two years off.

I find it hard to believe it was really all the same to you that whole time. A twelve-year ban?

Yes, it doesn't matter so much, really. I was happy with what I was writing at the time, and I was getting some productions in the West, in the Federal Republic.

That was enough for you?

Yes.

It's not that I doubt what you're saying. I really am just trying to understand it in human terms. It's enough for you just to write for the drawer.

No, it's not for the drawer. It's that I knew I was right. I was certain of it. It's all the same whether it's read now or later. It doesn't matter one bit. Literature is always right in the face of politics.

Kroetz in America

On an uncomfortably warm autumn afternoon, the man known as the playwright of the inarticulate stopped by and talked eloquently to me, in high German, for well over an hour. Franz Xaver Kroetz would have preferred to speak in his native Bavarian, but German "would do," he said, dandling his angelic baby daughter on his lap and beaming proudly as she spilled a box of tic-tacs, a jar of pencils and a glass of water on the floor. Publicity photos don't reveal that Kroetz is a muscular man, and as he peeled off his outer layers he didn't appear at all happy with the New York weather. In fact, at the end of his two-week trip here—a "stopover" on the way from Munich to Paris, he called it—he was in an animatedly aggressive mood.

Was this his first visit to America? "Well, I know Canada and Central America and South America. America—that's a little larger than just your country. No, I haven't been to the *United States* before." His first impression of New York? "There are worse cities in the third world, but it's a typical third world city. When you ride the subway, it feels as if you're riding in Calcutta."

Unlike his thewy physique, the author's facade of churlishness wasn't surprising—it fit perfectly with what is known about his background. Born February 1946 in Munich, during the most chaotic and difficult days after Germany's defeat in World War II, Kroetz had a frustrating and turbulent childhood. He once described his father tersely as "a pig-headed, foolish Nazi," and the son reportedly blossomed creatively only after the death of that taciturn, authoritarian parent, who wanted him to become a tax officer like himself and who granted permission only on his deathbed for Franz to attend acting school.

The immediate effect of his death in 1961 was to fan the flames of teenage rebelliousness: Kroetz become interested in opposition politics and later joined the German Communist Party. (He withdrew in 1980, but says "I am still a communist.") His acting career sputtered, partly because of his willfulness and impatience with school, and he ended up working as a manual laborer while continuing what had always been his secret midnight obsession, writing.

It would be years before anyone else took that writing seriously. In a 1985 interview, he described the period in the mid-1960s when he collected about 150 rejection notices: "Back then I wrote plays for the theater in a matter of hours, or a couple of days. I wrestled with every form, because I imitated them all. It was a terrible confusion . . . I wrote a new play every night." Gradually, though—doggedly—he developed a vigorous, original dramatic style and linguistic idiom, and in the following decade became the most frequently produced living German playwright.

Kroetz acknowledges a number of literary influences—Marieluise Fleisser and Ödön von Horváth, realists prominent in the 1930s who were rediscovered and revived in 1960s Germany; the "new realism" of Wolfgang Bauer, Rainer Fassbinder and others; the so-called absurdism of Beckett, Ionesco and Adamov, and the tradition of the German *Volksstück*—but to list these is to risk implying that his work has a derivative feel. It does not. The plays with which Kroetz first won acclaim in 1971—*Hartnäckig (Stiff-Necked)*, *Heimarbeit (Homework)* and *Wildwechsel (Game Crossing)*—provoked local scandals precisely because audiences had never seen a dramatic microscope turned on their society with this degree of magnification.

Kroetz's characters at that time were all unheroic outcasts, quintessentially ordinary and ignorant people who were so severely battered by circumstance that they became grotesquely aggressive: a pregnant schoolgirl who plots with her boyfriend to murder her father; a handicapped man who, denied his inheritance because of his handicap, thinks of killing his brother. In *Männersache (Men's Business)*, an earlier version of *Wer durchs Laub geht (Through the Leaves)*—the play whose revival at the New York Shakespeare Festival coincided with Kroetz's New York "stopover"—a man and woman play a macabre game of "chicken" with a rifle, stopping only when one of them drops dead.

The overarching themes of guilt and sexual frustration in these plays were hardly new, and other dramatists such as O'Neill and Gorky had used down-and-outs as characters before. Kroetz's figures were unique, though, in that they weren't given any ability to be articulate about their troubles. They had no eloquent language with which to speak beyond their fictional stations, as surrogates for the author-cum-social critic, and instead used clichés, banalities, phrases from billboards, radio and television—a manner of speech Richard Gilman has described as "not having been created by them but of having instead passed through them, as it were."

The young Kroetz became an overnight sensation, seen by the literal-minded as a spokesman for a stratum of humanity that had never before had a voice, and seen by the literary-minded as a deeply ironic and knowing minimalist in whose deceptively simple texts lay the profoundest of metaphors. Even taken together, the two positions offered an incomplete view of this bluff yet saturnine author, who in any case went on to progress far beyond the damaged language and expressionistic violence of his early plays. (He now calls those works "naive," which he means as a description, not a value judgement.) American theater people, as he is acutely aware, tend to know little about his work from the 1980s, and my conversation with him picked up on the question of remedying that situation.

"Since you have a theater system in which one can't earn money as a serious writer," he says, "I'm not interested in the United States, because financially there's nothing for me to accomplish. It really is financially uninteresting, 500 dollars here, 1000 dollars there . . . There's no system conducive to modern theater." Surely it doesn't *only* have to do with money, though. "What else should it have to do with?" retorts the communist. "What do you live on?"

And the productions that do take place here, such as JoAnne Akalaitis's *Through the Leaves*—is he at least happy about them? "I wrote that play in 1970. Do you really think it still interests me today? I find it good when it's done, that's okay, but it doesn't tear me off the stool." Lately, he's been busy with the premiere of his newest play, entitled *Bauerntheater* (roughly *Provincial Theater*, without the pejorative connotation) in homage to the milieu in which he began performing, and discussing old texts seems absurd to him.

I point out that, despite significant mountings outside New York of *Mensch Meier*, *Nicht Fisch Nicht Fleisch* (*Neither Fish nor Fowl*) and a few other plays, he has garnered most attention in this country from Akalaitis's versions of *Wunschkonzert* (*Request Concert*) and *Through the Leaves*, both of which originated at Women's Interart Center. What is his opinion, for example, of Akalaitis's decision to set the action of the latter play in Queens rather than Bavaria, for which a number of critics upbraided her?

"Thank God," he answers. "I find the worst thing is when I squeeze myself into an airplane, get out 10,000 kilometers later, ready to drop, get picked up, brought to a theater, and then see a production that, in fact, I could see done much better in Munich . . . I beseech the theaters, the translators, the directors: take it, if you can use it, for your political fights, or whatever other fights you have. When you choose a play by me, change it, bring it totally onto the level of your society. Just don't make a display case! That's the most repugnant!" His plays have been performed in forty countries and translated into twenty-seven languages, he explains, and he no longer has any desire to keep close tabs on what directors and theaters do. "My only desire is that it not take place in any empty cultural field."

Of course, he still hasn't really said whether he likes Akalaitis's production (recently restaged as part of a retrospective of the work of Mabou Mines). *Through the Leaves*, which deals with the chillingly unromantic love affair between an independent female butcher and a lazy, brutish packing-plant worker, is actually Akalaitis and translator Roger Downey's stage adaptation of a radio play Kroetz wrote in 1976, based on his own earlier stage material. "I was extremely impressed in Jerusalem," says the author, speaking of the first time he saw the production at a festival in 1986. "Now I think it's become a little too soft, a little too fast. Because it's in such a large house, it's somewhat changed, a little less mysterious, less poetic, more 'television.' But those are nuances. It is very good work."

Critics are fond of quoting a particular remark from early in Kroetz's career: "Language shouldn't be the central element in drama." Does he still feel that way? "I think that's changed," he says, "because over the past twenty years I've naturally come to see that the silence of the early plays . . . well, only a certain portion of humanity really does that. A much larger portion, right here in the cities, chatters incessantly. There's incessant talking, which is also another form of silence . . . In my last three or four plays, which have to do with intellectuals, artists, I've tried to unmask them by means of a lot of language—a lot of idle talk, a lot of articulation about themselves. So yes, the linguistic element in my plays has grown, the plays have become longer. They've become fatter."

Another standard critical assumption is that his attitude changes toward language have been directly connected to his political reversals—for instance, that he gave up "flat realism" when he gave up the Communist Party. He seems impatient at being asked about this. "In the past ten years the poetical has interested me far more than the political, if you want to take it that way. I write for myself. I write because for me it's a way of thinking. Writing is, for me, public thinking. . . . Theater really is no way to arouse society, to say nothing of offending it or changing it. That's just ridiculous." What is it, then? "Theater is a wonderful way of making questions experiential. You can't *answer* the questions, though; if you answer them, no one wants to know. I always mistrusted the theater as a political vehicle."

Political or not, Kroetz's vision of theater has, according to him, fallen "completely out of fashion" in Germany during the 1980s. "In the coming season, in the entire German-speaking world, I will be performed at only one theater, so it's safe to say that I'm completely forgotten in the German theater. I barely exist." He insists this is not because he has written less, although that is true, but because of changes in the theater itself. In the past few years, all the productions he's seen in and around Munich have been "boring," and he's left at intermission. To the question, "What directors are important to you?", he answers: "No directors are important. The theater isn't reacting to the social circumstances. The theater became a museum in the '80s. There are no contemporary dramatists, and if there are, they're seldom performed. I'm not interested in how someone like Shakespeare reacts to the problematic of the reunification. That's too soft for me. I find that dumb."

Interestingly, he says little about the reunification itself, though he does seem generally happy about the opening of Eastern Europe, where his work has only recently been played for the first time. (Noteworthy exceptions are Yugoslavia, where he has always had productions, and the GDR, where he was played up to the time of his withdrawal from the Communist Party.) Four books by Kroetz will be published in the next year: a travel book about Brazil and Peru, a book of poetry, a reprint of his earlier work on Nicaragua, and the play *Bauerntheater*—which he says isn't producible because it has small children in large roles. "In the past few years I've earned my money mostly as an actor, though, and a television actor at that," he adds.

Kroetz has not only performed on television in his own plays but has also had a regular role on the nationally broadcast series *Kir Royal* (named after a liqueur). New episodes of *Kir Royal* are no longer made, but the series was a blockbuster success from its beginning, is frequently re-run, and in his home country he is far more famous as the fictional high-society gossip columnist Baby Schimmerlos than he is as a real-life playwright. On the streets of New York, he says, German tourists approach him for autographs, calling out, "Hello, Herr Schimmerlos!"

How has his television career affected his writing? Not at all, he claims, apart from the obvious fact that he's written less. Others have quite vocally disagreed, however, saying that his rise to fame as a pop-culture star has indeed transformed him. A page-one article in *Theater heute* last October, entitled *"Kir Banal*: Franz Xaver Kroetz, An Obituary during Lifetime," denounced him by quoting (from newspapers and tabloids) sundry embarrassing off-hand comments he'd made over the years.

Kroetz is indeed a man who places no value whatever on being politic, on carefully measuring his words in the presence of journalists—and actually, there is an endearing quality in that candor. He appears to have been told so often during his youth that his authentic naiveté was a form of genius that, as he got older, he continued to embrace a certain careless behavior as a virtue. "My immortality is ensured," he told an interviewer in 1989.

And what are his newest plays like, the ones he has found time to write in recent years? One has the self-explanatory title *Der Dichter als Schwein* (*The Poet as a Swine*). Another is called *Bauern Sterben* (*Farmers Die*), a willfully unconventional "dramatic fragment" set "somewhere between Landshut and Calcutta" and written in an artificial dialect—a combination of East Tirolean, Bavarian, and Alemannic—that even Bavarians can't understand. The 1985 work *Der Nusser* is an epigrammatic, allegorical adaptation of Ernst Toller's *Hinkemann*, a 1922 expressionist drama about a man who all too literally loses his manhood in war. And still another, the title of which he doesn't mention, he describes at length.

"It's similar to *Request Concert* but with another premise. I've taken a writer—a huge monologue in his kitchen—who tries every morning, first of all, to write a good chapter. Then he tries to write a good sentence, then a good word would do, and at the end of the monologue he's drunk and hasn't written anything. A completely normal prose monologue: the situation of the writer. Why must we always depict the problems of the 'worker'? Why not a writer for a change? When a writer can't write he has it exactly as bad as someone who's unemployed. That was a problem. I've depicted simply the normal, daily misery of the unemployed, a writer who can't work, who goes to piss and misses because he's so drunk, who behaves completely like someone living in the filth on the street, and who goes to pieces."

Is this text—or any of the others, for that matter—autobiographical? It was in the aforementioned 1985 interview that Kroetz pronounced, "I don't want to hide anymore but rather write a play directly about myself, about a forty-year old in my present condition." "No," he now says quickly. "I haven't written a play about myself—but I *have* written about writers."

A Coupla White Guys Sittin' Aroun' Talkin'

A Conversation with Stanley Kauffmann

I've been asked to chat with you about what is or ever was valuable in the Off-Broadway and Off-Off Broadway theaters.* Do you detect a slightly funereal aroma in this?

I see the Off-Broadway and Off-Off Broadway theaters operating in the garments of legacy. There is a sense of continuing rather than propelling. In the earliest days of Off-Broadway and Off-Off Broadway—they started within seven or eight years of each other—there was a sense of bursting creativity, of things rushing into life. Some cheery souls even called it a new Elizabethan age. Those theaters blossomed for something over 20 years. The original impulses have long since waned, have been diluted by various factors, and there isn't much sense of pioneering about those theaters anymore. There's a sense of continuance, a feeling of persistence, and perhaps that's where the funereal aroma comes from. I have to add that I don't go to those theaters as much as I used to, but I get that feeling from reading the *Voice* and from conversations with people like you.

What was the most valuable contribution these two kinds of theater made?

The shift in values they brought about. When I was growing up, when I first began going to the theater before the Second World War, there were no such things as these theaters. There was some activity in Greenwich Village—the Provincetown Playhouse and the Neighborhood Playhouse, although these had withered—but anyone who wanted to work in the theater had only one place to aim toward, and that was Broadway. The latest, smart, commercially minded playwright aimed there, and Eugene O'Neill aimed there, too. That was all there was. The rise of these two other theaters brought a widening of the spectrum and a pluralism in opportunities so that a change of values could be put into effect. Before Off-Broadway and Off-Off Broadway arose, you might have decried and despised Broadway, but that was it. Now there were other options. Of the two most prominent American playwrights of the last twenty-five years, David Mamet never had a play produced on Broadway until very far along in his career. Sam Shepard not yet. Their goals were elsewhere.

These other theaters made possible the crystallization of different kinds of ambition—one of the most important crystallizing forces, incidentally, was Joseph Papp. Before the war you really had the feeling that there was a high, glistening steel wall around the theater, and only by luck could some people get over it or find a crack in it. By what he instituted, Papp made every young person interested in the theater feel: "If you have ability, you will find a place to use it." He changed what seemed to be a jealously guarded preserve into a field of open possibility that depended more on you than on approval from guardians on high.

Could you name some specific high points for you during the heyday of Off- and Off-Off-Broadway?

Something that's often overlooked is that their greatest achievements were not a result of jobbing around but rather the work of institutions like the Living Theater and the Open Theater. In the Living Theater, in its early days, you felt that a new kind of blood had flowed into the body of the theater, a new kind of enterprise, a new reason for being. One of the best-directed plays I've ever seen was *The Brig* in the early 1960s, done by Judith Malina, which gave me a glimpse of a vitality that wasn't available anywhere else in this city at that time. *The Brig* was the kind of production that you came away from with a sense of replenishment and a kind of surprise. The Open Theater's *The Serpent*, directed by Joseph Chaikin, still lives in my memory. I thought I was going to hate Andrei Serban's *Fragments of a Trilogy*, which he did with his La Mama company, but it was a transformative experience. I went back about eight times in the succeeding years. Serban would be waiting there when I came out to tick off the number on his fingers: "Number five!" "Number six!" That was one of the best things that ever happened to me in the theater. I thought that that company under Serban was going to be an exemplary force in the American theater. As I understood it, he went off on jobs and the company waited on unemployment insurance for him to come back and continue working with them, but he stopped coming back and they disbanded. I consider the disappearance of that company the greatest sin of the non-Broadway theater. This past January I went to France to see Mnouchkine's production of three Greek plays, and it was absolutely thrilling in every serious sense of that word. But it was also sad, because I thought, "This is what the Serban company might have been if it had worked together under one leader for as long as the Mnouchkine company."

People of my generation can admire certain achievements of those years, through books, films, or other sorts of reports, but we have trouble believing a lot of the lofty rhetoric. The communalist ethic, the sensualist ethic—it's all very hard to swallow after the fall of the Berlin Wall in the age of AIDS. Furthermore, whenever I hear the Off- or Off-Off Broadway theater described as a haven of cozy laboratory experimentation I have to laugh, because I've worked in some of those theaters and I know it's anything but safe or cozy there.

Yes. I'm sure that's true. Although some of them still talk about "the right to fail." How I hate that phrase.

So let me ask you: what was real and what was rhetoric in all those claims about using the greater intimacy between audience and stage to develop a new sense of community?

It's right for you to entertain doubts, because reminiscence is always tinged with a kind of ego. "You missed it; I didn't." But if I may reminisce, egotistically, it seems to me that there *was* a real sense of community there—a community derived from a simple proposition: there exists a hateful middle class which owns the commercial theater and we're here to uproot it, dynamite it. That simple war doesn't exist anymore. No one's revolting against Broadway anymore. In sheerly artistic terms, no one's revolting against the middle class anymore. I mean, what more trite kind of theatrical enterprise could there be today than to do something that exposes the Rotarian aspects of society? It would bore the avant-garde itself, let alone anyone else. Our vital theater is trying to finds ways to be healthily aggressive, healthily purgative, and the battlefield lacks terrain. Instead of fighting to cure this or that, most people are fighting to find out what to fight about.

Maybe you're right, but I don't feel that the problem is lack of talent. I know some extremely talented, even brilliant, people. A more important factor for me is that New York City has become a place where the sort of people who once supported this art can't survive. It used to be possible to maintain a bohemian lifestyle in the Village, working at odd jobs and so on. Now the ostensibly "alternative" scene is filled with people so busy scratching the rent together they barely have time to think about art, NYU students shooting film, and an army of recent college grads with rich parents willing to support their desire to act bohemian. For those not born to privilege it has become too harsh and unforgiving a place to concentrate on anything. I once said to Jim Leverett that people my age always had the feeling of arriving just after the party ended. He shot back, "Make a new party, Jonathan." I should have answered, "That's easy for someone your age to say."

You've put your finger on something very important. New York in the 1950s was more or less what it had been in the preceding part of this century—that is, a white, middle-class city. And Greenwich Village was what it had been historically in the days of O'Neill and Edna St. Vincent Millay, only brought a little up to date. We now live in a radically changed city, racially and in many other ways, and New York is really trying to find out what it is. In the midst of all this turbulence and turmoil there's no possibility of anything like a bohemian life. The demographics have changed, and consequently so have the cultural obligations.

Can we talk about those obligations? The word for all this is multiculturalism, which many people think should ideally involve a form of affirmative action, since certain people, even whole classes of people, were previously excluded from being heard. What do you believe?

Here's the time for a large pronouncement. I certainly do believe they were excluded and that something should be done about it, provided—and this is a heavy proviso—that artistic standards don't get lowered. Why shouldn't every racial group, every sexual group, every political group have cultural representation? These people have the energy to counteract the funereal air we were talking about at the start; they're greatly beneficial so long as they aren't praised just because they are of whatever race or persuasion they are.

Are you saying that you see a relaxing of standards for the sake of inclusion?

I certainly do, in education, in the theater, and everywhere else. We won't go into the subject of hiring faculty people by reason of gender and color of skin, because it inevitably sounds as if I'm against the other gender or certain colors of skin—which is not at all what I mean. It's a given that there's no going back for society. We're not going to return to a completely white, completely heterosexual (on the surface) city. What we have to do is go forward, keeping the *best* of what we've learned from the past in operation for the benefit of everyone concerned. Otherwise there's no point in the theater existing. Put the money into bridges and hospitals if we're not going to do this. The theaters must exist at their best according to the best of our tradition.

But you know the problem here. Whose standards are to be used in determining what is "best"? Those of white male Stanley Kauffmann or white male Jonathan Kalb?

No, it's myself and yourself as two of the inheritors of a world tradition that's funneled down and crystallized through centuries of the European American tradition. Of course, I'm not saying there are absolute standards of good and bad, but surely there's not much question about the areas of art in which the highest standards operate, where they come from, what they tend toward. When a group with a specialized interest says that other standards must prevail, they know they are rejecting the tradition, which has been growing for at least 5000 years in the Western world and which made them possible. The standards of X theater, which says that it is not going to be dominated by white, heterosexual, European inheritance, are consciously disruptive of a historical line, which I hope will always be open to growth but which I take to be fundamentally nourishing. It's very difficult to talk about this without sounding prescriptive, but any man or woman of whatever ethnic background or sexual persuasion who is cultivated in the Western tradition at its broadest, most humane, most liberal, most helpful, understands what this is about. And when they choose not to engage that understanding, they are often doing it for non-artistic reasons. And I think the theater is a poor place to do things for nonartistic reasons.

I marvel at your courage in defending the Western tradition so unrestrainedly. I guess you don't have to worry about being called "old." Lately, I find myself increasingly forced to answer questions like this in the most unfriendly circumstances. So many people my age or younger, white by birth, "of color" by conviction, believe that the Enlightenment is necessarily something imposed from above and enforced by institutions with exclusive policies. How do you respond to, say, a graduate student who believes he or she is of a revolutionary state of mind?

If you want to indulge in the 20th century pipe dream of revolutionary explosion, then you're bound to end up at an impasse. I think that's just a form of narcotic. I think it's been woefully proved to be so. Our world may disappear, but I doubt that it'll be through that kind of political explosion. Look, this is very large, very inclusive, very sweeping, and I suppose ultimately ridiculous, what I've just been saying, because it's so easy to ridicule. But in art it seems to me that the real triumph for all those groups—Asian people, black people, brown people, homosexual people—is not to splinter away from the best of the past but to enter into it, reshape it, renew it. This is obviously—I hope obviously—not to say that there shouldn't be black theater, Jewish theater, Asian or homosexual or feminist or any other kind of theater, each with its own thematic agenda. It's only to say that the artistic progress of those groups, in my view, is not in fragmentation. It's in taking possession of what there is to take possession of.

After centuries of abuse, though, it's perfectly understandable that disadvantaged groups would jump at real chances for power and hegemony, and the real chance for power in the theater lies in the smaller institutions of Off- and Off-Off-Broadway. The non-Broadway theater world is as preoccupied with power struggles as with aesthetic struggles, and that situation shows little sign of changing. What is it that you and I think we're upholding in such an environment?

Nothing about the power struggle—anyway, not as far as I'm concerned. But a good deal about the aesthetic struggle. We want the disadvantaged to have the best of what they've been shut out of, to add to it, not diminish it, to give to it and to get. To serve their causes by, so to speak, beating the mainstream at its own game. To take a foreign example: a woman who wanted to shake the theater awake, to dramatize political and social views, and who shamed the orthodox theater by beating it at its own game, Ariane Mnouchkine.

ENDS AND ODDS

The Mediated
Quixote

No epoch-making artist simply accepts his or her means of artmaking as handed down from previous artists. From Aristophanes to Michelangelo to Shakespeare to Molière to Picasso to Beckett, all can be seen (sometimes only in retrospect) to have engaged in lifelong critiques of their working media. This is never in itself a reliable indicator of greatness, and in 20th century art—which, high and low, good and bad, has been preoccupied with reflexivity—it is an especially poor one. Sometimes, however, an artist's critique is so confident, thoroughgoing, and persuasive that it causes significant change in the public's idea of what a particular medium is, or can be. As critics have frequently pointed out, Beckett's stage plays actually changed many people's notions of what can happen, or is supposed to happen, when they enter a theater.

Due to a number of factors, the same claim cannot be made about his works for radio, film, and television, which have had far less influence than the theater works. First, Beckett's media plays (as these are now irrevocably called; why and when theater ceased being a medium is a mystery) have had far less circulation. Rarely produced or rebroadcast after their premieres, they are largely inaccessible except as published scripts, which are in many cases coldly schematic guides to creating artworks rather than completed artworks themselves. Second and more fundamental, all three media are too young to have had much experience of significant change, their brief histories being dominated by distrust of alternatives to commercial programming, though this is less true in radio, and still less so in film. For an artist of Beckett's uncompromising temperament to turn his attention to any of them—especially television, in the second decade of its global domination— is for him virtually to ensure that his efforts will be marginal.

If one happens to be Samuel Beckett, however, marginalism isn't necessarily pernicious. "Success and failure on the public level never mattered much to me," he wrote to Alan Schneider, his American director, in 1956; "in fact I feel much more at home with the latter, having breathed deep of its vivifying air all my writing life."[1] In 1949, Beckett had argued in *Three Dialogues*, a text on painting, that a certain kind of creative failure had moral value: "to be an artist is to fail, as no other dare fail. . . failure is his world and the shrink from it desertion."[2] In other words, he seemed to say, lack of notoriety and influence mean nothing if they stem from monastic dedication, or from quixotic straining after some inner image of perfection. The novelist Robert Coover, comparing Beckett with the character Don Quixote, once described the enduring fascination commanded by "the impotent old clown caught up in the mad toils of earnestness"—implying that, even in those arenas where Beckett won worldly success, it might be more appropriate and fruitful to speak of his field of impotence, not influence.[3]

The point is, despite its relative lack of influence, Beckett's gaze at radio, film, and television was just as piercing as it was at theater; in fact, in some ways these media suited him better. In his perpetual search for purer and purer distillations of expression, the professional theater, with its endless ego-battles, financial hassles and publicity pressures, was never an ideal working environment. Now and then he would put up with the public eye, in an effort to see his works realized according to his original vision, but it caused him much discomfort; the experience of travelling to New York for a film shoot in 1964, for instance, was so hard on him that he never again considered working in film or returning to the United States. Two other points are probably of more crucial importance, though: (1) a perfectionist is better served by recordable media than by live media because the former offer the chance to freeze and preserve (nearly) perfect performances for posterity; and (2) the distinctive formal issues associated with these media— questions of subjective versus objective point of view, the benevolence or malevolence of the camera eye, and so on—coincide surprisingly well with many lifelong preoccupations of Beckett's, such as the agonistic themes of darkness and light, sound and silence, and the problems of veracity and subjective identity in fictional narrative.

Moreover, the progression from radio to film to television in his career also involves a movement toward increasingly pure distillation. To borrow a phrase from *Footfalls*, Beckett seems to have spent years "revolving it all" imperfectly in various genres and media[4]—"it" being that totalized or essen- tialized artistic statement usually achieved once, if ever, in an artist's life- time—until finding, in his seventh decade, a means of getting "it" right (or, again, nearly) once and forever. In what follows, my emphasis will be on what appear to be Beckett's general aims, the "it" or "its" he was reaching toward both in each medium and in the three media as a progressive se- quence.

Radio

The story of Beckett's introduction to radio drama has been told by numer- ous commentators, notably Martin Esslin and Clas Zilliacus, who provide valuable information about the circumstances of Beckett's first contacts with the BBC in the early 1950s and his subsequent "commission" to write *All That Fall* in 1956.[5] Between the lines in these accounts is the implication that Beckett's motivation for working in radio, and perhaps some aspects of his first radio play, were already clear in his mind when the BBC suggested he contribute something to its Third Programme. Disembodied voices, particularly the sort that act as goads to the imagination, had been an important feature in his prose fiction for years, and in retrospect it seems only natural that he would eventually make use of a medium in which dramas could be peopled entirely with invisible characters. The invisible as persistent prod to the visible, absence and silence as indispensable integuments for what is present and audible: these were trademark formal features in his work by the time he set about writing *All That Fall*.

"Whenever he makes the test of a new medium, Beckett always seems to take a few steps backward [toward naturalism]," wrote John Spurling in 1972.[6] At first it may seem strange to apply to radio a concept so bound up with stage pictorialism as naturalism, but anyone comparing *All That Fall* with the radio plays that followed it would understand at once what was meant. Unlike the later plays, *All That Fall* could be seen as a quaint aural picture of provincial Ireland around the turn of the century. To see it exclusively that way would be superficial, of course, but Beckett's free use of Irishisms (the play marks his return to English after a decade of writing in French) and the considerable trouble he took over details of local atmosphere cannot be ignored.

Also, as Esslin notes, in the prodigious literature of radio drama it would be difficult to find a work more concerned with visual textures than *All That Fall*. The play, which tells a relatively straightforward story set in a fictional but recognizably Irish town called Boghill, is dense with tactile references: "let me just flop down flat on the road like a big fat jelly out of a bowl"; "As if I were a bale"; "You are quivering like a blancmange"—all of these, incidentally, references to the central character, Maddy Rooney. The story follows old Maddy through various encounters with local residents as she goes to meet her blind husband Dan at the railway station, dwells for a while at the station as Dan's train is delayed, and then follows the Rooneys on their way home. The reason for the delay is the plot's one suspense element, and in the last line, when a subsidiary character reveals that an accident occurred involving a child who fell onto the tracks, the suspicion arises (due to scattered hints earlier) that Dan was in some way responsible for it.

Zilliacus has called this work "Beckett's *To Damascus*, a station drama portraying the passion of Maddy Rooney," and that description is helpful as long as one also understands that the "passion" is fraught with satire and accompanied by several other, peculiarly Beckettian structuring devices.[7] (The train-station/station-of-the-cross pun would certainly be typical of Beckett.) The play's first half is quite as much preoccupied with filling time and remarking on language as with revealing Maddy's personality—or soul, to continue the passion allusion—while she moves through her chance meetings-cum-stations, whereas the second half is a drama of delay on the model of *Waiting for Godot*: Beckett premises the action on a mystery and then makes it impossible for us to confirm or deny our suspicions about it. The play is constantly *not* satisfying the desire for information it generates and ultimately leaves us to discover for ourselves that the ambiguities and uncertainties surrounding the planted hints—such detective-fiction questions as whether or not the ball in Dan's hand belonged to the accident victim—are left intentionally open.

Informational considerations quickly become secondary, in any case, when one listens to *All That Fall*. The primary experience of the play in performance is of a sound-world that does not attempt to convince us of its veracity except as a product of Maddy's (and Beckett's) imagination. The "rural sounds" at the opening, for instance ("Sheep, bird, cow, cock, severally, then together"), which return later, are not only flagrantly artificial in themselves—they were radio drama clichés even in 1956—but are also continually used in ways that remind us of their radiophonic origin; animals and objects greet Maddy's mention of them with absurd efficiency and dispatch. Zilliacus writes that Beckett intends to contrast "the imperturbability of the animal sound systems" with the myriad anxieties associated with human language;[8] "Do you find anything. . . bizarre about my way of speaking?" asks Maddy of Christy, her first conversation partner. In any case, Beckett also clearly intends to suggest that the entire action may take place in Maddy's mind.

The quality of Maddy's voice in the first BBC production, directed by Donald McWhinnie, supports this. The actress Mary O'Farrell speaks closer to the microphone than the other actors, as if in confidence to the listener, and she often talks over the beginnings and ends of others' lines, delivering Maddy's numerous non sequiturs in a way that implies that others (including Dan) have no reality for her except insofar as they further her ongoing mental composition. As Esslin writes, Maddy's journey "has a nightmare quality; it might indeed be a bad dream"; we are never entirely sure, however, whether it is her dream or ours.[9] (It should also be mentioned that her nightmarish isolated condition is often said to be emblematic of the biblical fallen state. "'The Lord upholdeth all that fall and raiseth up all those that be bowed down,' " she says late in the action, after which she and Dan join in "wild laughter." The play's sundry references to falling mostly deflate the biblical conceit, reducing fateful misfortunes to clownish pratfalls, and death-and-damnation imagery to sexual innuendo.)

Maddy's conversations with her neighbors (and their dialogue exchanges with each other) notwithstanding, the action of *All That Fall* is propelled by her monologuing. As with many other Beckett works, the idea that the central speaker may really be alone generates a network of underlying questions and themes related to the notion of "company": can the imagination provide sufficient company to alleviate loneliness, especially the writer's special brand of that malady? When the artist is truly honest with himself, what can he say he knows for certain, or presume to depict outside the interior landscape of his skull? The subtext and formal features of *All That Fall* convey the substantial content, through means similar to that Pierre Chabert has identified in *Endgame*:

> Words emanate from silence and return to it; movement emanates from immobility and returns to it. All movements, all gestures move, so to speak, within immobility, are a victory over immobility and have value only in the tension they maintain in relationship to immobility.[10]

All That Fall, which begins and ends with the image of an old woman alone in a house, playing Schubert's "Death and the Maiden," emanates from lonely silence and returns to it, achieving forward movement as a victory over a sort of fundamental paralysis. Maddy is constantly on the verge of stasis, inanition, not going on, the local cause of which is fits of sadness associated with memories of "little Minnie" (apparently her dead daughter), the chronic cause of which is much more general and profound. "Oh to be in atoms, in atoms!" she says "frenziedly" at one point, as if her problems were traceable somehow to her existence as a coherently assembled human.

The play keeps on being detoured, derailed, by quasi-philosophical discourses that ultimately have to do with Maddy's fears, and the greatest of her fears is, apparently, of disappearance. Each time she feels ignored in a conversation she interrupts petulantly after a moment and asserts her existence: "Do not imagine, because I am silent, that I am not present." Anthropomorphically speaking, even language itself ignores her as it goes about its business, forming expressions that become common to others' ears but remain strange to hers. Like O in *Film*, however, Maddy also has a conflicting fear of "perceivedness," of being seen; confronted with a hinny that won't stop gazing at her, for instance, she suggests moving out of its "field of vision."

Beckett's primary focus in this uncharacteristically populous play, in other words, is a strange condition of precarious suspension between existence and non-existence, which radio is ideally suited to explore. "Only the present speaker's presence is certain [in radio]," writes Zilliacus; "the primary condition of existence for a radio character is that he talk."[11] Hence the author's famous objection to the idea of presenting *All That Fall* onstage: "whatever quality it may have . . . depends on the whole thing's *coming out of the dark*," he wrote in a 1957 letter to his American publisher.[12] Artistic constructions based on the solipsistic notion of people and things jumping willy-nilly in and out of existence simply cannot function in fleshy, concrete media.

Embers, Beckett's next radio play, is a transitional work in which conventional plotting and recognizability of place have been sacrificed even though a strong interest in tactile pictorialism is still apparent. Unlike *All That Fall*, in which a modest interpretive effort is necessary to see beyond the surface narrative about a nattering old woman, *Embers* has no surface narrative other than that of a haunted man talking about talking to himself, telling stories that he never finishes, and sometimes aurally experiencing (along with us) the ghostly people and things in his stories. Written in 1959, *Embers* opens with the sound of a man's boots "on shingle" and the sound of the sea, at first "scarcely audible," then incrementally louder. Henry, the man, is wrestling with his imagination—a spectacle we witness in the form of sound-effect commands barked out as if to obedient radio technicians: "Hooves! [*Sound of hooves walking on hard road. They die rapidly away. Pause.*] Again! [*Hooves as before.*]"

Henry, who may or may not be walking by the sea with his daughter Addie nearby, addresses his dead father, who may or may not have committed suicide in the sea. The father fails to respond—the text implies that he occasionally does respond at other times—and Henry tells a story about a man named Bolton (perhaps a father-surrogate) who has called for his doctor Holloway one winter night, for obscure reasons that may have to do with wanting to die. Henry then speaks to a woman, also apparently dead, named Ada, his former companion and mother of Addie, who speaks sympathetically but distractedly back to him. For most of the remainder of the action Ada and Henry reminisce about old times, some of which are dramatized as auditory flashbacks involving other characters. Henry complains several times of not being able to rid himself of the sound of the sea, and Ada suggests that he consult Holloway about both that and his incessant talking to himself. When Ada no longer answers him, Henry tries unsuccessfully to command the sound effects again, returns briefly to the Bolton story, and then ends by seeming to make a note in his diary: "Nothing, all day nothing. [*Pause.*] All day all night nothing. [*Pause.*] Not a sound."

It is probably safe to say that the word "nothing" in Beckett's work must never be taken literally. "Nothing" is invariably his way of referring to not quite nothing—his favorite designation for something depleted, waning, but still there, or else for that enormous, ineffable something always left to express after the artist's "power to express" has been exhausted. ("*Nothing is more real than nothing*," says Malone.[13]) The words "not a sound" are both a lie (after all, we listeners have heard a great deal and so has Henry) and the truth (the play ends at that point, and whatever Henry heard was something other than sound if it occurred in his head). In *Embers*, as elsewhere, Beckett employs linguistic duplicity as an example of, and metaphor for, all that is ephemeral and unverifiable in life. Like the hearthfire burnt down to embers behind Bolton—the word "embers," repeated several times in the play, is usually accompanied by the phrase "not a sound"—Henry's imaginative stratagems for fending off the looming maw of nothingness, symbolized by the omnipresent sound of the sea, are always growing thin but never exhausted.

Embers is also transitional in that it contains in embryo many of the reflexive formal games that Beckett would later focus on obsessively in the radio plays (the exception being *Rough for Radio II*), the television plays, and the middle and late prose fiction. Both Henry's closing lines and his opening line, "On," for instance, are as much simple technical references to the play's beginning and ending as they are orders to his mind or descriptions of its activities. In Everett Frost's 1988 production, actress Billie Whitelaw's singsongy, confidently feeble, self-consciously spectral voice made especially clear that Henry switches Ada on and off, and removed all possibility of her being understood as a physically present conversation partner independent of Henry.

The switching word, "open," which later plays an important part in *Cascando*, also appears in *Embers* and again recalls the issue of "company" mentioned above: after seeing Holloway through the window, Bolton "goes down and opens." To open one's house or mind, either to someone or to the memory of someone, is to interrupt the bliss of solitude and silence that the Beckett hero always longs for but never quite possesses (and never finds to be bliss after stealing a taste of it—e.g. after death). Like *Krapp's Last Tape*, in which a 69-year-old switches back and forth over the same bit of audiotape, listening to himself whispering "Let me in" to the memory of an old lover's eyes; like . . . *but the clouds* . . . , whose climactic moment is a man blurting out "Look at me" to the remembered image of a woman; like *What Where*, in which the main character punctuates the dialogue with the phrases "I switch on" and "I switch off" and, after obscure interactions with other characters who look conspicuously like him, says, "I am alone"—like these and many other Beckett works, *Embers* poses an irresolvable dilemma concerning the relative values of solitude and companionship. The protagonist wants his imagined creations to exist as concretely and satisfyingly as corporeal companions but then to go away, to switch off, at less than a moment's notice.

The explicit association of mechanistic switching with the engagement of the imagination, which would become one of the most fruitful metaphors of Beckett's later career, is one of two salient distinguishing features of the last three radio plays, *Words and Music*, *Cascando* and *Rough for Radio I* (the latter an early study for *Cascando* whose performance Beckett discouraged). The other feature is the introduction of music as an autonomous character, which also anticipates another important later development, primarily in the media work: collapse of faith in verbal language. The author himself drew attention on several occasions to musical structures in his plays (*Endgame* as "a string quartet," *Play* as "a score for five pitches," for instance[14]), and even if he had written nothing but novels and stories it would be clear from the cadences and phrasings of his prose that he possessed a highly developed musical sensibility. In the final radio plays, however, he does not so much embrace music as an overarching structural concept that subsumes writing as rather pit music against language in a dramatic showdown over their relative merits.

Written in 1961 as a collaboration with a specific composer, the author's cousin John Beckett, *Words and Music* begins with the sound of a small orchestra tuning up and a man's voice competing for air space as he too "tunes up," reciting sentences by rote describing "the passion of sloth." A crotchety man named Croak shuffles on, refers to Words as "Joe," to Music as "Bob," and enjoins them: "My comforts! Be friends!" Croak turns out to be an impresario of sorts who thumps a club on the ground and barks orders to Words and Music, alternately and together, to entertain him by illustrating first the concept of love, and then that of age. The two "comforts" or "balms" compete to satisfy him, Music playing love- and age-themes, Words reciting more rote formulations, poems and nostalgic descriptions of a woman's face, which cause the impresario to groan and cry out "Lily!" at one point. In the end he shuffles off as if unable to bear the memories the descriptions awaken, and Words and Music are left alone, Words sighing, Music repeating one of his last phrases (an illustration of "that wellhead" deep within Lily's eyes).

Unlike Dan or Ada, Words and Music prove to be at least partly independent of the central imagining agent in their play, Croak. They do not always obey him, they are heard before he enters and after he leaves, and it is possible in the end to read them as muses, creative forces in their own right living their own noumenal lives. This work, then, fits the general trend of the radio dramas toward focusing on communicative means, which muses (among other things) incontestably are. *Words and Music* also presents a special problem, however: its action consists of a relatively conventional dialogic exchange, but the dialogue is missing half its lines—lines that the play implies should match, sentence for sentence, in musical terms, the specificity and subtlety of Beckett's language.

It is hardly surprising that neither his cousin nor subsequent composers have been up to the task. In one case (John Beckett's score) the music proved unable to communicate ideas specific enough to qualify as rational lines, much less repartée, and in another (Morton Feldman's score for Frost's 1988 production) the composer came to feel constrained by the text's requirements. In the director's words, Feldman struggled "in the face of the imposed concisions." Frost adds:

> I do not mean to imply that I am in any way regretful . . . Such is emphatically not the case. But with this play more than the others, it will take several productions with a variety of musics before we can feel reliably that we have begun to get to the bottom of its complex and interesting possibilities.[15]

But the play's production difficulties run far deeper than questions of agreement in style; unless Music convinces us that it has at least held its own in the strange mimetic competition with Words, the action of the play lacks dramatic tension. Beckett once reportedly said to Theodor Adorno that *Words and Music* "ends unequivocally with the victory of the music."[16] Yet far from proving the superiority of music as pure sound, liberated from rational ideas and references, the play confines it to a function very similar to that of a filmic signature score. *Cascando*, written in French a month or so later, seems planned explicitly to overcome this mimetic limitation.

Cascando is also a collaborative work for which Beckett did not write the necessary music. This time his first collaborator was the Rumanian-born Marcel Mihalovici (who had previously written an opera based on *Krapp's Last Tape*) and the original *Cascando* on French radio (RTF) was considerably more "operatic" (meaning more extensively orchestrated) than any other Beckett radio production before or since. With this play, however, even a seemingly weighty matter like extent of orchestration *can* remain a question of style, because Beckett's text does not require music to function as a conventional conversation partner. In fact, the characters Voice and Music operate virtually independently of each other.

Like *Words and Music*, *Cascando* has a central imagining agent, named Opener, but he takes a much softer approach with his muses than Croak does. Instead of barking specific orders, Opener calmly speaks the generalized phrases "I open" and "I close," and the action that follows is more like tandem or parallel monologues than dialogue. Sometimes Voice and Music start and stop without Opener's explicit sanction, and some of Opener's lines imply that Voice and Music occasionally work together to a common purpose—"as though they had linked their arms"—although this is unverifiable in the text. Music's part is indicated only by dots extending across the page like a long ellipsis, and Voice's consists of a frequently interrupted story which he cannot finish and which he isn't sure is "the right one" (like the narrators in the novels) about a man named Woburn, one of those quintessential, stumbling Beckett figures walking by the sea in a greatcoat. Opener speaks haughtily between the story sections, scoffing at the notion that he and Voice might really be the same character ("They say, He opens nothing, he has nothing to open, it's in his head"), and, of course, the more he insists that there is "No resemblance" the more we listeners suspect that there is.

From the outset, the central question in *Cascando* is not "who may speak?" but rather "when may *I* speak and with which voice?" Unlike in *Words and Music*, the characters do not begin by tuning or warming up, practicing for some future performance that will be more authentic or significant than this one. Cooperatively, they plunge straight into a concerted, multiform effort to finish a story, giving the present-tense action a greater urgency and forward momentum than any of the previous radio plays had—primarily because listeners don't spend time wondering about plot questions, such as why Words and Music don't cooperate. Like *Embers*, *Cascando* contains Beckett's first rethinking for performance of formal techniques originally cultivated in his stories and novels. Voice's relationship to his subject (read: surrogate self), for instance, is the same as Jacques Moran's in *Molloy*, E's in *Film*, and the spotlight's in *Play*, one of pursuit; Woburn is as much chased as described. Also, Opener's repeated denial that he is the storyteller (or, by extension, the story's subject) and Voice's constant self-interruption—each two- to four-word phrase is followed by an ellipsis—prefigure the self-denying, fragmentary character Mouth in *Not I* and Beckett's habit through the 1970s and 1980s of using the fragmentary as a metaphor for a damaged whole.

Most important, though, *Cascando* contains Beckett's purest distillation of the essence of the radio medium. The stage direction *Silence* appears twenty times in the eight-page play (more than in any other radio play except *All That Fall*, which is over three times longer), and a significant part of listening to a production is the experience of being returned again and again to one's own sound-space. With only the thinnest of fictional conceits—actors pretending to be characters, actors and characters pretending to be in places and times other than here and now—the author transports the ephemeral products of his imagination by the most ephemeral means (electronic waves and sound impulses) and makes them oscillate in a sort of minimalist dance between presence and absence, between "going on" (the "obligation to express") and what professionals call, usually without Beckettian irony, "dead air time." Of all media, radio offered Beckett—to use his own wry description of his writerly efforts—the purest opportunity to put a "blot on silence."[17]

Film

Like *All That Fall*, Beckett's one work for cinema has been frequently described as a "commission." In 1963 Barney Rosset, his American publisher, decided to expand into film producing and invited Beckett (as well as Harold Pinter and Eugène Ionesco) to write something for the medium. As with radio, however, it is unthinkable that Beckett would have turned his attention to film solely because an opportunity arose for immediate production. The text of *Film* shows that he had given the medium hard thought for some time; indeed, according to Deirdre Bair, his fascination with it dates back to 1935 when, as a young man searching for professional direction, he wrote to Sergei Eisenstein in Moscow asking to be hired as an apprentice.[18]

Film is, as Linda Ben-Zvi writes, "a film about film."[19] Its very title is generic, like that of *Play*, indicating that the work will deal with fundamental qualities or principles of its medium rather than simply use film as an unobtrusive storytelling vehicle. Unlike *Play*, however, *Film* was the first and only work Beckett wrote for the medium, and unlike *All That Fall* and *Eh Joe* (his first work for television), it was not originally produced under state-of-the-art studio conditions. To be sure, the published text contains wisdom about the medium, but technical naiveté on both Beckett's and director Alan Schneider's parts prevented some of it from surfacing in the completed first version. (Schneider had never directed a film before.[20]) Yet *Film* is also a work of its time, displaying many of the same formal obsessions as the French New Wave, just burgeoning in the early 1960s: a reflexive concern with the staring camera eye, an invocation of Hollywood icons such as Buster Keaton along with a general consciousness of film history, and a resistance to montage in the Bazinian tradition (surprising considering Beckett's early interest in Eisenstein, but not surprising considering the absence of montage and cross-fading techniques in the radio plays).[21]

The deceptively simple action of *Film* consists of a cat-and-mouse game played by a single protagonist "sundered into object (O) and eye (E), the former in flight, the latter in pursuit." E is the camera, O the character onscreen, and E pursues O from behind, trying not to exceed a 45-degree angle beyond which O "experiences anguish of perceivedness." It is "a variation on the old Keystone Kops chase,"[22] writes Ben-Zvi, which Beckett says should have a "comic and unreal" climate. Comedy aside, much in the film depends on establishing two different visual "qualities" clearly distinguishing between O's point of view and E's—one of many details that proved far more technically complicated than either the author or the director realized. Only in the end do we see O's face (Keaton with a patch over one eye), after which a quick cut to E (another view of Keaton, with the opposite "quality") reveals that "pursuing perceiver is not extraneous, but self."

The three-part, silent, black-and-white action moves from a public to a private milieu, with most of part one omitted in Schneider's production because the footage turned out to be unusable and reshooting prohibitively expensive. The printed text of part one ("The Street") calls for O to come into view "hastening blindly" along a wall, dressed ponderously in a "long dark overcoat," as surrealistic couples in summery costumes rush by in the opposite direction. A woman he jostles "checks him" with a firm "sssh!"—the film's only sound—which communicates humorously that the work is silent by conscious choice, perhaps even out of homage, not for want of resources. (Beckett rarely uses a technical means simply because it is available; in fact, he is likely to reject as a "gimmick" any technique that lends an air of adroitness or ingenuity to his terra *in*firma.) The woman and her companion then express horror upon looking straight at the camera, establishing the convention of "agony of perceivedness."

Part two ("The Stairs") consists of another brief encounter leading to horror of the perceiving camera, this time by an old woman carrying flowers. Finally, part three ("The Room") deals with O's fate when he relaxes in an "illusory sanctuary." After an extended, comic section in which he covers a window and mirror and ejects or covers anything with eyes or resembling eyes (dog, cat, goldfish, an envelope with round fasteners—an early title for the work was *The Eye*), O sits in a rocking chair and inspects seven photographs of himself at various points throughout his life—as compact a biography as the one told when Krapp listens to his taped self describe an earlier taped self. O destroys the photos, as well as a print of "God the Father" hanging nearby, before falling asleep, and then E creeps round along the wall and ends up in position to stare O in the face. "Search of non-being in flight from extraneous perception breaking down in inescapability of self-perception" is Beckett's summary of the action.

Much critical commentary on *Film* has centered on the work's Latin epigraph—"*Esse est percipi*," to be is to be perceived—from the philosopher George Berkeley (1685-1753), who believed that the material world had no independent existence outside sentient minds, which in turn exist only because God perceives them. Two lines after this quote, however, Beckett, in typical fashion, backs off from fully endorsing it: "No truth value attaches to above, regarded as of merely structural and dramatic convenience." Anyone familiar with his language games, or with his famous statement that "it is the shape that matters," understands that issues of "structural and dramatic convenience" are invariably metaphysical concerns for him, and questions about the pertinence of Berkeley's dictum are inevitable for those studying the work.

Some, recalling that Berkeley was an Anglican bishop, suggest that Beckett intends to give a religious maxim an atheistic twist. Vincent Murphy, for example, regrets that "E becomes a kind of surrogate of God in a world in which God no longer perceives"—a desolate view that overlooks, among other things, the degree to which Beckett's humor undercuts all definite, and therefore overly serious, identifications, such as E with God.[23] Others point out that O and E are partly blind and therefore imperfect perceivers (recall the eye patch), suggesting that Beckett is well aware of the devalued sort of being conferred by terrestrial perception such as E's, and that his intention is to underscore that fallen state; Sylvie Debevec Henning, for instance, writes that "there can never be full unity of the self, nor any perfect self-identity—not, at least that we would ever be aware of."[24]

Still another reading might focus on the eye/I pun (later made central in *Not I*) and on the way Beckett again pursues a metaphysical meditation through critiquing his working medium. The pun hangs on the notion that E may or may not be ultimately equivalent to O and that the seeing "eye" is primarily occupied with acquiring self-knowledge, the problem of clearly seeing an "I." In contrast to Bishop Berkeley, who would say that such clarity is impossible without the perceiving light of God, Beckett wonders about the validity of all neat subject-object distinctions, divine or human (that notion of "company" again). A contemporary theorist might add that neither a film's characters nor its narrator-surrogate (the camera-eye as subjective "I") really *exists* until a machine shines incandescent light through celluloid, generating sharp, ephemeral images that fool viewers into believing that the camera-eye is perceiving in the present and that perceivedness is necessarily desirable. Decades before the word "scopophilia" became fashionable, driven partly perhaps by his abhorrence of publicity and blood-houndish critics, Beckett was asking essential questions about the invasiveness of the camera and the use of it as an ontological validator.

Television

That Beckett wanted to write for a medium like television at all is as interesting as any of the works he made for it. As mentioned above, television has been dominated by the narrowly circumscribed formats of commercial programming since its birth, and those formats have contributed to egregious, worldwide psychological changes: shrinking attention spans, discouraging reading, and encouraging passive, narcotized habits of viewing art of all kinds. Unlike radio and film, television has not (yet) been through anything like a Golden Age in which individual artists could exploit it for idiosyncratic purposes. Apart from the efforts of a few quixotic souls like Beckett, whose art always distinguished itself by demanding a greater than usual level of viewer/reader concentration, the medium's high-art potential remains untested. "In being popular culture's *raison d'être*, television is . . . identical with power," writes Alan M. Olson.[25] Beckett, the inveterate outsider, used it to consider his lifelong issues of powerlessness: "I'm working with impotence, ignorance. . . I think anyone nowadays who pays the slightest attention to his own experience finds it the experience of a non-knower, a non-can-er."[26]

Some academic critics, wishing to protect these works' canonical position by treating them exclusively as "video art" (i.e. for privileged viewers in gallery and museum contexts), may bristle at this way of introducing them; and it must be conceded that, though Beckett did own a TV set, there is no proof he was reacting against any specific object. The five works he created for television (six counting *Was Wo*, his adaptation of *What Where*) contravene common preconceptions mainly by answering to standards of compositional precision that we have come to expect only in other media, such as painting. From the vaudeville gags in *Godot* to the casting of Keaton in *Film*, however, Beckett has a long history of mixing high- and low-culture (one reason why he so often figures in debates about postmodernism), and the subtitles and original production circumstances of these works make clear that he thought of them specifically as "television plays" for mass broadcast.

Predating his next work for the televisual medium by a decade, *Eh Joe* (1965) is a transitional piece in which Beckett is still using the camera as an antagonistic pursuer, as in *Film*, but the setting has become entirely interior and sound has returned, literally with a vengeance. Generally, the main difference between a film image and a television image is that the latter is fluorescently back-lit, cruder in resolution and confined to a small box; taking this into account, Beckett now poses ontological questions not by "sundering" a highly mobile protagonist on a big screen but by setting up ambiguities about the relation of a spoken text to a relatively still visual picture. These plays contain very little physical movement—and certainly no chase scenes, except perhaps *Quad*, in which the figures seem driven by some inner demon. Unlike *Film*, *Eh Joe* is an insular, inward-referring work designed for a medium typically watched by supine viewers isolated in intimate spaces.

The play begins with a man sitting on a bed, seen from behind, who peremptorily inspects three rectangular openings—window, door and cupboard—locking each afterward and drawing a curtain over it, as if to ensure he is alone. He returns to the bed and the camera approaches within a yard of his face, stopping when a woman's voice begins speaking: "Joe . . . Joe." For approximately twenty minutes this Voice—which insists that it is not coming from his mind and identifies itself as one of his discarded lovers—harangues him about his past womanizing and other personal failings, and we watch the reactions of his face, which Beckett says is "impassive except insofar as it reflects mounting tension of *listening*." (From *All That Fall* to *Ohio Impromptu*, Beckett worked from the premise that the act of listening holds inherent dramatic value.) The words stop only for a few seconds at nine specified points, during which the camera pulls in closer to his face, so that by the final section only a fragment, from brow to lower lip, is visible as Voice finally fades out.

Eh Joe has never been a favorite of Beckett's critics, some of whom dismiss it outright as melodramatic and obvious: a lecherous man haunted by guilt in the form of a torturous voice from his past. As I have explained at length

Heinz Bennent in Samuel Beckett's **He Joe** *(**Eh Joe**), directed by Beckett at Süddeutscher Rundfunk, Stuttgart, Germany, 1979.*

elsewhere, however, such analyses neglect formal features and ambiguities beneath the clichéd surface that prefigure fundamental aspects of his subsequent, admittedly richer, television works.[27] Added to the standing uncertainty over whether Voice really comes from Joe's mind is an uncertainty over the relation between Voice and the camera: are they equivalent, allied? The camera never moves while Voice speaks, and it sometimes seems like a separate, perhaps subordinate, entity. After twenty minutes, the closeup of the man's face (the play was written for and originally produced with Jack MacGowran) becomes far more eloquent than Voice's monotonous verbal assault. Among other things, her loquacity may act as a smokescreen, designed to distract viewers temporarily from the complex depths of a portrait, making those depths all the more impactful when they are noticed later, and this effect is only heightened by the portrait becoming fragmentary in the end. Beckett's aesthetic of wholeness-in-fragmentariness is pursued on television by means of rectangular framing.

Ten years later, when he began *Ghost Trio* (1975), the author had already made the transition to his later stage dramas, and there is a complex mutual influence, which may never be fully teased out, between those dramas and his mature television work. The later stage dramas generally dispense with the provisional naturalism used in the plays up to *Happy Days* (as well as in *Eh Joe* and *Film*, for that matter), presenting rather meticulously sculpted tableaux at which the audience stares while a musical flow of words with some enigmatic relationship to the tableau emanates from the stage. They are also populated with characters who are not only ephemeral (Maddy-as-sound impulse, O-as-light image, Joe-as-collection of fluorescing dots) but downright ghostly, possibly dead—"not quite there," Beckett once said about May in *Footfalls*. The television plays from *Ghost Trio* on also fit this pattern, the difference being that the visual images become more and more finely wrought, the texts increasingly sparing with speech.

Ghost Trio takes its name and mysterious, ethereal atmosphere from a Beethoven piano trio (op. 70, no. 2) entitled *The Ghost* (written for an opera based on *Macbeth*), parts of which Beckett specifies should be heard at various points in the action. In the first of three sections ("Pre-action") we see a seated male figure (F) bent over a cassette player, "clutching hands, head bowed, face hidden," and hear a female voice (V) describe the environment in tones that range from neutral to sardonic:

Good evening. Mine is a faint voice. Kindly tune accordingly. [*Pause.*] Good evening. Mine is a faint voice. Kindly tune accordingly. [*Pause.*] It will not be raised, nor lowered, whatever happens. [*Pause.*] Look. [*Long pause.*] The familiar chamber. [*Pause.*] At the far end a window. [*Pause.*] On the right the indispensable door. [*Pause.*] On the left, against the wall, some kind of pallet. [*Pause.*] The light: faint, omnipresent. No visible source. As if all luminous. Faintly luminous. No shadow.

The room, of course, is not at all familiar, to us or (apparently) to F, and as Ben-Zvi points out, the more V describes it the stranger it seems.[28] V instructs us to "look closer" at "the kind of wall . . . the kind of floor," and the camera responds (sometimes) by showing different grey rectangles, so plain we would take them for simple geometric cutouts if V did not name them. "Look again," she says. "Knowing all this, the kind of pallet. . . the kind of window . . . the kind of door. . . Look again."

Part two begins with V's statement "He will now think he hears her," which reveals that F is waiting for some woman (an early title for the piece was *Tryst*), though it also reveals, in light of the author's previous uses of waiting, that the woman is unlikely to arrive and introduces questions about the identity of V. Is she the awaited woman? F's reluctant muse? Death, "who will not come to release him from a life to which he barely clings?" (James Knowlson's suggestion).[29] As V narrates—"Now to door. . . No one. . . Now to window"—F rises and, moving soundlessly in an almost puppet-like manner, inspects the room's various openings, including a dark, grave-like corridor outside the knobless door, then returns to his seat and music. In part three V does not narrate and F goes through similar but not identical activities (examining his face in a mirror, for example), eventually opening the door to find a boy in a glistening black oilskin, who "shakes head faintly," then "turns and goes."

The imperative "look again" in part one applies not only to the rectangles but also to the rest of the play and, by extension, to the other television plays, all of which (except *Eh Joe*) employ cyclical repetition: "look again," Beckett seems to say, not only at the picture at hand but at the way you looked the first time, at how that may have been inadequate. This might be called the model of the "double-take"—contrasting distant and near views of the same scene—and it is another example of Beckett incorporating the viewer's process of viewing into his drama. Like many other Beckett works, *Ghost Trio* is partly about the failure of a central agent to perceive clearly. F seems to have been in this "familiar room" for some time, yet he moves soundlessly about the space, looking distractedly at his own face, as if everything were foreign; only at the end, after the boy has left and the Beethoven piece finishes, does he raise his head and smile, as if finally freed from anticipation. Similarly, viewers are distracted by the rectangles and the playfulness of the voice, which seems to say little that is vital for understanding the action, although, as Ben-Zvi writes, that distraction turns out to be vital:

> Each rectangular shape is seen against a still larger rectangle: the window against the wall, the door against the wall. . . All these rectangles, of course, are subsumed in the framing rectangle of the television screen, possibly being viewed in the rectangle of 'the familiar room' of the viewer. . .[30]

Beckett's play, in other words, is partly about the fact that television itself has grown too familiar.

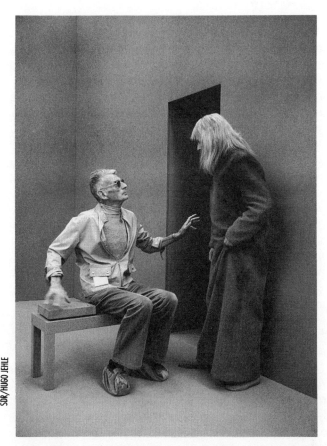

Samuel Beckett directing Klaus Herm in Beckett's **Geistertrio** *(**Ghost Trio**),*
Süddeutscher Rundfunk, Stuttgart, Germany, 1977. Cloth shoe-wrappers were
worn on the set to preserve the pristine cleanliness of the floor.

. . . but the clouds . . . (1976) was first broadcast by the BBC together with
Ghost Trio and an adaptation of *Not I* in a program entitled *Shades*, but its
elegaic, rueful tone recalls *Nacht und Träume* (*Night and Dreams*, 1982) more
than the earlier television plays. The title is a phrase from the closing stanza
of W.B. Yeats' poem "The Tower," which Beckett could recite from memory
and which concerns reconciliation with the decrepitude of old age and death:
girding himself for a final bout of plying his "sedentary trade" in a tower
sanctuary, the indomitable poet half convinces us that, there, "the death of
friends" and similar losses can "Seem but the clouds of the sky/When the
horizon fades/Or a bird's sleepy cry/Among the deepening shades." Beckett
never completely relinquishes his sardonic tones, but there is a greater than
usual level of earnestness in *. . . but the clouds . . .* and *Nacht und Träume,*
as if whatever mental censor had previously prevented his works from
becoming saturated with emotion had suddenly disappeared.

. . . but the clouds . . . begins with a brief, obscure view of a man (M) bowed

over an invisible table, a view the camera subsequently returns to fifteen times. As his voice (V) narrates, M is repeatedly seen moving in and out of a lighted circle surrounded by darkness, V explaining that the movement is his daily routine: arrival from "having walked the roads since break of day" (entrance at left of circle), change into his nightclothes (exit and re-entrance at right of circle), and exit to his "little sanctum" (top of circle), where he crouches in the dark and "beg[s], of her, to appear." This "her" is a woman (W), presumably a lost loved one, whose face appears briefly on the screen whenever he speaks of summoning her. Pedantically distinguishing among four cases—W not appearing, appearing, appearing and lingering, appearing and speaking—V becomes emotional near the end and addresses her directly ("Look at me. . . Speak to me") before reciting Yeats' closing lines in synch with her inaudible lips.

Nacht und Träume also begins with a view of a man (Dreamer) seated at a table, "right profile, head bowed, grey hair," only this time there is no narrator; the story is told entirely in pictures (as were the stories that seemed most reliable in *Eh Joe, Ghost Trio* and . . . *but the clouds* . . .). The only speech is a barely intelligible line from a Schubert *Lied*—"Hölde Träume, kehret wieder" ("Lovely dreams, come again")—sung by a male voice, which lulls the Dreamer to sleep. In a square cloud above him we see his dream: himself seated in the other direction, being visited by disembodied hands that touch him gently, offer him a chalice, wipe his brow, then join with his hands to form a cushion for his head. This sequence is then repeated, except that the second time the camera pulls in close so that the dream cloud fills the screen, revealing details not perceivable before. Among them: a distinct religious flavor and a congeries of references to classical painting. "Look again," the work seems to say, not only at its particular action but at all secular and art-historical assumptions about this author.

Along with *Quad*, a compelling work completely without language, these two plays mark a great wordsmith's break with words near the end of his life, instances of him working more as a composer or painter than a traditional playwright. Indeed, Beckett took a painterly, "hands on" attitude toward all his television plays, directing them himself and refining them at Süddeutscher Rundfunk in Stuttgart after assisting with the original BBC productions, ensuring that the images, sound and pacing would be preserved on tape exactly as he had imagined them. . . . *but the clouds* . . . and *Nacht und Träume* are also particularly significant in his oeuvre, however, because they use his real emotions about death unashamedly as artistic grist. Beckett was known for being tactically old his entire career, preoccupied with creating narrative personae who joked about death and half seriously praised the glory of ending. Where his personae exist in worlds peopled only by ghosts, may in fact be ghosts themselves, the mental distance necessary for irony is harder to achieve.

There is a gem-like, iconic quality to all the television plays, particularly Beckett's own productions, which stands as a tacit criticism of all art that is made less painstakingly, with less monastic obsessiveness. Acts of formal originality such as the model of the "double-take" are the closest Beckett ever came to explicit political critique, but, as with so much he said quietly and subtly, the power of the acts is extraordinary once they are understood. Beckett takes a medium famous for destroying the capacity of humans to think rigorously and perceive clearly and uses it to make plays about the infinitude of the soul and the grandeur of the smallest mortal memory. As a painter of miniatures employs a magnifying glass to achieve an impression of perfection, Beckett uses technical instrumentation to augment human perception and, by inference, dignify it, sending his ghostly emissaries from the humanist "heap" through the air waves into people's living rooms.

Gender and
the Void

Women in Beckett is a belated and inevitable book. As is well known, Samuel Beckett was canonized in our universities with unprecedented dispatch, but until now no concerted effort has been made to focus critically on gender issues in his work or to question his canonical position by way of them. After all, Beckett's vision is universal, isn't it? His stripped-down panoramas, his gnomic, abstemious relationship to language, his punctiliously wrought ambiguities, are all products of deep meditation on the *human* condition, strategies for focusing on those venerable questions of birth, death and the great void—aren't they? Perhaps yes, but after the appearance of Linda Ben-Zvi's groundbreaking if uneven collection, it will be a bit more risky to make such sweeping statements without first acknowledging that part of his pandemic wisdom was purchased during fierce intellectual struggles with the daemon of gender.

Ben-Zvi, author of a 1986 study on Beckett, began assembling these essays by chairing an MLA panel a few years ago, and like many other books that begin life at panels, *Women in Beckett* is marked by wide quality swings. Reading it from cover to cover is a bit like following a sine wave, the most extraordinary originality alternating with the most embarrassing superficiality. It is divided in two, "Part One: Acting Beckett's Women" and "Part Two: Re-Acting to Beckett's Women," and some of the sine wave effect could have been allayed simply by switching the parts around. Part One, a series of interviews with (or brief texts by) thirteen women who have acted Beckett roles in seven different countries, has a few exceptional entries: those with (or by) Billie Whitelaw (England), Nancy Illig (Germany), Hanna Marron (Israel) and Martha Fehsenfeld (USA). In most of the others, however, as in so many actor-interviews, the gemlike insights are hidden under discouragingly high mounds of platitude, adulation and flummery. If nothing else, Ben-Zvi made a rhetorical misstep in following her fine introduction—a lucid summary of the main issues to come as well as an original argument about them—with a long section bound to worry readers about the book's level of discourse.

Women in Beckett really starts gathering steam on page ninety-one with

Susan Brienza's "Clods, Whores, and Bitches: Misogyny in Beckett's Early Fiction." Methodically, a tad gleefully, Brienza provides persuasive evidence for a reading of the early prose works—*More Pricks Than Kicks, Dream of Fair to Middling Women, Murphy* and *Watt*—that emphasizes their "disturbing negative depiction of female characters." Brienza points out that, at the beginning of his career, Beckett—at least in his writing personas—adopted wholesale not only the old Western *agon* of "woman as body versus man as mind" but also the conviction of Shaw, Wilde, and others that marriage (i.e., family life) and true artistry were incompatible: "women as a clod of earth impedes intellectual man" as he strives for creative solitude. According to Brienza, Beckett is more objectionable than his predecessors on this score because of "the overwhelming mean-spirited tone of [his] male narrators," and the strength of her conclusions is disturbing indeed:

> Overall, several . . . generalizations are unavoidable: disparaging depictions of female protagonists often seem gratuitous; attacks on women emerge from cruel physical descriptions; and insistent derogatory remarks about female characters take on the cumulative force of dogma. But dogma of what sort? Not a clear male supremacist one since Beckett's men suffer physical disease and decay and possess a complex of various faults that leave them scarcely more attractive personalities. Beckett's men, however, transcend their imperfect bodies: as limbs decay and parts descend, the mind grows more alive.

This is a point many readers of the early works undoubtedly perceived but may never have formulated for themselves quite so starkly. Essentially, Brienza is saying that, had this Nobel Prize-winning author died after writing only his first few books, he'd likely have been forgotten as a bitter, misogynistic Joyce-imitator, and Rubin Rabinovitz, author of a book on the fiction, proves largely the same point in the following essay, perhaps without intending to. The traditional argument against those who would accuse Beckett of antipathy toward any particular group is that his disgust is omnidirectional, universal (that word again), and Brienza demonstrates in exhaustive examples that this claim is patently untrue in the early fiction.

For all the rigor of her analysis, however, she concludes with a disappointingly facile whistle-stop tour through the later fiction, attempting to extend the misogynistic stigma to it by lifting quotations out of context from *Malone Dies, Imagination Dead Imagine* and *The Lost Ones*, and by deliberately understating points that don't fit her argument: e.g., the significance of Winnie in *Happy Days* (certainly a central female character who "transcends her imperfect body") and the degree to which Beckett's world-view evolved during his long career. That is unfortunate, especially since the reader is well-primed by then to pore through the rest of the book and find out whether its collective narrative will ultimately redeem the author of his youthful shallowness.

To be sure, Beckett, like all men, perhaps all people, grew up possessed of a measure of culturally ingrained misogyny, and perhaps his measure was larger than others'. Along with everything else in his personality, however, at some point in the 1940s or early '50s the misogyny got tossed into a sort of sacrificial cauldron and boiled over a heat of self-scrutiny few other humans could have tolerated. Katharine Worth makes the interesting observation, for instance, that "women began to come into their own in Beckett's theater at about the time he discovered the attraction of writing for radio." But regardless of genre, the terms of debate about misogyny and gender representation must change to accommodate the critical creative transition Hugh Kenner once called "the siege in the room."

As Martin Esslin writes in his essay, "Patterns of Rejection: Sex and Love in Beckett's Universe," the author's trajectory may move through rejection of love and the Shavian Life Force toward absolute stillness as envisioned by Belacqua, even in the post-"siege" works—"What about hanging ourselves?" (Estragon); "Better than nothing! Is it possible?" (Clov); "The earth might be uninhabited." (Krapp)—but it never reaches a point of satisfaction or transcendence in stillness. "Whatever the object," Esslin writes, "our thirst for possession is, by definition, insatiable," and that insatiability—the fact of Beckett's ruthless self-scrutiny, his refusal to endorse any notions of wholeness or healthiness—is the central problem not only for Brienza and others in this collection but also for most critics approaching Beckett from a Marxist perspective. Yes, male characters such as Murphy, Hamm, and Krapp jettison females, as well as stuffed dogs, black rubber balls, and other "dear ones" of variable animation, for the sake of the religion of art, but as Beckett's career progresses, the fact of the jettisoning acquires far more semiotic weight than any stated or implied deficiencies in the jettisoned objects, the world, or the stage-as-world. And that is not merely an opinion of one male reader/spectator but also the *consensus doctorum* of Ben-Zvi's collaborators.

Keeping to the crests, I found particularly impressive an essay by Ann Wilson entitled "'Her Lips Moving': The Castrated Voice of *Not I*," which, along with a short piece by Peter Gidal, inaugurates a debate on the subject of *Not I* that makes the last sixty pages of *Women in Beckett* the most engaging of all. *Not I* is the play in which a mouth (called Mouth), surrounded by darkness and situated eight feet in the air upstage, delivers a disconnected, torrential monologue—both describing *and* constituting a trauma—while repeatedly denying that she is talking about herself. ("What? . . . Who? . . .no! . . .she!" she says five times, as if responding to a speaker, inaudible to us, who urges "I" on her.) "*Not I* is ur-Beckett, the image that underlines all other Beckett works," writes Ben-Zvi in an excellent essay on the 1975 television version with Billie Whitelaw, and perhaps it is only to be expected that a work that communicates so much through synecdoche should come to be treated synecdochically by critics wishing to generalize about the author's oeuvre. That a play whose only speaking character is a vagina dentitia should become a central battleground for scholarly combat over the vexed question of universality, however, is remarkable indeed.

Wilson begins by lucidly recapitulating the arguments already made about this work by Gidal (in his 1986 book *Understanding Beckett*) and Julia Kristeva, whose eloquently sententious essay, "Le père, l'amour, l'exil" (*Cahier de l'Herne*, 1976; trans., "The Father, Love, and Banishment," *Desire in Language*, 1980) is a sort of *locus classicus* for many critics in the collection. "It is tempting to read Mouth's relation to language as paradigmatic of the relation of woman to language," writes Wilson, summarizing the view of Jacques Lacan and other psychoanalytic critics that language in general is phallocentric, belonging to the Order of the Father. Since Mouth's speech is not only fragmentary but also marked by repeated refusal to employ the first person pronoun, it turns out to be ideal material for Lacanian analysis, practically oozing questions of subjectivity and otherness. Wilson, for her part, greatly prefers one such reading over another:

> . . .the status of [Mouth's] refusal needs to be called into question. Does it mark, as Gidal argues, a refusal to locate herself within a patriarchal discourse? Or is it a mark of humility, the erasure of the self by someone who is before God? Kristeva argues that Mouth's tenacious clinging to the third person "postulates the existence of the other. Here, since it is 'not I,' not *you* either, then it must be a *He beyond communication.*" . . . She argues that Mouth does not refuse the discourse of the Father but in fact submits so fully that, standing before God, the Father who is Presence beyond representation, Mouth denies herself.

In fact, Wilson is more severe than Kristeva, arguing that *Not I* not only places its protagonist in a predicament similar to final judgement but also "effect[s] the denial of woman by establishing a textual economy within which feminine sexuality is erased." I must confess to not understanding fully this latter part of her argument. (It uses, as self-evident truth, a quotation from Luce Irigaray implying that lesbian sexuality is the quintessence of the feminine.) The bulk of the analysis is admirably rigorous, however, and convincing to the point where the reader begins toying with notions of simultaneous discovery: *Not I* dates from 1972, exactly when this sort of gender-based analysis was gaining acceptance.

Moreover, the implications of observations like the following (about the TV version) extend far beyond the boundaries of one play:

> The sexual overtones of the image are obvious: Mouth is aroused. The viewer's position as spectator is that of the voyeur watching the lips/ labia, a position which replicates that constructed by pornography, in which the object of desire (usually female) is the site onto which the spectator (usually male) can project his fantasy. The very ambiguity of the image in *Not I*, and the fact that on video (and, to a lesser degree,

in the theater) our position relative to the image is not disrupted, facilitate the element of fantasy. We are constructed as subjects within a structure of desire, which is masculine. What we desire is knowledge, in all its complexity, of Mouth. Key to this structure is the impossibility of desire being sated.

From one point of view, the experience of watching a Beckett play, particularly a later one, is a beautifully enigmatic process of dealing with the unverifiability of information, ambiguous relations between reported histories and observed events, the collapsing of expected connections between signifiers and signifieds, but from another point of view, all those parameters function within unbalanced power equations. What does it *mean* politically, for instance, to keep audiences perpetually guessing about character identities? As Walter Kendrick, Susan Sontag, and others have written, pornography is an extraordinarily frequent and apt figure in modern culture: Beckett the Great Reducer once again distills the essence of a plexus of questions. We have, of course, much to learn from this sort of inquiry. Problems arise only when those conducting it lose touch with its limits, as when Wilson closes her essay with a comment about Mouth's "unproblematized inscription of gender" that belies all that has gone before about how profoundly problematized it is.

The jewel of Ben-Zvi's collection is unquestionably Elin Diamond's "Speaking Parisian: Beckett and French Feminism," an essay whose declared purpose—to show that "reading Beckett through a feminist theoretical lens foregrounds often-overlooked features of his gender representations"—is anomalously modest compared with its memorable conclusion:

> Samuel Beckett's own posture as venerated twentieth-century author has been continually to link mastery to failure, speech to silence, syntax to gap. He has, in other words, "feminized" his writing, permitted the other to invade his discourse; and at this historical moment, as Parisian women theorists have been writing (of) the feminine, the Irish-Parisian writer has theatricalized their theory, ruptured and challenged *their* discursive mastery through powerfully denatured stage images.

I suspect other critics in the book would passionately challenge this circumspect statement, which stands out partly because of its explicit refusal to veer off into conspiracy theorizing. Diamond declines to employ feminist terms for the preordained purpose of unmasking or embarrassing Beckett, and her text further distinguishes itself through the level on which it engages with Beckett's later poetic language, recognizing and interpreting its peculiar intricacies and humor.

Clearly uncomfortable with extreme positions taken by several prominent feminist theorists, Diamond sets herself up as a sort of colluding mediator. She argues, for instance, with what she calls the "polemic" of Hélène Cixous and Catherine Clément concerning feminine hysteria—"They insist that the inability of the female to say 'I' . . . is precisely the symptom, incurable in Western culture, that betrays and unravels the patriarchy"—preferring a much more ambiguous and complex reading grounded in the idea of mimesis: "The hysteric uncoils and unleashes her antilanguage, a derisive somatic mimicry of the father's lexical and syntactic order." At another point, she establishes a contrast between Cixous and Jane Gallop (specifically Gallop's comments in *The Daughter's Seduction* [1982] about "the anxiety of/between women concerning phallic privilege") in order to make some incisive observations about *Footfalls*, a play she says "stages a crisis posed by feminist theories of the maternal." In *Footfalls*, a woman named May paces slowly downstage while talking with her offstage mother, who asks several times, "Will you never have done . . . revolving it all?"

> Perhaps this "it" [phallic privilege] has nothing to do with May's "it"— the privilege to escape from the mother-daughter dyad. Is May's pacing perhaps *not* the result of a mysterious "it," some veiled trauma about ghostly semblances, but rather the very image of that engulfing bond that keeps mother and daughter in paralysis so that "one can't move without the other"? Is that "it"? Gallop's analysis of the phallic mother—she who engulfs, who is in command and all powerful—belies Cixous's vision of the deep, productive (milk-giving) intimacy between the mother's voice and the listening daughter/writer. Beckett's *Footfalls*, itself an unstable, overdetermined "it," partakes of and produces both visions . . ."

This essay, along with Ben-Zvi's "*Not I*: Through a Tube Starkly," ought to be required reading from now on for anyone interested in the potential of feminist theory to illuminate not only Beckett but also any other great modernist work with the reputation of transcending presumably parochial questions of gender. Though she never makes the point explicitly, Diamond's perceptiveness and eloquence, the sheer strength of her observations and formulations, ultimately amount to an articulation of *Women in Beckett*'s best *raison d'être*, which is: universal or not, many of this author's most resonant and powerful imaginative creations find their most vital performative energy in and through constructions of the female. Toward the end of his life, as he honed his vision down to skeletal essences, concentrating more and more on an art of omission, exclusion, suppression and repudiation, the misogynistic author of *More Pricks than Kicks* apparently came to see that questions of male and female identity, particularly when focused on language, *are* fundamental questions of birth, death, and the great void.

Krapp at the Palast

Brecht never completed his infamous 1956 project to rewrite Beckett's *Waiting for Godot* as a socialist allegory, and it is not known whether he gave it up because of ill health or second thoughts. Perhaps he eventually came to see value in the play as written, but that is not a popular view among Brecht devotees, who continue to believe that the finished adaptation might have been extraordinary in its own right, like *Edward II*. In the 1960s and 70s, that intended adaptation became the spiritual impetus for a number of "Brecht/Beckett evenings" in Western Europe, prominent among them Peter Palitzsch's 1971 *Godot* in Stuttgart, which was influenced by Brecht's plans, and Ralf Langbacka's 1979 four-hour double-bill of *Godot* and *The Exception and the Rule* in Helsinki. Until 1986, however, I had never heard of such an evening in the Soviet block, where Beckett's works were rarely seen in any context.

Ekkehard Schall's *Lebensabende*—which combines the East German premiere of *Das Letzte Band* (*Krapp's Last Tape*) with a musical version of Brecht's poem *Die Erziehung der Hirse* (*The Education of Millet*)—might be seen loosely as part of the tradition, though one must remember to speak of affinity rather than influence when comparing across East-West boundaries. In this case, the existence of Beckett on the program at all was more noteworthy than the combination of Beckett with Brecht, for it was one among several examples of increasingly lenient censorship in the past East German season, which also included (several months later) the triumphant premiere of *Godot* in Dresden.

Krapp was particularly interesting for Westerners, however, because of the glaring questions raised. How would Brecht's son-in-law, star actor of the Berliner Ensemble, fare in a Beckett role? What does he know of Beckett and how it is usually acted, and how would his skill with Brecht help or hinder him? Beckett has had a profound underground influence on many East German writers, but his works still are not for sale in the GDR, and the majority of theatergoers have had no exposure to them. What would they think of an actual play by the legendary "greatest living playwright of the West?"

As it turned out, for spectators from both sides of the Wall, the evening was embarrassingly bad, and would ordinarily deserve merciful obscurity. Being a kind of unwitting confession of cultural isolation, however, it also had a certain instructive value.

Theater im Palast, where the production took place, is not really a theater. It is a corner, subdivided with plain gray tarpaulins, of a convention hall on the fourth floor of Palast der Republik, a monstrous building that also houses the Volkskammer of the German Democratic Republic (the highest representative body of government). The Palast—which shares a large public square with the headquarters of the Volkspolizei (police), the Staatssicher-heitsdienst (secret police), and the Communist Party—is an ostentatious marble and glass structure built on the site of an old Prussian Royal Palace, which, having stood for centuries and still structurally sound after the war, was nevertheless dismantled as a symbolic gesture of victory for the new order. Thus, the new edifice has a peculiarly ambivalent atmosphere, part self-serious, professional and bombastic, part slipshod, scrimpy and counterfeit, and that feeling is somehow compounded by this choice of plays. Imagine Artaud's *The Jet of Blood* playing at the Lincoln Memorial and you have some idea of the incongruousness of Beckett in this place.[1]

When Schall enters the dark stage, a row of florescent lights at the rear of the hall remains lit, and he halts abruptly, calling, "*Das Licht! Das Licht muss erstmal ausgemacht werden!*" Nothing happens, he grows annoyed, and eventually leaves in a huff. The audience thinks it is part of the play, even after an apologetic announcement. But it is ten minutes before the light can be extinguished.

When the performance restarts and the stage lights rise, I am momentarily startled by Schall's makeup. It is not the clown-face that Beckett specified in early drafts of the play—"White face, Purple nose"—but rather a plain, completely gray base, thickly caked onto his thin hair and bushy mustache in a haphazard manner, which gives not the slightest impression of clowning. There seems to be a conscious attempt to make him appear as filthy as possible, as if Schall or the costumer had fixated on Beckett's word "disorderly." This is by far the most decrepit Krapp I have seen, which becomes an obstacle for the actor, not because the character is supposed to be clean but because the general tone of disorder also affects his movement.

The opening mime, an impeccably chosen series of odd activities that provides a sort of miniature portrait of the character, usually sets the tone for the whole performance. Schall's version is driftless and unfunny, composed of casual movements that do not seem well-drilled, or even particularly rehearsed. It is slow to the point of tedium and, despite several cuts, lasts twenty minutes. Schall seems to believe that Krapp is a sluggish old man, so he plays the idea of "sluggish old man," employing unconvincing grumbles and stiff limb movements in utterly commonplace repetitions. Schall's movements are devoid of strangeness. Every time he rises from his chair, he acts as if it's in his way and bends down to push it aside, but he does this in exactly the same uninteresting way each time, so the audience soon learns to expect boredom from the bit. And the same is true about the peeling and petting of bananas, the exits for drinks and atextual bits such as Schall's fumbling with keys and his five or six extra glances at the crumpled envelope. All of these are wholly indicated and predictable. Even the slipping on the banana skin with the huge white shoes, which I have never seen fail before, falls flat in this performance.

So where was the director? The program identifies him as "David Leveaux, Grossbritannien," and his bio lists no previous experience with Beckett. Following that bio are two short German paragraphs informing us that he feels most Beckett criticism is "obtrusive meddling" in a relationship that should be "consummated exclusively between the poet and the conscience of the individual," and that Beckett is not an "ideological" writer. Thus we can surmise that at least one of the production's problems was that this man ought to have read a bit more of the criticism he criticizes, but it is difficult to say for certain what influence he had on the actor's choices.

The remainder of the printed program is worth another moment's digression. After a four-sentence quotation from Beckett, the source of which is not given, opining that "the theater is not a moral institution," one finds: a four-page text by Christoph Trilse, who speaks of Beckett's roots as "bourgeois" and of his literary context as "the blind alley of late capitalism"; a three-page excerpt from the story by G. Fisch that Brecht used as his source for *The Education of Millet*; a two-page excerpt from a recent magazine article about a farmer who became a hero of Soviet agronomy; two pages from Käthe Rülicke-Weiler's book on Brecht, which describe the planned adaptations of *Godot* in language similar to Trilse's; and a photocopy of Beckett's polite note declining Barbara Brecht-Schall's invitation to the opening. But despite this barrage, there is nothing explicitly political in the Krapp production itself; Schall *does* try to do justice to the material.

The performance continues and some reasons for its flaccidity suggest themselves. Schall has two types of reaction to his taped voice: wholly internal and invisible, or very broad and gestural, as if exaggerated for spectators far away. There are few eyebrow twitches, tiny smirks, or other moment-to-moment psychological reactions such as were seen by the score in the original Krapps: Patrick Magee, Jean Martin and Martin Held. One sees rather large arm-swings ending with the hand behind the ear, implying partial deafness, or violent tosses of the head, perspiration flying every which way, implying frustration and anger. Schall does everything in his power to ward off realism, but it arrives anyway. To be sure, *Krapp* is not a realistic play, not wholly so at least, but it does involve a kind of voyeurism that cannot be made clear unless the actor portrays some degree of aloneness. From the start, Schall's externalized actions work against any private images—he even cuts the masturbatory gesture of the banana in the mouth, although clearly not because of fastidiousness—so in the end all of his signing and gesturing is without referent. Ultimately we have only a realistic image of an actor's *Gestus*, which hangs in the air like a badly told joke.

By the time he comes to making his new tape, the stiffness of movement seen in the opening has becomes a worsening paralysis, and he has worked himself into such an emotional frenzy that he drools and spits copiously on every line. The point, subtle as Molloy's knocks on his mother's skull, is that Krapp is dying, and dying men are not pretty. I venture to suggest, however, that it is obvious from Beckett's words, even from his title, that Krapp is dying. That is the given situation, the condition of the play, and it need not be hammered home with morbid gymnastics. Furthermore, as S.E. Gontarski writes:

> [Krapp's] final motionless stare may signal less death than postcoital, rather postmasturbatory, emptiness and loneliness . . . The ultimate image is again of failure; Krapp cannot control his passions, again.[2]

The significant questions for performance have to do with what else, besides death, is happening to Krapp. What occurred in the past to cause these circumstances? And what kind of man has perpetuated them, is now living with them, before our eyes?

In the words of Pierre Chabert, whom Beckett directed in this role: "In fact, Krapp is not an old man, but rather someone who has grown old

*Ekkehard Schall in the East German premiere of Samuel Beckett's **Das Letzte Band (Krapp's Last Tape)**, directed by David Leveaux, Theater in Palast, Berlin, Germany, 1986.*

MARIA STEINFELDT

conserving a certain robustness at all times; the stage directions give him a cracked voice, an indication more psychological than physical, but always difficult to produce."[3] The death is most effectively presented through subtle indications such as this voice, and what Chabert calls Krapp's "carnal relationship" with his machine. Moreover, the character is a writer and has, in a way, a carnal relationship with words, which makes all the more poignant his onstage discovery of what his words mean, and have always meant, about his capacity to love. Something Beckett once said about *Endgame* might also apply to *Krapp*: it has the ability to "claw" spectators because it lures them into a high degree of concentration on an action that appears clown-like at first, but then slips into an almost unbearable tension within the character himself.[4] Schall's performance does not deal in such subtleties; it seems built on the assumption that audiences would not understand them. His broad characterization, together with his slow pace (the performance lasts eighty-five minutes, about twenty minutes longer than usual), effectively clip the play's nails.

The relevance to *Krapp* of the title word, *"Lebensabend,"* which means "the evening of one's life," is obvious, but let us not forget *The Education of Millet*, which plays to some forty percent fewer spectators after intermission. The stage is empty except for a burlap grain sack, and Schall enters, tastefully dressed in a casual jacket and a boyish skullcap. With piano accompaniment, he sings and recites fifty of the fifty-two verses, well-known to East Germans from their school lessons, of the story Tschaganak Bersijew, nomad from the Kasakstan desert, who discovered the secret of reaping huge millet harvests: watering seeds whenever they want makes them grow up weak, like spoiled children, but selective, occasional watering creates a tough, hearty grain. When *"Sowjetmacht"* came to his land, Bersijew "joined" a collective farm, whose harvests then became so large they were the wonder of the Moscow Science Academy, and in the fight against Hitler, millet became the staple of the soldiers' diet. Now Bersijew lies buried beneath a sea of swaying millet, and is remembered for the way he shared his seed.

Perhaps there exists in some East German periodical an ingenious analysis of the relationship between this work and *Krapp's Last Tape*, but I have not yet been able to discover one myself. I suspected at first that permission from the Culture Ministry to perform the Beckett was granted on condition that it be paired with the Brecht—which calls up a mental picture of plays as alchemical laboratory beakers filled with colored liquids that can neutralize each other if mixed according to mysterious formulas—but Schall denied that in an interview with me.

> I don't think at all about playing Brecht off Beckett or Beckett off Brecht, using them that way. I polemicize with the contents of the texts about my experiences with reality; that's enough.[5]

Whatever the reasons for the pairing, the audience seemed to detest both halves of the evening equally; an air of dutifulness during *The Education of Millet* was unmistakable even in Schall's performance.

It is tempting to spring from these observations to a detailed analysis of the differences between acting Brecht and acting Beckett, to examine why skills that are helpful for the former are hindrances for the latter—and to an extent that is relevant. Unfortunately, this *Krapp*'s problems were nowhere near so complex. At a few points, Schall seems to employ a different performance philosophy from what is known to work in Beckett—e.g., his broad arm motions indicating deafness, and all the movements contributing to his exaggerated exertion. These are the moments when the production is most interesting, when I can see Schall thinking as a Brecht actor, trying to delineate Beckett's character in broad outline in order to clarify the presumably larger questions in his story. Ill-fated as that effort may be, it is at least worth exploring, and Schall is not the first actor to do so. Much more unsettling than that attempt, though, is the impression Schall leaves of not taking it fully seriously.

I have seen him perform works by other authors on at least four occasions, and I came to this *Krapp* with a preconception of a master-actor whose distinguished career has provided, among other things, a sort of standing vindication of Brecht's idea of *verfremdet* acting. Schall's usual technique is to inhabit fictional characters in an apparently offhand manner, creating a deceptive patina of casualness over the "deeper substance" of his specific, calculated actorly comments on the action, which almost always *do* leave an impression of seriousness. I have seen this technique work equally well in plays as disparate as Brecht's *Caucasian Chalk Circle* and Strindberg's *Dance of Death*. With a quasi-naturalistic role such as Edgar in *Dance of Death*, the context of the *Verfremdungseffekt* is altered, but it can still work brilliantly (and ironically) inside the play's fiction by amplifying the character's disingenuousness. In Beckett, that casual technique becomes a hindrance, or rather a blinder, leading Schall to underestimate the intricacy of the text and the attention to detail necessary to bring out its subtleties of meaning.

Had Schall not shown me his production book during our interview, carefully notated with thoughts about Krapp's speech and movement, I would have assumed the production was under-rehearsed. Actors typically practice the mime in *Krapp* for weeks, until every moment is as precisely crafted and timed as an acrobatic act, and audiences laugh uproariously at the result, following the actor's every muscle movement as if it were part of a visual poem. But rehearsal is obviously not the problem.

The weaknesses in this *Krapp* more likely have to do with a certain aesthetic naiveté. Schall has read Beckett before but has never seen a Beckett production during his numerous performing tours to the West, and the truth is that, stylistically, his performance is decades behind the times—Western times, that is. It displays an ignorance not only of Beckett but of a whole tradition of post-war performance that sees ambiguity as a positive value and rejects direct focus on actual political process. Its English director notwith-standing, this production bespeaks a poor understanding of an entire theater vocabulary that includes Pinter, Ionesco, Pirandello, Handke, and a hundred other writers whose works were lumped together as "formalist" and de-nounced as "bourgeois" by the official mainstream of Marxist criticism.

It must be extremely difficult to approach these writers cold, so to speak, especially when one is busy with repertory performances at the Berliner Ensemble and has precious little time to grow accustomed to a new dramatic universe. One does expect, however, at least a production true to some non-Western standard. I can easily imagine, for instance, a *Krapp* interpreted politically along the lines of Brecht's planned *Godot* adaptation: perhaps a historicism of the play's Manichaean opposition of light and dark, leading to ideological contrast between events onstage and the tape recorder's evocation of a world that is, in Chabert's words, "at the same time lost and present."[6] Strangely, though, ideology does not dominate, despite all the ideological gestures. The production was very likely as foreign to the East Germans as it was to me.

The Other
Avant-Garde

Until the publication of John Rudlin's 1986 book *Jacques Copeau* in Cambridge University Press's "Directors in Perspective" series, Americans with no French had to be library moles to find much detailed information on one of the most influential theater artists of this century. (Grotowsky, Barba, Mnouchkine and Strehler are among those who speak proudly of being Copeau's progeny.) The better reference and survey books contained sections on Copeau and the Vieux Colombier, but it was always difficult for English-speakers to see this artist as more than a collection of earnest testimonials and encyclopedic phrases about bare stages and the training of actors from childhood. Now, with Rudlin's earlier study recently out of print, he and Norman Paul have given us another side of Copeau—the critic, diarist and theoretician—and the central themes of their collection suggest a possible explanation for his relative neglect.

Copeau: Texts on Theatre consists mostly of translated passages from *Registres*, or *Account Books*, the sprawling, multi-volume collection of Copeau's writings in French, compiled after his death in 1949 according to his own unfulfilled plan. In 1943 he wrote:

> For a long time now, I have been burning with the need, not to narrate my life-story nor to write my memoirs in well-ordered chapters, but to throw pell-mell into a series of volumes everything I have done and not done, learned and thought about, imagined, composed, failed at, succeeded in; that is, to confess completely to myself and to God, for posterity if it preserves this jumble or, lacking that, for my friends and family; the whole thing under the title of *Registres*.

Mercifully, rather than attempting to duplicate the French jumble, Rudlin and Paul made a judicious selection and added brief, informative editorial texts throughout, producing a book as important, unique and useful as Edward Braun's *Meyerhold on Theatre*—which, in certain ways, it complements.

Copeau's voice is quintessentially French, marked by that strange mixture of braggadocio and modesty that wins the reader's confidence after a while by speaking plain good sense. Some would call Copeau a conservative, the editors use the word "traditionalist," but both terms are misleading for an artist who established his reputation in the course of withdrawing from the mainstream boulevard theater. Copeau *was* an avant-gardist, but he represented a branch of avant-gardism, whose roots reach back to André Antoine, that we now have difficulty recognizing as radical: the one that didn't set out primarily to destroy, or to advocate impracticable revolutions, but rather to teach. Copeau was a creature of the Enlightenment, and if his occasional journalism, his quickly jotted notes to himself, still fascinate us, it's because they reveal him immediately as the real thing—the quixotic modernist who still believes in something called "authenticity" and bothers to fulminate against its opposite (which he names *cabitonage*).

The spectacle of Copeau's "belief" may have an edge of religiosity at times, but it's never quaint or tepid. He started out as an acidic critic who articulated his disgust at the Paris theater, the superficiality of its star system driven by personality cults, in publications such as the *Grande Revue* and the *Nouvelle Revue Française*, which he helped found in 1909. In 1913, without formal training but with the support of powerful literary friends, he penned a manifesto, gathered together a group of like-minded young people, moved to his mother's home fifty miles outside the capital, and formed a company dedicated to an ideal unknown at the time in France: total immersion in, and monastic commitment to, theater art.

The Vieux Colombier was founded as a theater, but Copeau made clear that that was only a necessary expedient for the founding of a school. Unfortunately, World War I intervened, forcing a temporary exile to the United States, and the school didn't get started until 1920, by which time the company and its leader had acquired a distinct style and a reputation for upholding certain values in production. Perhaps most prominent was the idea of the *tréteau nu*, or bare stage, stripped of all but the most minimal furniture and props, which describes only one of many stylistic phases but has nevertheless become known as a trademark. It is certainly, for instance, what Strehler has in mind when he speaks (in an appendix to this book) of Copeau's "severe, Jansenist moral vision."

Because Copeau was an enemy of flashiness and technical gimmickry for its own sake, he had from the beginning to fend off accusations that he imitated Craig, Appia, Stanislavsky and others. Rudlin and Paul deal with this drily and respectfully, gathering the relevant texts in sections entitled "Ideas in Common: Edward Gordon Craig," "Ideas in Common: Émile Jaques-Dalcroze," and so on, allowing readers to decide the originality question themselves. This reader comes away with an impression of a man who simply was far more worried about quality than about priority or authority of ideas, an extremely perceptive, selectively absorbent sponge who knew exactly what he wanted and exactly whom to ask for advice on how to elicit it from his company members. Moreover, he did graciously acknowledge his debts, at least later, after he was established, and the accounts of his first meetings with Craig and Dalcroze in 1915 are among the most engaging selections in the book.

Also distinctive are his texts about acting, especially his "Preface" (it ought to be called "Rebuttal") to a 1929 edition of Diderot's "Paradox of the Actor," which argue for the living performer, rather than inanimate elements such as costumes or settings, as the prime medium of expression onstage. Copeau says that this primacy can be achieved only with certain actors who understand—either by native insight or through work with him—that a capacity for "simplicity, honesty, comradeship and firm discipline" is more important to their art than appealing personality, skill at impersonation or talent for display. Copeau's "complete education" of the actor would ideally be free of charge, begin about age ten or twelve, and involve a comprehensive, self-sacrificial cultivation of the imagination and spirit. "Education is a more important factor than vocation," he writes in the 1921 brochure for his school, which will function (he says in another text) "without scientific pedantry, without scholastic theories," and will take its aesthetic cues from children's play.

There is much more of interest—Copeau's ideas of recovering the classic Chorus, for instance, which he abstracts and generalizes in order to make comparisons with less ancient types of performer-groups such as *commedia* troupes and circus families—but nothing in the book is more enduringly provocative than the texts on the proper treatment of authors. Here is Copeau speaking in Lyons in 1920 to a crowd that clearly contained the three-year-old JFK: "When a director finds himself in front of a dramatic work, his role is not to say: 'What am I going to do with it?'—his role is to say: 'What is it going to do with me?' " And here are stronger words from fifteen years earlier, which sound almost hypocritical coming from a man who dissolved the Vieux Colombier company in 1929 rather than relinquish autocratic rule over it, a man whose name arises in nearly every informed discussion of the ascendancy of the *metteur en scène*:

Vain and arrogant, [directors] are the true masters at the present time. Their whims and despotic ignorance rule the stage. In their hands, a work becomes unrecognisable. They modify the text, adding or crossing out lines at will, remake entire scenes and change the endings of plays. They are considered to be the writers' collaborators while they are in fact their hangmen.

The hypocrisy is skin-deep, though. More fundamental is that Copeau was uncomfortable with anyone who viewed the relationship between director and dramatist as a struggle; he chose not to see the issue primarily in terms of authority. Again, for him the significant question was quality of thought: Who has the better ideas? Who has done the primary research, the really hard thinking about life, and formulated it in a way others can share and learn from? In his experience, that invariably turned out to be the dramatic poet, not the director, and the latter's work was thus properly subordinated to the former's. For some readers it will be difficult to accept that ideas like these continued to flourish in the French avant-garde through the 1930s, as Artaud's theoretical essays were appearing and Meyerhold's auteurial practices were gaining worldwide renown.

That may be the most significant contribution of *Copeau: Texts on Theater*, however: ultimately, it reaches beyond one artist to illustrate a neglected point about the historical avant-garde. The closer we get to the turn-of-the-millennium, the greater the temptation to think of the 20th century as monolithic, distinguished by certain singular, consolidated trends, and in the theater the most famous trend is the disassociation of the Author, which repeated mention has granted an aura of moral rectitude. How timely, then, how deliciously politically incorrect, that this book should appear in the same year as Jean Chothia's *André Antoine* to remind English-speakers that the range of ideas represented under the aegis of avant-gardism was, from the beginning, wide enough to include notions we think of today as irredeemably *arrière*.

The artistic values upheld during what historians now refer to as the "first avant-garde"—associated with Naturalism and beginning with Antoine's founding of the Théâtre Libre in 1887—did not, contrary to common belief, suddenly disappear with the advent of Symbolism and the appearance of Reinhardt, Stanislavsky and the other great fin-de-siècle directors. As Chothia points out, all the independent theaters directly inspired by the Théâtre Libre flourished by discovering and associating themselves with particular dramatists: the Freie Bühne (Hauptmann), the Intimate Theater (Strindberg), the Moscow Art Theatre (Chekhov), the Irish Players (Yeats, Synge, O'Casey) and the English Stage Society (Shaw, Galsworthy and Granville-Baker). In other words, from these theatres to the Provincetown Players to the Royal Court to Circle Repertory Company, those values lived on. Indeed, the independents—specifically, their common idea of a small, intimate theater that seeks to create and educate new audiences while ignoring accusations of elitism or marginalism—served as model and inspiration for our Off- and Off-Off-Broadway houses. All survived in no small measure because they shared one bit of hard-earned practical knowledge: that, the evils of logocentricity notwithstanding, it ain't so easy to identify and nurture good new writing, even after you declare that producing it is your main goal.

Chothia describes Antoine as the spiritual father of Copeau and says that the central paradox of the older man's artistry is that "the first exponent of playwright's theatre was the creator of director's theatre," a point he goes on to demonstrate with numerous examples from a mysteriously truncated career (the years between 1921 and Antoine's death in 1943 are a blank). As with all the books in the "Directors in Perspective" series dealing with directors who worked before film and video, the research is especially impressive, a result of burrowing and sifting through letters, press statements, manifestoes, prompt books, still photos, contemporary journalism, and more in the interest of piecing together reconstructions that give the flavor of productions. For the time being, though, the greater value of both *André Antoine* and *Copeau: Texts on Theatre* is in their inadvertent revisionism.

Antoine was, among many other things, the founder of what might be polemically called "the other avant-garde," which has been driven deep underground during generations of directorial hegemony. The Parisian "pocket theater" (Ruby Cohn's apt term for the independents), model of nearly every stage today that offers food for the mind, was also the seedbed of an avant-garde tradition that didn't get stuck in the famous nihilistic cul de sac, perpetuating an endless cycle of anarchistic rebellions that feed on the corpses of previous rebellions and, as time goes by, bequeath less and less in the way of formal discoveries. Certain notions—such as granting authority to the person who has the most living ideas, even if it's not the director—can be appreciated, it seems, only in an atmosphere of mature judgement where decisions may be considered in terms of principle, something beyond the nervous needs of the unaccommodated self. That is rare indeed in a contemporary avant-garde scene dominated by adolescent energy. Domination isn't absolute conquest, though, and it's worth reminding ourselves that some of the warriors who fought so that we might scream were interested not only in slaughtering 19th-century fathers but also in growing up and founding schools.

Mayakovsky's Tragic Comedy

All roads led into the mire in my time.
My tongue betrayed me to the butchers.
There was little I could do. But those in power
Sat safer without me: that was my hope.
So passed my time
Which had been given to me on earth.

—Bertolt Brecht, "To Those Born Later"[1]

Certain revolutionary societies have produced artists who felt cosmically liberated—freed from the very way that civilization had moved through history before them. These artists extolled their new social orders with a moral fervor that shocked even their leaders, and inevitably, the revolutions that produced them killed them. With some, such as F.T. Marinetti, the inability to leave a political movement gone sour changed their fervor into self-righteous, amoral ecstasy. Others, such as Vladimir Mayakovsky, retained their moral standards at the cost of professional success and official sanction; they could then only channel their energy into negative forms, creating a literature of attack.

Manifestations of such attacks have a tendency to become time-bound, and according to general opinion, Mayakovsky's last play, *The Bathhouse: A Drama in Six Acts, with a Circus and Fireworks*, is a case in point. A satire on Soviet bureaucracy, it focuses on familiar Russian situations and character types, and contains a great deal of *na litso*, or barbs against named people of the era. If one is to believe the few critics who have offered judgments, this topicality relegates the play to historical obscurity.

In spite of the occasional flashes of Mayakovsky's genius that are in it, *The Bathhouse* is now quite dead, and probably could not be revived.
(Edward Brown)

Plot is secondary in both *The Bedbug* and *The Bathhouse*; the poet's meanings depend on caricature and on parody understandable only to contemporaries.
(Vera Alexandrova)[2]

But undue neglect aside—much of the significance of *The Bathhouse* clearly lies in elements that supersede topical references—the play is something of an icon of cultural-political stasis in the Soviet era. It is not naive, as the simple label "topical satire" implies, but is a work of tragic proportion whose ending contains profound ambiguities concerning reward, punishment, and inanition.[3] Moreover, *The Bathhouse* and the features that distinguish it from Mayakovsky's other plays are central to any full understanding of why this author attained quasi-mythical stature among artists sympathetic to socialism from Pasternak to Brecht and Müller.

The setting is Russia, 1929-30. The "compromising" capitalism and relative freedom of NEP (a palliative measure that Mayakovsky hated) had been over for two years, and the industrial surge of the first Five-Year Plan was in full swing. Stalin, having consolidated his power, was in a position to clamp down firmly on peasant opposition to mass collectivization, and in the next several years an estimated 10 million people would be killed or displaced. In literature, official encouragement was given to RAPP (Russian Association of Proletarian Writers), which favored psychological approaches to character. For years Mayakovsky had been violently opposed to RAPP, but on February 6, 1930—when the script of *The Bathhouse* had been delayed by the censor for over two months—he was finally forced to join. Permission to produce the play was granted on February 9.

By that time the Soviet bureaucracy had become such a huge, sprawling monstrosity that strict measures had to be legislated to curb its waste. Strangely, as James Symons points out, in this one sense *The Bathhouse* was consistent with Party policy.[4] On a banner in the Meyerhold State Theater in Moscow (where the play opened on March 16, 1930) Mayakovsky wrote:

> You can't wash away at once the whole swarm of bureaucrats. There just aren't enough bathhouses or soap. And besides, bureaucrats get help from the pen of critics like Ermilov.[5]

V.V. Ermilov was a shallow and doctrinaire critic who had viciously attacked *The Bathhouse* in a *Pravda* article (March 9, 1930) after having read only part of it. He was a member of RAPP, which subsequently pressured the Meyerhold company into removing the banner. 1930 audiences would have associated Ermilov's name with the popular debate on "psychologism versus theatricalism" (forerunner of the later "realism versus formalism" scrimmage). To Mayakovsky, "psychologism" had become a bugbear for all the superficiality to be found in ideological art; and the allegorical action and spectacle in *The Bathhouse* were, among other things, a rebellion against that naiveté.

The play's characters are divided into two camps, parodying the simplistic classification of people into types in official speech. An "honest worker," Chudakov (the name means "eccentric"), invents a Wellsian time machine and needs government funding to complete his project. He is opposed by the "bourgeois opportunist" Pobedonosikov ("nose for victory"—connotation: overbearing), head of the Federal Bureau of Coordination, who only inhibits with red tape "those struggling to build Communism." The zeal of Chudakov and his worker friends (which both exemplifies *and parodies* the ideal of the new Soviet citizen, whose motto is "The Five-Year Plan in Four Years") is suppressed by the utterly corrupt bureaucrats. Thus, the plot comes to an almost clichéd stalemate mid-way through the play—"petty-bourgeois ignorance and vulgarity" at loggerheads with "true Soviet ambition."[6]

Chudakov's machine, however, becomes functional prematurely, and a Phosphorescent Woman from "the Age of Communism" appears, announcing that she will take back with her to the year 2030 "anyone who possesses even one trait making him kin to the collective of the commune."[7] Though Pobedonosikov then tries to take credit for the invention, the Phosphorescent Woman installs herself in his office and listens to petitions, which reveal to her the inequities of the 1930 system and Pobedonosikov's hypocrisy. When the time comes for the select group to leave, all the characters (including the bureaucrats, who push their way in) gather in Chudakov's workshop and sing a rallying chant, "The March of Time." Then the machine explodes and the bureaucrats are left alone onstage. Pobedonosikov delivers the last line: "She, and you, and the author—all of you! What have you been trying to say here? That people like me aren't of any use to communism?"

The comedy of the play centers on the satire of bureaucrats, who manifest machine-like behavior so intractable and insensitive it could serve as an illustration for Henri Bergson, with his theory of a comedy built solely on the principle of "mechanical inelasticity."[8] Pobedonosikov and his secretary Optimistenko, run an organization through which every official proposal must pass but which has no real purpose except to perpetuate itself. The Bureau is like a robot with Pobedonosikov at its head. He is a clownish caricature, the main butt of the satire, who performs meaningless official tasks with mindless reflexivity. He dictates importantly about arbitrary subjects:

TYPIST. We stopped on: "And so, comrades . . ."

POBEDONOSIKOV. Oh, yes. "And so, comrades, remember that Leo Tolstoy was a very great and never-to-be forgotten wielder of the pen . . .

TYPIST. Pardon me, comrade. Before, you were talking about a streetcar, and now for some reason you've put Leo Tolstoy in it while it's moving along . . .

POBEDONOSIKOV. What? What streetcar? Oh, yes! All these continual greetings and speeches! . . . Where did we stop?

TYPIST. On "And so, comrades . . ."

POBEDONOSIKOV. "And so comrades, Alexander Semyonich Pushkin, the peerless author of . . .

At times, Pobedonosikov's relentless mechanical behavior becomes more than ridiculous, even evil, like a disease people catch when they come too near him: e.g., the petitioners in the line outside his office "imitate one another's movements like so many cards being shuffled."

The play also has another, non-satirical aspect that centers on the general sense of hopelessness, the feeling that the social situation may never improve. Chudakov speaks of his invention in Act I in a tone that is not wholly optimistic:

> I shall compel time to stop . . . People will be able to climb out of days like passengers out of a streetcar or bus. With my machine you can bring one second of happiness to a halt and enjoy it for a whole month—or until it bores you. With my machine you can make long-drawn-out years of sorrow flash by like a whirlwind . . . thus bringing your days of gloom to an end.

His compulsory ambition to serve the state is mixed with a rejection of the present, an impulse simply to escape. In subsequent scenes he and his worker-allies occasionally appear to be normative characters, because their bureaucratic opponents are so ridiculous, but none of them ever displays a clear, exemplary moral standard against which we may measure the other characters' iniquity.

Thus *The Bathhouse* is something of a dysfunctional satire almost from the opening curtain. For it also contains something of the tragic—the old agon of vision and possibility, the real and the ideal, framed in a way that cannot be reconciled with sanctioned criteria for Soviet dramatic art (such as Socialist Realism).[9] Tragedy, that hallowed rundle of ideas about the transitoriness of life and the immanence of failure in human designs, is in fact inconsistent with any world view that treats socialist enlightenment as inevitable. Yet here is Mayakovsky, in the year local authorities were empowered to confiscate the property of "kulaks" and send them all into exile, balancing an almost totally iniquitous dramatic environment (questions of immorality) against an ecstatic hope for the future (questions of immortality). The theory of tragicomedy formulated by Ionesco, arch-enemy of programmatic art of all stamps, would seem to apply:

> . . . it seems to me that the comic is tragic, and that the tragedy of man is pure derision . . . I tried . . . to confront comedy and tragedy in order to link them in a new dramatic synthesis. But it is not a true synthesis, for these two elements do not coalesce, they coexist: one constantly repels the other, they show each other up, criticize and deny one another and, thanks to their opposition, thus succeed dynamically in maintaining a balance and creating tension.[10]

Unlike his earlier plays, *Mystery-Bouffe* and *The Bedbug*, *The Bathhouse* places the comic and tragic in a tension that is never resolved; the comic and tragic refuse to "coalesce," and the play ends with an ambiguous view of the future, another red flag to Party ideologues (though clearly not red enough).

Some of the humor in the first two acts is based on exaggeration and enlargement, but more of it is based on frustration. Chudakov's opening conversation with his friend from the Young Communist League, Velosipedkin ("bicycle man"), is an example of the former type:

VELOSIPEDKIN. (*rushing in.*) What's new? Does the vile Volga still empty into the Caspian Sea?

CHUDAKOV. (*waving a blueprint.*) Yes, but it won't for long. Better pawn your watch or sell it.

VELOSIPEDKIN. I'm in luck—I haven't even bought one yet.

CHUDAKOV. Well, don't. Don't buy a watch under any circumstances! Before long those flat, tick-tocking things will be more . . . useless than an ox team on a highway.

The language is inflated to exaggerate enthusiasm and to create a framework for the sci-fi terminology that goes with the time machine. But as Optimistenko remarks in Act II (a line with sharp personal edges for Mayakovsky): "Nobody needs your enthusiasm." Much of the action shows the workers' inflated rhetoric, indeed all individual enterprise, being damped by the bureaucrats' bullying. This kind of humor of frustration dominates both Mezalyansova and company's visit to Chudakov in Act I and the workers' visit to the Bureau in Act II:

CHUDAKOV. . . . If we can't shift our experiment to the space above the city, there may be an explosion.

OPTIMISTENKO. An *explosion*? That's enough of that! Don't you dare threaten a government agency! It's not proper to get us all worked up and nervous. And if there *is* an explosion, we'll report you to Certain Competent Authorities.

One might expect the character of Chudakov, who is introduced as the protagonist, to be developed further through contact with his chief adversary, but in Act II he is reduced simply to the "persistent knocker," as cardboard a figure as Pobedonosikov. The drama becomes wholly preoccupied with depicting the bureaucrats as entirely without social value; they commit one after another of the most flagrant abuses, and Mayakovsky spares them no malice.

Though all satire is born of moral rage, the rage in the first two acts of *The Bathhouse* is unusually close to the surface. Mayakovsky's anger is so fierce that it threatens to burst the formal confines of the play, which it actually does in Act III. Its urgency might be illustrated by comparison with *The*

Inspector General, a more realistic play than *The Bathhouse* but nevertheless based on some of the same satiric principles. In Northrop Frye's words, "Satire demands at least a token fantasy, a content which the reader recognizes as grotesque, and at least an implicit moral standard."[11] In Gogol's play, the grotesquerie or fantasy (far from token) lies in the magnification of the townspeople's corruption and philistinism. Within that framework the plot is fueled by an internal logic (based on a mistaken assumption) that causes a sequence of events to continue unmasking new aspects of vice until the guilt and shame of the society, represented by the townspeople, stand "naked" in the final tableau.

In Mayakovsky's play, the represented society is "naked" almost from the beginning. Since the piece is theatricalist, fantasy elements such as the endless line of petitioners and the declamatory language are expected, and grotesquerie exists in the exaggerated caricatures of the bureaucrats. The plot, however, is only sporadically logical. Until the entrance of the Phosphorescent Woman, the characters are powerless to affect their situation even in slight ways. The same (or nearly the same) hypocrisy regarding the socialist ideal is seen in character after character, and the same problem of Pobedonosikov's obtuseness is demonstrated in situation after situation, as if Mayakovsky needed to flay the society he had already stripped bare. Sometimes the dialogue degenerates into insults: "NOCHKIN. All you care about is following precedents and paragraphs, you old stuffed briefcase! You paper clip!" In fact, the play becomes almost unbearable by the end of Act II—not because of boredom (there is too much laughter based on recognizable foibles for that) but because of the futility one feels in watching any helpless situation.

Act III surprises, however, by taking a different line of attack on the bureaucrats and diffusing the audience's sense of frustration. Pobedonosikov and his entourage are seen attending a performance of *The Bathhouse*, and during an ostensible break in the action the Chief admonishes the play's director, who appears as a character: "We don't have officials like that. It's unnatural. Not lifelike. Not the way things are." The Director listens for a time with strained patience, but then answers with an outburst by staging, on the spot, a sarcastic symbolic ballet in mockery of the type of theater officially seen as "appropriate" in 1930—which, of course, Pobedonosikov likes. An abrupt change of tactics: Mayakovsky turns the guns of the theater on the critics before they have a chance to criticize his play, showing the real bureaucrats in the audience their own reaction to *The Bathhouse* while they are having it. The symbolic ballet is a satire of Reinhold Glière's *The Red Poppy*, recently performed at the Bolshoy and considered by Mayakovsky and Meyerhold to be typical of the simplemindedness of Soviet drama.

An understanding of Act III's structural relationship to the play as a whole, however, does not depend on recognition of this topical reference. The beginning of the act reads as follows:

(The stage represents an extension of the orchestra seats. There are several empty seats in the first row. A signal: "We are beginning." The audience looks at the stage through opera glasses, and [actors on] stage look back at the audience through opera glasses. People begin to whistle and stamp their feet as they shout, "Time to start!")

DIRECTOR. Comrades, don't get all worked up! Owing to circumstances beyond our control, we've had to delay the third act a few minutes.

A Pirandellian mirror is turned on the spectators, and their viewing of the play now becomes part of the play's subject. Mayakovsky, perhaps finding himself incapable of sustaining the black humor of Acts I and II, exchanges oblique cynicism for direct address. Topical satire alone is insufficient to contain his bitterness, and he must go beyond it. It's as if the issues are so urgent to him that they burst out of the plot into a metatheatrical grimace. Up to this point readers or spectators are likely to have wry responses due to the lack of potential for change, but now the possibility of change arises. The sudden shift in technique invites them to perceive a sense of option, if not hope, for the first time.[12]

Accompanying that sense, however, is a parallel one of dark foreboding. Like Mayakovsky, the Director loses composure in the face of arrant hypocrisy. He says, apparently placating Pobedonosikov, "I see what you mean, of course. So we'll make the necessary changes in the play, introducing cheerful and graceful supplementary scenes." But later he adds to Velosipedkin, who corners Pobedonosikov at the theater in order to ask him for money, "Comrade Velosipedkin, please don't make a scene! . . . Please! I don't want them to catch on. You'll receive full satisfaction before the play is over." His words might be seen as a threat: a note of defiance against the bureaucrats and a kind of curse on the rest of the play. He invests Acts IV through VI with an undertone of vengeance, saying in effect, "I'll make this play mean what I want it to mean, even at the most extreme risk."

R.C. Elliot has written that the origins of satire in Greek literature before Old Comedy were magical rites in which invective, ridicule, and other violent language were used ritually to kill off evil spirits that plagued the society; the phrase "stinging satire" was once used literally.[13] Metaphorically, modern satire's purpose is also to kill, the act of writing it being an aggressive attack with the weapons of wit and humor. The Act III reversal of *The Bathhouse* turns this aspect of Mayakovsky's satire inward, against itself. Formerly clear distinctions between subject and object are distorted, and the satire's target now must include the satire (more specifically, its present performance), and under this pressure it dissolves. No longer sustaining a pretense of storytelling, the satire criticizes storytelling itself. A metaphoric attack becomes a direct one, made with "homicidal" viciousness while also acting as a self-criticism that is not so vicious but does ask an apt question: can the Soviet theater, under present conditions, still serve significant social ends? The answer may well be "no," and for the remainder of the play, a suspicion of futility accompanies the apparent prevalence of hope.

In a sense, Acts IV through VI shrug off the objections made in Act III by returning to the metaphoric satire. Now the element of hope (which remained indispensable to cultural bureaucrats like Ermilov right up to 1989) has been firmly introduced, however, through the presence of the Phosphorescent Woman. She creates a stir in Pobedonosikov's former office (now called the "Bureau for Selection and Transfer to the Age of Communism) that resembles "all the excitement and disorder of combat conditions, as during the first days of the Revolution." The workers treat her as their socialist Messiah, pleading for each one's individual redemption and admission to the Communist Heaven of 2030:

> POLYA. Please forgive me for intruding but I have no hopes at all. What hopes could I have? It's ridiculous. But I just wanted an answer to one question: What is socialism?
> . . .
> TYPIST. Can it be that where you come from, people will notice a girl even if she doesn't use lipstick? If that's true, then give me a look at that life there . . . please send me right now.

The bureaucrats, when they can gain access to her, treat her as a very senior official, fawning on her as if she determined their next job promotion:

> POBEDONOSIKOV. Greetings comrade! Forgive me for coming late—awfully busy, you know. But I still wanted to drop in on you for a minute. You see, at first I declined to make the trip. But nobody would hear of it. "Go," they said, "and represent us!" Well, since the collective had asked me, I had to agree. But you must bear in mind, comrade, that I'm a top-level executive.

The Woman, for her part, sees through the Chief's arrogance fairly quickly: "No matter what you talk about, it's always 'I don't,' 'I don't,' 'I don't.' Isn't there anything you 'do, do, do'?"

One of the funniest ironies in the play is that all the characters, bureaucrats and workers, hope to leave with her and be free from their era. In Act VI they gather in a provisional brotherhood and sing "The March of Time" together like old friends:

> O
>   Time,
>   march on!

Quicken your pace,
> dear land of mine,

Old ways
> are dead
> > and gone!

March
> on-
> > ward,
> > > Time!

When that song ends, Pobedonosikov bullies his way aboard the machine like a misguided Ubu blurting out demands for his personal comfort even after he is deposed, and starts articulating his own foibles as if a malfunction had occurred in his mechanical mind:

> The apparatus of liberated time was invented in my apparatus, and nowhere else, because in my apparatus there was as much free time as you could want. The present, current moment is characterized by the fact that it is a stationary moment . . .

Sponging has become such second nature to him that he leeches onto every new opportunity without even thinking about what it is. Thus, he comes almost inadvertently to *want* the Communist utopia (which would presumably deny him his present bourgeois excesses), and the audience gets to feel that justice is done when he is denied something he wants. The society marches off ecstatically to an age of perfection, leaving the evil ones to suffer the most horrible of punishments: staying in their world.

Neither that justice nor its benevolent quality, however, is guaranteed. They are never more than desired possibilities, as in classical tragedy. The final gesture is ambiguous, rapture colored with negativity, and the elements of that ambiguity are present earlier in the play. Consider, for example, the speech of justification that the Phosphorescent Woman delivers when she is installed at the head of the Bureau:

> Comrades, our meeting today is rather rushed. But I'll be spending years with many of you, and I'll tell you many other details of our joyful experience. Almost immediately, when we learned of your experiment, our scientists went on continuous watch. They helped you a lot, anticipating your inevitable miscalculations and correcting them. You and we came toward each other like two crews of workmen digging a tunnel, until we met—today . . .

Her speech has the oddity of containing no information about what solutions the future holds. In fact, one cannot tell from anything she says whether she really knows more about the future than the people in 1930. She speaks in generalities, and the righteous, immaculate air that surrounds her seems to forbid close questioning. Furthermore, except for the promise of the time machine, the political situation in Act V is almost exactly the same as in Acts I and II; only the top authority has changed, and Pobedonosikov is now among the disadvantaged. We are back in a chaotic urgency similar to that of the opening acts, modified only by the hope the characters place in the time machine and the Woman.

Both the time machine and the Woman mean much more to the characters, and the author, than is explicitly stated. To read their functions in the story only literally (i.e., as the instruments of an actual journey through time) is to miss much of their resonance. A science-fiction fantasy is predominantly important for what it reveals about the people who must cope with it. The Woman herself says, "I came here only to convince you people of our existence," and she might be seen as coming from their imaginations. As a wish fulfillment she can satisfy several pressing desires: miraculous assurance that the toil of building socialism will ultimately end in success; the consolation of a confessor, to whom the workers unburden their present frustrations; and immediate gratification of the general desire to escape. The time machine, too, is a kind of wish fulfillment. Invented by Chudakov as a solution to the world's ills, it might even be seen as the play's protagonist. What or who else could be the "bathhouse"? In this interpretation, the Phosphorescent Woman is the volitional force behind the time machine, and whether this force is benevolent or evil depends on how one views Mayakovsky's idea of Time.

The theme of Time always figured prominently in this author's work. In *Mystery-Bouffe* Time is seen as the Heroic Destroyer, Revolution's greatest ally, which will eventually kill off all its enemies. In *Vladimir Mayakovsky: A Tragedy* and *The Bedbug*, it is also a destroyer but its ally, Revolution, does not improve Man's condition; Time is the Indifferent and Somber Gravedigger, independent of any socio-political design. In all three earlier plays, however, Mayakovsky shows the future, if not as proof of socialism's triumph then at least as proof of its survival. In *The Bathhouse* we never see the time machine's destination. After showing the Communist Paradise in *Mystery-Bouffe*, after showing the year 1979 in *The Bedbug*, Mayakovsky, significantly, declines to use his penchant for futurism at the end of *The Bathhouse* to show the year 2030. *The Bathhouse* contains no vision of the past, only a hypothetical vision of the future, and a present action that is aborted at the moment when Time is about to leave it behind. The resulting feeling of incompleteness may be easily seen as a critique of the notion of progress, in violation of politically sacred ideas of historical teleology. If Time is a metaphor for the act of writing, then Mayakovsky is indeed saying, as suggested above, that neither can achieve progressive goals any longer.[14]

To Soviet authorities this was of course heresy, evidence of an unforgivably aporetic disposition. It is easy to be misled by the fact that official denunciations of Mayakovsky near the end of his life tended to be couched in the terms of the fashionable theatricalist debate. Since he never denied the Party's position that the theater *should* be a didactic forum for exhorting particular political behaviors, direct attacks on his ideological fidelity were avoided. (The great majority of his writings after 1917 were for propaganda purposes, and no one could reasonably question his belief that, to use Friedrich Wolf's maxim, "art is a weapon.") It was Mayakovsky and Meyerhold's insistence that plays also be entertaining spectacles, a criterion they thought the Moscow Art Theater, by then a national treasure, did not meet, that made them politically vulnerable, and *The Bathhouse* presented their enemies with a perfect pretext for attack. Not only did it employ the frivolous model of a circus; its action, the world-of-the-play-as-world, was so distressing it turned the theatricalist subtitle *A Drama in Six Acts, with a Circus and Fireworks* into a satirical fillip. Mayakovsky's official detractors were right about him from their perspective; this time, he *had* stretched "self-critique" to the point of dissent.

In the context of his career as a whole, however, an even more fundamental schism was at work. A basic contradiction always existed in Mayakovsky's use of non-realistic theatricalist forms to communicate the Messianic ideals of Communism, and the reasons for his tenacious hold on those forms reach beyond Marxist problematics of "individual versus collective interest" or "subjectivism" to older questions of romantic identity. A central thesis of socialist cultural theory from Lunacharsky to Lukács consistently held that, since modernism was attributable to 19th-century social inequities presumably alleviated in revolutionary societies, its "inaccessible" forms and the "elitist" and "alienated" attitudes behind them were irrelevant in the socialist world; socialist art should be "people's art" made by artist-workers who were fully integrated into society. Today, it seems almost commonplace to point out that this thesis was based on false assumptions: among them, that the romantic heritage subsuming modernism, more than a century old and wielding massive psychological influence on artists, could be summarily erased by a *theoretical* utopia.

Even the Mayakovsky of the early 1920s, the most steadfast of Bolsheviks, lacked sufficient "collective interest" to expunge his former self entirely from his personality: the lonely Futurist touring provincial towns where no one understood him had been a veritable model of quixotic Byronism. That fortuitous insufficiency is why *Mystery-Bouffe* remains stageworthy seven decades after its premiere; utopian and iconoclastic in equal measure, it enjoys the bizarre reputation of being, simultaneously, the greatest Bolshevik and the greatest Futurist drama. In the late 1920s, faced with overwhelming opposition to his aesthetic impulses but with his idealism intact, Mayakovsky had nowhere to turn for inner direction except to the iconoclastic heritage of his youth. If *The Bedbug* and *The Bathhouse* were theatricalist "Slaps in the Face of Public Taste," twenty years displaced, they were also effulgent appeals, one hundred years displaced, for the masses of Man to rise in mystical communion with the artist's alter-ego (now appearing as worker-hero *manqué*): "Why am I alone in the cage? Dear ones, my people! Come in with me! Why am I suffering? Citizens!" (Prisypkin, *The Bedbug*).

The parallel with ecstatic Expressionism, that naive, quasi-Communist branch of the early avant-garde, supposedly "overcome and surpassed" after the Russian civil war, is salient. What distinguishes Mayakovsky's work is the way ambiguity is woven into the pattern, as in *The Bathhouse*'s final implication that it is equally likely that 2030 will bring perfection or nothingness.[15] Again, Ionesco's terms are apt; this is not a case of ambivalence but of teeth-grinding self-control by an artist bent on fending off despair by "balancing" tragedy against comedy. As a propagandist, Mayakovsky preached hope almost automatically (his role of satirist is a grotesque distortion of his deep impulse to articulate proper goals for his society), but some time before *The Bedbug* he began to experience horror and desperation as well (sentiments of which Marinetti, the "other" sort of Futurist, would seem to have been incapable). By the time of *The Bathhouse* Mayakovsky could not breathe, could not talk freely about his inability to breathe, and the result was a tragic play about suffocation written with the lighthearted trappings of regenerative farce—"breath" in this case understood as a trope for the self-expressive impulse the proletarian artist tries heroically to subordinate to the needs of the commonweal.

It is the knotty problem surrounding that word "heroically" that gives the case of Mayakovsky its stature as a paradigm. The process of working to destroy the conditions that make romantic heroism possible transforms the artist into a romantic hero. Far from having offered him a viable alternative identity, the socialist order under Stalin treated him as either a useless, lazy bourgeois or an entrepreneurial charlatan (as in the caustic caricature of the "painter" Belvedonsky)—that is, if it didn't succeed in making him a mouthpiece for *realistic* state propaganda. As is well-known, the grim effects of this treatment lasted until the breakup of the Soviet Union and beyond. It was inevitable that the most talented artists, invariably fierce socialists in their youth, would react to persecution and marginalization by turning their personal tragedies into metaphors, mythic or otherwise.

The young Jerzy Grotowsky, for instance, left the leadership of the Polish ZMS (Union of Socialist Youth) in 1957 amid accusations that he "undermined its integrity"; within the following two years he produced *Orpheus*, *Hamlet* and *Faust*. Heiner Müller, expelled from the East German writer's union for "historical pessimism" in the early 1960s, turned to mythic allegory and then burst onto the Western scene in 1977 with a play called *Hamletmachine* in which the central action is the tearing of his photograph. A dozen other examples would fit as well, including Brecht, whose "To Those Born After," quoted at the outset, is a magnificent poem of seventy-four lines, forty of which contain first-person pronouns. Again and again, for these and many other figures, Mayakovsky became the dream of the unified self, the impossible model of an unshakably moral creative spirit who, at least once in this century, died refusing to choose between chiliastic passion and idiosyncratic vision.

One Thing
After Another

. . . one must reject composition in favor of shape (or
something else)

—Richard Foreman, 1972

My work is always a tale of anguish, the picturization of a
free-floating anxiety that I believe IS the daily world in
which we all swim together . . . I am drawn to those
situations which evoke the quake and vertigo of
psychological shipwreck.

—Foreman, 1979

You have to start out speaking . . . in the art, and then let it
drift, fall apart—so that a begun trajectory splinters, gets
lost.

—Foreman, 1981

If you shut your eyes and point at random in any essay or manifesto by
Richard Foreman, you're likely to come up with an illuminating epigraph for
Georg Büchner's *Woyzeck*. It's as if all Foreman's thinking about the thea-
ter, all his preternaturally articulate exhortations over the years about what
performance ought to be, led ineluctably to his present directing project at
Hartford Stage.

   Woyzeck—based on an actual case from the 1820s of a common soldier
who murdered his lover after learning she'd betrayed him—holds a special
place in the modern consciousness. Found after the author's death (in 1837,
at age 23) as an unnumbered jumble of scenes, apparently unfinished, perhaps intentionally abandoned, the play wasn't produced until 1913 in
Europe, until the 1960s in America, largely because it was seen as too
gloomy, and is generally recognized as the first drama dealing with a protagonist lacking any social status or dignity whatsoever. Much more important
for our century, however, has been its fragmentary nature. Its very incompleteness, the fact that even the ordering of its scenes is uncertain, has come

to mean as much to us as its themes: the injustice of a universe that seems to require the victimization of man, the absurdity of notions such as madness, sanity, and normalcy in the face of that cruelty.

Foreman, too, holds a special place in our consciousness. A maverick among mavericks who has paid the price of isolation (perhaps not entirely unwelcome to him because of his shyness), he is the avant-gardist who sometimes directs classics, a one-man movement even when he collaborates. We think of him as unusually courageous not only because of his independence, but also because he has risked awakening that most insidious of American prejudices, anti-intellectualism, rebelling against received theatrical ideas by writing with the merry disregard for conventions of a *belle époque* European. A hundred years ago, he would surely have been an expatriate. Today, he is the closest the American theater has come to a German-style intellectual in the pattern of Büchner, Kleist, and Heiner Müller. "I'd rather be thought of as a French-style intellectual," he says, "but that's only because I prefer France to Germany."

Before the first reading of *Woyzeck*, the actors sit rapt, some bewildered, some terrified. One of them confesses that he almost turned down his role after speaking with a friend who'd been in *Penguin Touquet*: "There was just no freedom, he said. You were told where to move every minute, and I thought: he doesn't want an actor, he wants a robot." Only David Patrick Kelly, who plays Woyzeck, has worked with Foreman before; the body language of the others implies defenses ranging from wariness to panic—a condition hardly ameliorated when someone from the literary office deposits a six-inch-thick packet of background materials on the central table.

Foreman has an upstream paddle, and knows it, and I am immediately impressed at how quickly he finds his way to an easier current. "I know I'm known as a person who has a lot of theories and so on, but for me making art has to do with getting up on your feet and trying things." His introductory speech is remarkably practical-minded, and it succeeds in reassuring the actors. Shoulders relax, eyes return to their sockets, and he goes on to speak about ideas in the context of his own startling admission: "I have no idea how to do this play."

"The truest and most incisive thought for our time must be aphoristic thought," he says. "Thought in fragments. Fragments appeal to us. Fragments are relative to the situation we're in because the world, in a sense, if it's not falling apart, at least it's mixing up, ready to give birth to something else." He is talking about *Woyzeck*, but he could be describing one of his own Ontological-Hysteric Theatre plays, or his erstwhile intention as a director to break stage action down into smaller fragments or "atomic" units. His primary connection to *Woyzeck*, he explains, is with its language, the way Büchner's lines leap from idea to idea, jumping logical steps. "It's totally that particular, stylistic use of language," he tells me. "I mean as far as the first tragedy about a poor little guy . . . [laughs] . . . you know, that's fine, but we've seen that. That's not even too extraordinary."

Foreman has written out his major concerns in a one-page document for the program with the characteristically talky title "3 Things I make myself remember while working on WOYZECK," but he doesn't refer to it in his speech. Instead he speaks to the actors conversationally, taking pains to explain how his perceptions about the text apply to them. For him, the play "is about clairvoyance, in a way . . . Insight pours through Woyzeck in spite of the fact that he's untutored, in turmoil, schizy, and everything else." And the benefits of that insight belong not just to the protagonist, but to everyone in the play's world. "The very things that Woyzeck says, the very way he uses his language, puts us in touch with some basic building blocks in our own unconscious, in our own spiritual orientation, and I think we can find that. I think we'll be able to find that truth for all the rest of you miserable screwed-up people in this play."

Finally—and this point seems essential to him—he says that the drama, for all its depressive qualities, for all the suffering it depicts, is ultimately redemptive. "Sometimes evil is the gasoline that ignites something that drives through an insight, or a way of looking at things, or a realization. It is of use to humanity in the long run." "Suffering is the great educator, sad to say," he elaborates in his "3 Things." "Pain is the unwelcome stimulus to self knowledge. . . . It is unfortunate that there exists a dangerous and seductive mix of evil and ravishing, poetic, visionary beauty, but it is the way of this fallen world. Every character in the play echoes this unholy union between the devil and the angel in man."

"So, with dread and trepidation, let's start reading," he says, motioning to a technician to switch on one of the tape-loops that, as usual with him, will accompany nearly every moment of rehearsals and most of the production. As much as anything else, these loops, with names like "Violin Whine," "DumDum," "Ringtone" and "Yid Glitter," are a sort of Foreman signature. They are emotionally manipulative, of course, as is all background music, but so flagrantly so, due to an obsessive, plangent pounding of the same sound, that their effect is ultimately ambiguous, like a half-serious critique of manipulativeness.

Privately, I ask if *Woyzeck* functions from him as an exploration of the workings of consciousness, as do his own plays. "It sort of does when I read it," he answers. "I mean, that's what appeals to me about it when I read it." But he adds: "In spite of what some of my critics have said, I do not believe in taking classical texts and trying to turn them into one of my plays. I believe in just doing the play and not getting in the way . . . *too much*." Indeed, his fidelity to the text—or, more accurately, to current scholarly opinion about what Büchner's intentions were—is clearly evident. It is so evident that, when he arranges a high platform for his chair at the back of the rehearsal space, I decide not to ask whether he intends to reside there during performances, as he habitually does at his own plays.

Two weeks later, I return and see a run-through during which I cannot stop thinking about the quirky rightness of the casting. There is something slightly "off" about each actor, or at least that's what I glean from the half-realized performances. Kelly, with his slightly haggard cheeks and knife-straight facial lines, has already reached a level of intensity uncomfortable to watch. Spinning and skittering about in short, jerky movements, waving his arms, he seems always to be thrashing in flight. And Gordana Rashovich, who plays Marie, is equally laserlike, with an air of inner agitation and torment that eliminates any possibility of audiences seeing her character as an ingenue. Both she and Tracey Ellis, who plays all the other female characters, convey a strong and troubling sense that things are not all right with them, deep down, and never will be.

The cast has clearly overcome any lingering apprehensions about Foreman and moved on to the much more formidable problem of *Woyzeck* itself, this monstrosity of a masterpiece in which actors must enter, achieve the pinnacle of energy and stylization in two or three lines, and then exit. The six-inch-thick packet is now dog-eared, and well-thumbed paperbacks of Goethe, Nietzsche and Lenz lie about the lounge area. Foreman has just had a talk with the performers in which he explained that there are really only two "fully dimensional characters" in the play; the rest are more or less cartoons. Woyzeck and Marie are "discordant," he explains, switching metaphors, whereas everyone else constitutes "this choral fact that they're trying to escape." The point is hardly calculated to win the hearts of American actors, but the cast has plainly developed a genuine respect for him. They are trying hard, in Ellis's words, "to become the painting he sees in his mind."

Easier for some than for others, though. As William Verderber, the Drum Major, asks, "How do you play a two-character love scene where she is a full character and you are a cartoon?" Verderber has no answer. He says simply that he'll continue to bring in suggestions for the character's personality and leave it up to Foreman to edit out what he thinks is too much.

During the first few rehearsals, I had been surprised not only at Foreman's fidelity to Büchner but also at the extent of his discussions about psychological motivation, which contradicted most of my preconceptions about his working process. There was talk about the nature of Marie and Margret's rivalry, talk about the position of women in society at that time, talk about religion and superstition in relation to Woyzeck and Andres—all extremely detailed and surprisingly sensitive to what actors ordinarily perceive as their needs. In the course of the next few weeks, however, according to several cast members, those discussions all but disappeared. The more the play's frame, the outlines of the composition, became clear in Foreman's mind, the more he told actors exactly what to do.

"It's like a series of haikus," he says, describing the effect he wants. "Something is said, you sort of catch it, and then it's gone." He asks the actors to start sitting out front to watch when they're not onstage, to get a general feeling for what he needs them to fit into. He doesn't want puppets, he says, but he is looking for a more "Bressonian" texture in which a schism appears to exist between speech and demeanor. "Try to get a sense of what a sad world this is. I still have the feeling that a lot of you are feeling an obligation to make more happen than has to happen. Your presence counts more than what you do with your lines. . . . You just have to be saturated with the world that produced *him* . . . Try to savor the syntactical joy, the syntactical weight of the words. Just let them reverberate in your head without your having any effect on them."

It has been an exhausting run-through. He is greeted with a chorus of blank stares, and he searches for an image that will lighten the atmosphere and make his point clearer. Suddenly, his face lights up: "In a sense, you're all zombies. That's overstated, but it's sort of like putting sauce in a stew. Obviously, you're not all zombies, but it needs a little zombie sauce!" General laughter, followed by more blank stares.

"This century found it necessary to invent *Woyzeck*," wrote Timothy Wiles in 1972. The statement has proven true again and again. In effect an honorary 20th-century artwork, the play didn't meaningfully *exist* in theater history until Eugen Kilian staged the world premiere, and since then it has often served as a vessel for other artists' ideas. In 1925, Alban Berg adapted it into the opera *Wozzeck*, which became more widely known than the play. In 1969, Ingmar Bergman used it to start his controversial "open rehearsal" program at the Royal Dramatic Theatre in Stockholm. Joseph Chaikin acted the title role in 1975, after a long absence from the stage, in a production incorporating many ideas from the Open Theater. And now Foreman, grown "older and mellower" by his own admission, finds it necessary to invent a drama of logical leaps and language fragments.

Upon entering the theater for the performance, the first surprise is *Woyzeck*'s setting, particularly for anyone familiar with the way this director typically outfits a stage. He had said at the beginning: "For many years I've been doing plays that are overloaded with props and dreck and I'm trying to do this very simply." I had seen a scale-model of his design, which he called "a kind of theatrical laboratory bullring dissecting room constructivist machine." None of that prepared me for the desolate emptiness of this black space, which sucks up light—white, for preference—as absolutely and indifferently as Woyzeck's surroundings suck up his words.

Outlining the small thrust stage is a low, U-shaped ramp, inside which a semicircular flat space leads to a steep rake and, atop the rake, another flat playing area with an angled ceiling. Most of the floor surfaces are padded, all are black, and a wall lined with white, tilelike squares occasionally flies in and out upstage, leaving an impression of a psychiatric cell. Lining the edge of the U, however, are tall, thin, black poles with bulbs on the ends that suggest street lamps and leave a non-institutional impression of a deserted highway or alley. Numerous other references also come to mind—a boxing ring, an examination room, a stage—but dominant always are the loneliness and colorlessness. The air of desolation is mitigated only by a few skulls, taut strings and rusty chandeliers, which hover up near the flies like a composite logo conveying that complete abandonment of the Ontological-Hysteric was never Foreman's intention.

The second surprise is the extent to which the director has succeeded in achieving his much-discussed "zombie" quality, a sense of true seediness and decrepitude, with a group of actors who, two weeks earlier, still seemed conspicuously healthy and college-educated. Only now do I fully understand what Foreman meant in rehearsals when he spoke of this ubiquitous, menacing chorus of dull-witted people. The faces of the ten performers comprising it are made up in ghoulish white with red eye sockets. Their presence generates an ambient fogginess—despite the plentiful white light, you're never quite sure if you're seeing everything clearly—which eventually reads as a metaphor for the impenetrable fog between Woyzeck and everyone around him.

Strangely, it's this fog, this background of *un*clarity, that sets Woyzeck's isolated condition in a meaningful frame. No question of madness whatsoever, his visions are indeed a form of insight, clarity. The impression is that his eyes are too much open for his own good, and he isn't safe in his world. A capacity for real feeling is a liability where numbness is the prevailing ethos, so he becomes a victim through a process that seems almost automatic, natural. Foreman denies him and everyone else privacy onstage; no one is ever alone. In every scene, someone looms in the background, someone left over, or arrived early, or someone listlessly eavesdropping for no apparent reason: Woyzeck's friend Andres shuffles around on the upper platform during the scene between the Doctor and Captain; Karl the Idiot and a little boy lounge about on the rake during the scene where Woyzeck give Andres his personal effects.

On the one hand, the extraneous people are calculatedly distracting. They make it difficult for spectators to concentrate on Woyzeck's romantic poetry without immediately recalling the disagreeable truth about his world. On the other hand, they serve as visual segues, helping to propel the sixty-seven-minute action forward with a smoothness even greater than what I had noticed at the two-week run-through (attributing it then to the actors having internalized the tape-loops as a form of tonal direction). Woyzeck's crushing understatement about what has happened to him, "One thing after another," could also summarize the breakneck pacing and the choreographed movement. Scenes fit together like collapsing tubes, and a ritualistic sense of tragic inevitability soon builds around the coming catastrophe—a sense, I notice in passing, at odds with the bulk of Foreman's theoretical writings.

This tragic propulsion is also partly attributable to the cohesiveness of the small, tightly knit choral group. For instance, due to budget restrictions, the eternally strange Grandmother's tale was given to Karl the Idiot, played by Brian Delate, a decision that seemed at first unfortunate because the surprise of the story's morbidness is lost if it's told by a character we expect to be

*Georg Büchner's **Woyzeck**, directed by Richard Foreman, Hartford Stage, Hartford, CT, 1991. David Patrick Kelly as Woyzeck, attended by the "choral fact."* (Overleaf)

morbid. Delate makes it into such a moving cameo, though, that it ends up seeming like a fleeting moment of genuine self-knowledge, or sanity, not only for him but also for the world he typifies. A few others don't fit so neatly into the package: Michael J. Hume, for example, who was already playing near performance tempo two weeks earlier, is now far beyond the median level, as if, having found the right attitude for the Doctor too early, he started distrusting it and fell into overacting. Kenneth Gray plays the Captain with a maniacal, Nazi-like machismo I had never seen at rehearsals, and his shaving scene with Woyzeck is now one the production's weirdest sequences. He is a large, fair-skinned, blond man with slicked-back hair, and when he's covered with a sheet and sprawled over backward on a chair nailed to the center rake, he resembles a pig awaiting slaughter.

Holding it all together is Kelly, whose performance is one of those brilliantly aberrant gems that come along only once or twice a decade. He is the opposite of a conventional leading man, short, quirky, unhandsome, violent-looking yet something of a nebbish—in short, the perfect Nobody—and Foreman makes fine use of his idiosyncrasies, taking innumerable choreography cues from the way he manifests Woyzeck's chronic strain: the tense neck muscles, the darting eyes. The best example is the production's most lasting image: Kelly lying upside-down on the rake, convulsing rhythmically as he says, "Stab, stab the bitch to death? Stab, stab the bitch to death." Similarly, when he actually stabs Marie, he comes up behind her and does it in quick, sharp jabs, after which she rolls logwise down the rake and a dozen blazing klieg lights all but blind the audience. The action convulses itself beyond visibility, as it were, an example of the "basic metaphysical paradox" Foreman has spoken of. "There's some other energy that you cannot fathom, cannot scan," he says, "so the more you try to see things clearly, i.e., more light, the more invisible the truth of the situation becomes."

Kelly's performance is, in fact, so central that it ends up suggesting that the play really contains only *one* "fully dimensional character," Foreman's earlier statement notwithstanding. In rehearsal, Rashovich's intensity seemed as if it could easily have been a match for Kelly's, had Büchner given Marie a bit more to say and do. As the play stands, though—especially in this relatively short version—the actress playing that role cannot help but become a part of the "choral fact." For one thing, she understands Woyzeck as little as the others do, and for another, as Rashovich's performance demonstrates, doing justice to Marie's bewilderment and simplicity means sacrificing much of her prominence as a lead. The occasional stare and gelid tone of voice, no matter how resonant, hasn't a hope of competing with Woyzeck's sweeping expressive range.

The real revelation in this production, though, is its reaffirmation of what we knew all along about *Woyzeck's* unique openness, its adaptability to widely differing ideas about theater. Foreman did try to serve the text, and to that end he sacrificed many of his theoretical ideas, but some of them crept in anyway, as if the text itself had called them back. There was, in the end,

despite the logic and fluidity of the action, a strong flavor of "pearls"—
Foreman's traditional framing devices that create what critic Kate Davy once
called "a sequence of static pictures," his version of Gertrude Stein's "contin-
uous present"—implying an affinity with the material deeper, perhaps, than
even the director imagined. Ironically, the seamlessness ultimately served him
as a framing device; for it made the audience all the more anxious to catch
and examine the dozens of immaculately staged moments that were continually flying by.

The resulting amplitude of those details—a momentary glimpse through a
doorway of Marie and the Drum Major dancing, brief cut to a pinspot on
Woyzeck's "double-vision" speech—brought with it a pathos that extended
beyond the fictional story. It's as if the ephemerality of the theater event were
made part of the subject matter, and the impossibility of catching it all
became the key to a more essential fragmentariness that *was* poignantly
preserved. And oddly, as with the isolated "pearls," this effect was ultimately
given extraordinary impact by being framed by its opposite.

In the last scene, Kelly, after running three complete laps of the stage at
full speed, winds down to a stop near some loose boards in the U-shaped
ramp. Lifting them, he finds pools of water underneath, into which he slowly
wades, mumbling, and the play's frantic, panicked action comes to final rest
amid the contemplative sound of lapping water.

ON THE FRONT LINE

Why I Write For
THE VILLAGE VOICE
(Part One)

Moron! Vermin! Abortion! Morpion! Sewer-rat! Curate!
Cretin! Crritic!

— *Waiting for Godot*

Streithammel! Querulant! Stinkstiefel! Giftzwickel!
Brechmittel! Pestbeule! Parasit! Ober . . . forstinspektor!
      — *Warten auf Godot* (German translation by Elmar Tophoven,
      in consultation with Samuel Beckett)

Occasionally I'm asked why I return to Germany every year on a theatergoing pilgrimage. It's a naive question, but the answer is pertinent to the
"Crritic" series.[1] I go to Germany because I need to remind myself regularly
that theater people do exist who can see that George Steiner's comment, "To
read well is to take great risks," has theater application. I need the balm, at
least for a few weeks, of contact with a theater world not dominated by
middlebrow aristocrats who believe that artistic utterances should be im-
mune from contradiction and counterstatement and by "artists" who expect
genuflection simply because they call themselves that. I need to remember
what it's like to be among spectators who need the theater as much as I do,
people prepared to shout and boo and whine, determined that their voices be
taken into account.

As is well known, thinking has an entirely different status in the German
theater. To be in an audience there is to feel you are among people approaching a carefully constructed puzzle. They're there to enjoy deciphering or
solving it, teasing out the questions posed by events onstage. Hence, the
critics come as highly experienced puzzle-solvers whose solutions may not be
right in any absolute sense but are at least considered interesting by dis-
criminating readers. The critic is there to match wits with the director,

author, and designers—and sometimes the actors. Critics are embraced as thoughtful observers of the era, the Über-puzzle, of which the theater is a mirror and a lamp.

In my country, as is also well known, most directors and authors, after some success, lose interest in matching wits with critics or any other observers not directly compliant with their will. Notwithstanding Michael Hillyer's refreshingly candid "The Privilege of Being Judged" (*Voice*, May 14, 1991), they don't see critical feedback as worthwhile even when it's intelligent and astute. We American critics practice our craft in an atmosphere of zealous anti-intellectualism, and no counterargument from me, regardless how lucid and airtight, will change that. "Beware the Egos of Critics" (*Voice*, April 9, 1991), by choreographer and former reviewer Wendy Perron, offers a pure illustration; "Nothing I have done is more difficult than choreography," she writes, unaware that her statement reveals more about her criticism than her choreography.

As Eric Bentley observed back in 1964, the atmosphere in our theater contains something contagious, corrupting even the heartiest of intellects— "Reviewers of plays in the English and American theater may be expected to be anti-intellectual from the very nature of their position in society"—and that is largely why uptown reviewing so often deteriorates into verbal slugfest. The writers sink to the perceived level of a public whose highest mental and spiritual capacities are thought to be directly and accurately measured by its newsstand purchases. Perhaps that's a workable definition of reviewers as distinct from critics; in any case, Bentley now seems to believe that the *Voice* is part of the problem. "To hell with your writers' opinions," he says in the voice of Jerome Clegg. "To hell with their usually overpowering wish to say something devastating, smart, and dismissive." (*Voice*, May 7, 1991)

His curse is especially strange, because he knows better than most how to make distinctions in this field and because it comes from the man who once wrote: "The voice that tells me it is *un*necessary to throw bricks is the voice of opportunism." Surely there's a way to be honest about the critic's circumstances without negative exaggeration or false humility. We downtown reviewers allow ourselves the conceit that we're different from, more idealistic than our uptown colleagues, that our purpose really is to help people see better, see more, that the bricks we throw can be picked up and used to build something better than what they have destroyed. The truth is, though, we often aren't given the chance to do that. What Bentley curses—and again, he knows this, or ought to—is primarily a result of forced brevity. Space pressure makes you mean, makes you put things in severer terms than you'd prefer, makes you express opinions backed by insufficient description. After that admission, however, is the proper response to dismiss opinion per se, or to launch an attack against the circumstances that transform it into a blunt instrument?

Look at any critic who brought dignity to theater criticism over the past two centuries, from William Hazlitt to Alfred Kerr to Bentley, and you see that he had the space to write detailed description and to comment on seemingly peripheral matters of craft and atmosphere. Bernard Shaw could spend 1000 words comparing two actresses' complexions; G.H. Lewes, in the same space, could compare two actors of the same role who died almost a century apart; Paris journalists of the 1920s and 30s who are otherwise forgotten appear in our histories because they were able to digress a bit about the incongruity of evening dresses and diadems in the audiences at avant-garde premieres. As recently as twenty years ago, the United States still had journals in which my teachers Stanley Kauffmann and Richard Gilman could build their reputations with columns written as think-pieces and could collect them in books.

Today very few American critics have a regular forum, other than in quarterlies, to publish that sort of detailed prose. Commenting at respectable length on a theatrical event while the event is still running has become one of the rarest of writerly privileges, and publishers and editors, preoccupied with ad-to-text ratios and similar matters, have little leisure to worry about what is respectable. The most well-meaning invariably reduce the question to this: how much can be shaved off before a hypothetical quorum of p.c. intellectuals would definitely say "stop"? Over half a century ago Walter Benjamin observed that "modern man no longer works at what cannot be abbreviated." Today that "modern" condition is accepted as preordained. Ours is an age of strangled possibility masquerading as technological pleni-tude, in which an entire generation has come to maturity *never having had the chance to choose* whether it wants everything byte-size or not.

Leonardo Shapiro, in an otherwise lucid article (*Voice*, August 27, 1991), suggests that indifference or laziness on the part of us critics in writing Choices [one- or two-sentence recommendations of what to see and do each week] is responsible for making the contemporary scene seem listless and lacking in excitement. I submit that the almost complete exclusion of "scene" from our theater reportage, driven by precisely the confusion of criticism and PR that creates a demand for Choices and Cameos [100- to 150-word mini-reviews], is a much more significant factor. Theater people complain all the time about a lack of community feeling. What causes what, though? Cer-tainly excitement is possible without criticism, but critics in the past have been highly instrumental in giving people a sense of occasion, tradition, and community. Again, let's not confuse low ambition with lack of opportunity. Do we not care because we don't care, or because nearly every media form we've ever encountered has treated us as people who don't care?

The proper response to publishers who nod understandingly and then point to the bottom line is the same as it has been since Dickens' age: that there is also a spiritual and ideational bottom line, too often, and danger-ously, ignored. Does that sound absurdly idealistic? I certainly hope so. One of the *Voice*'s more bizarre peculiarities is its readiness to package and sell idealism, in the form of critiques of itself, without changing its policies in the slightest afterward. It's like a little dance in which the partners tussle over who will lead while the public pays to laugh at the discord. My idealism and griping extend far beyond the *Voice*, though. I have an almost irresponsibly high opinion of my contemporaries in general and my readers in particular, malnourished as they are, to the point where I believe that even a modest dose of Germanness—in the form of frontal attacks on anti-intellectualism on both sides of the curtain—could work almost instant miracles.

For over two centuries the Germans have faced directly a truth we still resist accepting in this country: that most theater, and particularly the kind that needs substantial technical means, doesn't pay for itself; it needs subsidy to exist in anything but the most superficial form, so we must decide as a society whether we want it or not. Ultimately, in the arena of editing rather than government, the same is true for theater criticism. Measured against, say, theater advertising receipts, criticism doesn't earn its space in any paper, and a decision must be made at the policy level whether readers want it. As Kauffmann once wrote: "Not one newspaper or magazine, however high-minded, would carry criticism one day after the editor became convinced that the public had stopped reading it." The truth is, people do read it, and the only sensible argument is over what it should be.

For reasons of space (!), my opinion on the proper handling of published opinion will have to wait until next week.

(May 12, 1992)

Why I Write for
THE VILLAGE VOICE
(Part Two)

The truth is closer to Ubu than to anything else.
    —Anonymous *Voice* senior staff member speaking of upper management.

Over the past two decades antagonism toward opinion has acquired a sort of phony cachet in the United States because of the prevalence of science envy in the arts. The most implacable enemy of evaluative criticism has been Michael Kirby, former editor of *TDR*, whose argument always seemed to me half-extremist and half-valid. The extremism had to do with the idea that publishing opinions about other people's work was, *a priori*, immoral—as if value judgement hadn't been under scrutiny for the duration of this century by formidable minds such as T.S. Eliot and Northrop Frye, and as if Kirby did anything to advance the debate by retreating to 19th century delusions of absolute exactitude in observation.

This aspect of *TDR*'s editorial policy played straight into the hands of the sort of predatory poetasters who, in every generation since Dr. Johnson, have made themselves feel large by trying to pressure critics into timidity. To imply, as did several of the contributors to the "Crritic" series, that, because financial realities make it unprecedentedly difficult to produce plays, we critics should relax our standards and temper our language, is to call for dishonesty and tergiversation. Of course we care that the funding outlook is desperate and that fledgling ventures can be easily killed, but critics aren't advocates for the financially disadvantaged or any other special group. Nor are we affirmative action agents. Nor would the poorest of practitioners, after an hour's quiet thought on the subject (what a luxury!), want us to be.

We are just people possessed by two passions that may ultimately stand in mutual contradiction, for the theater and for telling the truth. The latter makes us more or less natural pariahs in a field with so many huge, fragile egos, where no one is ever sure whether actuality is preferable to illusion—and that is especially pertinent in a land where the mind has little independent standing. A fair analogy is Sartre's clown "who releases man from himself by an ignominious sacrifice for which no one thanks him," only in our case laughter is replaced by scorn. The ignominy of the clown and the critic would be indistinguishable if people didn't mistakenly assume that critics were necessarily comfortable bourgeois wage-earners. To set the record straight, a young would-be critic pays just as high a price in poverty, rejection, and discouragement as any would-be playwright, director, or actor, and generally acquires much less wealth and stability than they do after becoming established.[2]

Very early on, though, a young critic does develop a certain righteous anger, not from weakness or ill intent but simply from going to the theater 150 times a year; and anyone who fails to develop this anger probably lacks a crucial job qualification. Shaw wrote the authoritative piece on this somewhat masochistic (his word was "inhuman") activity. "The cardinal guarantee for a critic's integrity is simply the force of the critical instinct itself," he wrote, and like all instincts it's unavoidable. In other words, either you're a critic or you're not, and if you are then you're inextricably bound to your inner vision of what the theater *can* be—and, yes, that supersedes people's feelings. "If my own father were an actor-manager," Shaw went on, "and his life depended on his getting favorable notices of his performance, I should orphan myself without an instant's hesitation if he acted badly." It's not a question of cruelty in the name of an abstract ideal, but rather of making a Sartrean choice for the theater over the father. Perhaps that's partly what Borges had in mind when he said that "torture is the mother of metaphor."

Artists feel they must protect their egos by playing a half-serious game of rejecting standards set up by critics, saying in response to any objection, "But I meant it that way." Somewhere in all of them, though, is a deeper awareness that neither they nor humankind have truly evolved beyond the condition of making judgements in the presence of works of the imagination—most of which (pomo theories be damned) still reflect or record the strivings of individual souls toward some sort of transcendence. To twist a formulation of Artaud's, we are not nice, and the judgement of others can burst through our earplugs at any moment, and the theater has been created to teach us that first of all. Criticism only records what is always already occurring in the house at every theatrical performance.

Returning to Kirby, though, the aspect of his objection that was always much more substantial and disturbing than his *a priori* argument was his claim that shorthand subjective accounts are worthless as documentation, the truth of which grows more shamefully apparent every day. I remember an article in the *Voice*'s 30th anniversary issue expressing pride in the simple fact that the paper had been *there*, reporting on hundreds of important avant-garde events when no other publication was. The pride was justified. As a theatre historian, I've found many old *Voice* articles (and *TDR* reports, for that matter) extremely valuable, but it's difficult to see how any future researcher or practioner will be able to make use of the Cameos, or even the ten- and twelve-inch reviews that currently appear in these pages.

Since the topic calls for full disclosure, I'll answer the obvious question frankly: why, then, do I agree to write Cameos at all? First, because once in a while I do see something I think is best addressed in 100 to 150 words. Second, and this is the crux, because I need the health insurance, for which we *Voice* contributors have to write a minimum number of pieces per year in order to qualify. Again, most of us aren't comfy, complacent institutional employees but rather writers who scratch by as narrowly as those we write about. And anyone who thinks health insurance is only a personal matter and not one of the most terrible and resonant metaphors of our time should think again. The shabby state of American theater criticism has to do with our failure to accommodate fully human forms of journalism, which in turn has to do with our failure to support institutions that fully accommodate humans.

The *Voice*'s senior editors say that shorter reviews are necessary in order to "cover more," but I wonder: what's the value of "covering more" at the expense of critical substance? Here's a dirty little secret I can let readers in on: the Cameos were originally an experiment. When they started, the editors half expected bags of mail condemning them as an outrage, but, as it happened, no one complained, and the assumption was naturally made that theater people were so grateful for those scraps of free publicity they deemed the sacrifice worthwhile. Now, seriously, is that true? Did readers ever think at all about what was sacrificed or, unaccustomed to true choice of any kind, did they just accept what was served up?

This "Crritic" series was and is, among other things, a chance for *Voice* readers to demand more from their theater section, and at the risk of sounding apocalyptic and paternalistic, I can't help chiding: you are blowing it, darlings. Ross Wetzsteon's initial piece seemed to me clear and courageous, but maybe he asked his questions too nicely. Here are some blunt reformulations. Do you think 100 judgmental words, often by a writer with slender credentials, in response to a production that has taken months to prepare, are in fact better than nothing? Do you think Michael Feingold should be the only theater writer who can regularly write 1000 words or more? Do you approve of the fact that, over the past two years, the median length of "full reviews" other than Feingold's has shrunk from 750 to 500 words?

If you're still reading this, there is hope for you, and for this paper too, which responds to its public more directly than many believe. It is derelict just to shrug and say that our generation didn't inherit a *Voice* like the one that documented the 60s avant-garde. The *Voice* will be only what we demand that it be. For those interested in serious, timely commentary on the theater from more than one strong voice, this shrill, smarmy, infuriating newspaper, which has never been only a newspaper, is *all we have*. Compromised as it is with Ubu, it's the closest thing that exists to what we need—a fact now so obvious it no longer needs to be proven by bashing other journals.

For ten years I wrote regularly for the theater quarterlies and have yet to receive my first postcard in response. At the *Voice* at least I get hate mail (mostly), which gives me the illusion that the abyss out there has a bottom. To enemies and friends alike, I propose a deal. If you keep protesting the philistine backsliding of this publication—my work included, certainly—then I promise to do the same, and to keep on doing so, at least until the day the theater section is taken over by some puff-mongering cretin who won't let me talk about Germany.

(*May 19, 1992*)

Wilder Than Thou

The Matchmaker, by Thornton Wilder, Roundabout Theatre Company
The Skin of Our Teeth, by Thornton Wilder, Jean Cocteau Repertory

More than with most other authors, to criticize Thornton Wilder is to give yourself away. Almost regardless of his talent as a dramatist, he has become a touchstone for everyone's credentials as an American. Sure, there's lots of heady stuff written about him, both for and against. The bulk is unbearable today, not because of the rightness or wrongness of the observations but because of a certain torpid, "why bother?" quality, even in the praise from the 1940s following his third Pulitzer Prize. The critics sound positively tired describing his "radical formal innovations": the bare stages, the actors addressing the audience directly. Wilder is a bottom-line man. All most people really want to know, even cosmopolitan theater types, is whether you're a bellyachin', smart-aleck intellectual or someone who can appreciate the optimism and the down-home wholesomeness.

Of course, Wilder himself was one of those intellectuals his humbler-than-thou defenders love to scoff at. His provincial Wisconsin origins notwithstanding, he was as well-read, well-traveled—as Europhilic—as any author of his time, an inveterate name-dropper more at home in a first-class steamer cabin en route to Paris or Buenos Aires than in any sleepy New Hampshire town "just across the Massachusetts line." And it's precisely *because* his works communicate his ambivalence about the life of the mind that he can continue to function (along with O'Neill) as a repository for chauvinistic anxieties about whether we have a real indigenous drama yet.

Harold Clurman's quip that "he arranges flowers beautifully, but he does not grow them" remains an apt trope for Wilder at his worst. For anyone with his education to write a play like *The Matchmaker* is to ask to be seen as the anti-intellectual's intellectual, the guy who went off to read all the books in order to reassure us there wasn't anything in 'em we couldn't have learned on grandpa's knee. *Our Town*, with its gentle gibes at "scholars" who haven't "settled the matter yet," occupies a middle ground on this score, but even *The Skin of Our Teeth*, the great paean to human resourcefulness, the play that ends with a triumphal march of quotations from famous philosophers, takes a somewhat condescending tone toward Mr. Antrobus' desire to save his books. Wilder built a reputation as a sort of dilettantish Martin Luther of letters, an apostle (or heretic) in the religion of art so mistrusted in his native land, and he had to live up to that image even when possessed by an impulse to make drama from *Finnegans Wake*.

The Matchmaker, a flower arrangement from 1938, began life as *The Merchant of Yonkers*, an adaptation of an adaptation. The world premiere, directed by an exiled Max Reinhardt in the doldrums of the Depression, closed after 28 performances, but a production by Tyrone Guthrie in the pabulum-sucking '50s was a popular success in London and New York, and a decade later Gower Champion and others transformed the play into *Hello, Dolly!* Perhaps the strangest revelation of this revival by Lonny Price is that the text comes off utterly devoid of wit. What anyone ever found funny in a sloppily structured farce about a thoroughgoing virago bullying an uncouth, miserly merchant into marrying her is truly a mystery.

There are a few fine performances, notably Jim Fyfe and Rob Kramer as the merchant's clerks, and Lisa Emery and Lisa Dove as the milliner and assistant, but they stand no chance of clearing the dust away. The few pseudo-serious ideas Wilder inserted—enjoy life while you can, have adventures once in a while—were pedestrian to begin with and are now little more than maudlin. Wife jokes, hair-dye jokes, mock anguish over elopement—it's all so unsustaining I sat there wishing the actors would break out into songs from *Hello Dolly!* All except the truck-like Dorothy Loudon, that is, who is too unappealing as Dolly for anyone to want her to do anything.

A more imaginative director might have helped: Price went straight for the standard museum reconstruction, sprinkled with ostentatious 19th-century costumes and set in an overenthusiastic mandible of interlocking curlicue frames stretched with lacy pink and apricot cloth. The problems are ultimately more fundamental, though. This is a play that instructs the audience to think but reproves it if it goes to far. Laugh for two hours at the expense of the parvenu merchant and his vulgar manners, but don't balk when the plot goes on to strut as a grand vindication of the Common Man. Feel bad if you haven't dropped everything for the sake of adventure recently, but look the other way at the fact that everyone in the play lands on nice fat financial cushions after they do. Hardly new hypocrisies, alas, even in 1938.

Whatever immortality Wilder may have today comes from his earnestness, those fleeting moments of porchside eloquence in *Our Town* and *Skin of Our Teeth* that create an astonishing sense that maybe this really was a man who saw divinity in every mundane moment and fact of life. The most cynical will buy into his buoyancy for a while, if only as a curiosity, as long as it's not belied by a play's form—which is why these two plays are such dependable workhorses for small, poor, and amateur companies that only do "just the facts" productions.

Robert Hupp, working with a small fraction of Lonny Price's budget, has created a plucky, exuberant fantasy world for his version of *Skin of Our Teeth*, the set for which consists of simple arrangements of speckled wood slats. In fact, if I weren't one of those bellyachers who questions the basic assumptions of this type of balsam-theater—"All I ask is the chance to build new worlds and God has always given us that" (Antrobus in perpetuum)— I'd recommend that Roundabout audiences rush down to see it before *The Matchmaker* has a chance to tarnish their image of Wilder.

A blithe announcer reporting epochal events in human history in the form of local New Jersey news, importunate whimpering by domesticated dinosaurs, a presidential address to "fellow mammals" convened in Atlantic City: these are extremely durable stage items. Wilder knew how to push clichés to the brink of tolerability and knew how to jerk a tear, and there's nothing more affecting than watching actors who believe implicitly in him pour their hearts into his clever allegory. Everyone in this production is well cast—no small praise for a tiny company—with particularly strong and detailed work by Jeanne Demers as Sabina and Craig Smith as Mr. Antrobus. At one point in the largely geriatric matinee I attended, a rapt spectator shouted out, "You bet it is!" when Antrobus in the ice age exclaimed, "It's cold."

From one perspective, there's no arguing with that sort of proven effectiveness. From another, though, there's an obligation to challenge it, especially with an author who has at least one major character advise the audience "not to think about the play" and never makes clear exactly what his attitude is toward the advice.

(September 3, 1991)

Awakening

When We Dead Awaken, by Henrik Ibsen, American Repertory Theatre

Upon leaving *When We Dead Awaken*, by far the most satisfying Robert Wilson experience I've had, I couldn't suppress a smile at the thought that this production will likely seem abominable not only to the cemetery-keepers of naturalism but also to the pundits of postmodernism. The former, who have always thrived on the lingering aroma of William Archer's corpse, would hate any willful interpretation of this play—whose naturalism is problematic in any case. The latter, though, who simply hate interpretation, usually sing Wilson's praises, and they will be shocked to see the panache with which their lance-bearer has engaged in the taboo exercise of assigning meanings.

Substantial cuts and interpolations notwithstanding, Wilson has *directed* Ibsen's play, which is either recidivist or courageous depending on your point of view. Why courageous? Well, because this is an artist who's been told for years that his historical uniqueness consists in devaluing texts—even classics by Euripides and Shakespeare—in favor of large, slow-moving images superimposed without conscious regard to correspondence. For him to turn around now and blithely subordinate those images to a language framework determined by Ibsen is to risk hurling his constituency into throes of discomfiture. May the spirit of Artaud rain blessings on gurus who betray their proselytes.

Actually, Wilson has hinted at this shift for years. Despite his denials, numerous pieces such as the Act IV Epilogue of *the CIVIL warS* (1985), *Alcestis* (1986), and *Swan Song* (1989) have contained extended bits of literariness. The surprise of *When We Dead Awaken* is that the bits have become the whole. Gone are the trite and bombastic tableaux, though the technical marvels remain to serve subtler ends. Gone is the use of text as a verbal equivalent of banal and annoying movie background music, though words are sometimes intoned, distorted, or repeated as formal embellishments to meaning—that is, when they aren't being spoken naturalistically by

When We Dead Awaken
by Henrik Ibsen, directed
by Robert Wilson,
American Repertory
Theatre, Cambridge, MA,
1991. From left to right,
Mario Arrambide
(Ulfheim), Stephanie Roth
(Maya), Elzbieta
Czyzewska and Sheryl
Sutton (both Irene), Alvin
Epstein (Rubek),
Margaret Hall (Maid),
Charles "Honi" Coles
(Spa Manager).

Ulfeim, Rubek and Maya
*in Act III of **When We***
***Dead Awaken**, set design*
by Robert Wilson and
John Conklin.

actors with obvious and profound investments in the psychology of their characters.

When We Dead Awaken is usually described as a two-protagonist drama about a reunion, after many years, between a famous, aging sculptor (Rubek) and the ethereal, slightly unstable model (Irene) who inspired his masterpiece, *Resurrection*, culminating in an ambiguous epiphany involving an avalanche and a mumbling nun. In Wilson's version, a third character becomes equally, if not more, central: Maya, Rubek's young wife, with whom he has grown bored and hence willingly surrenders to a bear-hunter named Ulfheim. With the bare-chested, clubfooted Ulfheim dressed as a cartoon, and Rubek and Irene (whom Wilson conflates with the nun, creating a composite character) unable to transcend their pallid and sedentary states, Maya becomes the only truly living spirit onstage, often appearing to control events, even entering at one point with an electronic box that makes the set pieces move.

What an exceptional opportunity for an actress, and sure enough, Stephanie Roth runs with it, finding as great an expressive range within Wilson's precise vocal and choreographic requirements as any performer I've seen. Instructed to alternate between mechanistic and everyday speech, she makes the alternations function as surprising character information about Maya. Told to hop on one foot when declaring in neutral tones that she doesn't know how to talk about art, she moves so gracefully it become ambiguous whether her words are sarcastic. For similar reasons, Alvin Epstein is a lucid, strong Rubek, equally adept at playing a haughty character and an elegant cipher. More than anything else, this frequent, abrupt shifting, which also extends to the music, sets the production's tone, and Wilson's decision not to apply it to the very capable Mario Arrambide (Ulfheim) prompted my only significant objection. Caricatures can't play reversals, and without some crack in Ulfheim's ursine demeanor in the last scene, Maya's final actions and lines about freedom are incomprehensible.

It has long been clear to critics that Symbolism could be an ideal vehicle for Wilson's talents—all those mystical, rarely performed turn-of-the-century works by Maeterlinck, Strindberg, Hofmannsthal, Yeats, and others, dealing with intimations of worlds beyond ours—and now, seeing the intensity with which his moodiness, his nonconversationally directed voices, his meditational backdrops illuminate *When We Dead Awaken*, I'm more convinced than ever. And it isn't merely a case of somber bedfellows making a somber marriage.

Wilson took his biggest risk in inserting three vaudevillesque knee plays, each of which diffuses the built-up heaviness with jazzy dances to songs by Charles "Honi" Coles (who also plays the Spa Manager). These vignettes are so corny, so unapologetically focused on love, that the audience's skepticism is palpable when they begin; imagine the whole cast, in a kick line, rhythmically chanting the play's title in counterpoint to Cole's bluesy lyrics, "I did it. So what? I fell in love." In the end, though, it all seems thoroughly justified, not only because of the weathered dignity of Cole's voice, but also because of Wilson's earnestness, the fact that he declined to undercut or mock Ibsen. It's as if he saw this as a play about love and simply wanted to direct it that way. Perhaps there's hope for us yet, when we postmodernists awaken.

(March 19, 1991)

Reckonings

Parsifal, by Richard Wagner, Hamburg Oper

Robert Wilson has withstood a formidable array of chilly adjectives over the years—cerebral, obscurantist, glib, bombastic, inarticulate—but rarely has anyone been able to accuse him of wearing his heart on his sleeve. His recent productions of Ibsen's *When We Dead Awaken* and Wagner's *Parsifal*, however, seem to mark a significant change in attitude, not only toward text but also toward all those mucky, warm emotions that so often flirt with sentimentality. Thomas Mann once described these two works as "farewell mystery plays. . . apocalyptic climaxes, majestic in their sclerotic languor, in the mechanical rigor of their technique, their general tone of reviewing life and casting up accounts." For Wilson to direct them back to back—despite the fact that his interest in *Parsifal* dates from years ago—is virtually to urge several knotty questions on us.

Why the interest in last plays? Could they possibly be serving as a composite funeral for his earlier career, culminating opportunely in this Hamburg production in which, to borrow Mann's phrasing, his infatuation with the merely monumental and grandiose may be blamed on someone else for a change? And why the sudden (inadvertent?) modesty? As was Ibsen's, Wagner's aesthetic vision is allowed to remain the center of attention the entire time—conductor Gerd Albrecht and the singers doing a superb job that, if heard as a recording, would bear no trace of any modernist gimmicks more contemporary than Wagner's.

Better to reassure the panting Wagnerites right away about the emotionalism: Wilson offers no pathetically wailing Kundry, no boo-hooing youths beside the dying Titurel, no soft-porn titillation by Klingsor's magic maidens. If anything, his *mise-en-scène* is more rigorous and austere than ever, as if he were so afraid of falling victim to his reactions that he ended up revealing them through overcompensation. He is obviously uncomfortable with even the small amount of interpretive decision-making necessary to apply his images neutrally. How can anything be "neutral," after all, until some extreme thematic poles are defined—be they Good and Evil, Christ and the Devil, or modern and postmodern?

Gurnemanz and the other Knights of the Holy Grail, for instance, having been wounded in their sides, singly and collectively, during various slip-ups of the flesh with Klingsor's enslaved seductresses, stand with their left hands pointed stiffly downward, right hands raised stiffly at chest level in a gesture of half-prayer: a visual reminder of tentative piety and weakened faith that disappears only at the end when Parsifal becomes Grail King and the black round table turns white. The Knights and attendants also wear severe, angular black gowns, presumably to set them apart from Parsifal, who enters in a white, sleeveless, open-chested pants-suit that—what with his blow-dried hair—makes him look like a quack dentist from L.A. There's nothing fundamentally wrongheaded or un-Wagnerian about these touches. They're just so irredeemably oversimplified in the name of essentialization that they end up discouraging thought. And in a five-hour opera whose predominant quality is stasis, the mind needs more prods than snags.

Wilson clearly made a decision from the outset to match stasis with stasis, opening the field for audience interpretation as wide as possible. It's as if he were trying to outpurge Wieland Wagner, the composer's grandson, who shocked Bayreuth audiences after World War II with his spare stagings purged of the trappings of Teutonic myth. Wilson's response to all the big directorial questions posed by the libretto—what is the Grail? what is the spear? what do the kiss, the collapse of Klingsor's castle, the healing of Amfortas, mean, and how should they look?—is to run the other way. Most of the opera's classic problematic moments are either missing or might as well be.

The reference to the attempted murder of Kundry, for instance, comes and goes while Parsifal is lying face down on the stage, hardly in form to strangle a passing insect. The kiss, too, the famous peripeteia that isn't one, never arrives, the closest contact between Parsifal and Kundry in Act II being an indolent jab with a small metal rod she happens to carry. The idea that all of it, everything magical—the spear, the castle, the wounds, the sins, the redemption—exist *only* in the characters' minds is Wilson's strongest claim to conceptual originality. He literalizes and pushes to an extreme the frequent critical trope that *Parsifal* is really an opera of internal states. The trouble is, the production isn't nearly so open or free from coercive devices as he seems to think.

The ubiquitous black and white costumes (Kundry, draped unsexily in brown, is the only exception among the main characters) and the obsession with coffin-shaped set pieces (Amfortas' litter, Klinsor's tower, and more) aren't even the most heavy-handed signposts. The Grail shrine turns out to be a sharply jutting erection of iceberg that slides on from the side just in time for the giant ring-shaped table to descend onto it from the flies, the descent stretched out over a long, teasing, secretion-inducing interval. The actors, it

Parsifal by Richard Wagner, direction and stage design by Robert Wilson, Hamburg Opera, Hamburg, Germany, 1991. Dunja Vejzovic as Kundry and Siegfried Jerusalem as Parsifal.

*Kundry, Gurnemanz (Kurt Moll) and Parsifal accompany foreplay of round table and Grail shrine in **Parsifal**.*

seems, may not touch each other, but the stage may fornicate with itself, apparently quite satisfactorily since the orifice-table is left aglow after Parsifal's final exit, a healthy flame burning in the ice's place. The meditative value of his beautiful, nearly still pictures notwithstanding, Wilson lurches into cliché at the borderlines of meaning, whenever the incremental movements the plot does make force him to define his terms.

That is overstating the case, but only a bit. There are moments when Wilson ignores Wagner sufficiently for his visual conception to take root on its own: at one point, dozens of Knights in black cocoonlike wrappers line up across the forestage, aggressively confronting the audience and obscuring the scene behind until they gradually part (like Wagner's cliff-walls) to reveal the Grail Temple. That's exactly the sort of outright challenge to the theater of narcosis that, multiplied a hundredfold and applied equally to the music, could have made this indeed a historic meeting of Napoleonic minds. As it is, funeral or not, Wilson seems to lack the stuff necessary for genuine renunciation. In marked contrast to his production of *When We Dead Awaken*, he fails to fully accept or abdicate interpretive responsibility, and his *Parsifal* lacks the quality of ruthless self-scrutiny characteristic of art truly charged with "casting up accounts" before the great reckoning.

(July 23, 1991)

Chaikin Through the Flames

The only language I know how to speak is English, although
I've always felt it isn't my tongue. Until I find another, I
make do.

—Joseph Chaikin, 1972

. . . new things . . . new . . . after my . . . aphasia . . . and
many people . . . agree with me . . . I was . . . only . . . on
earth . . . I can't talk . . . no good . . . I was . . . self . . .
one.

—Joseph Chaikin, 1991

What is it in us that needs to impose meaning on catastrophic illness, view it as a metaphoric frame that casts the patient's past life into profound relief? Susan Sontag has written several books on the question, but they apparently haven't made interacting with her old friend Joe Chaikin any easier since a stroke left him aphasic in 1984. "She's afraid . . . now . . . to talk with me

... still," he says, without rancor or remorse, in his distinctive, involuntary *Telegrammstil*. Is it cruelty, cleverness, or something nobler, then, that makes us look back on this artist's Beckettian obsessions, his lifelong dallying round ineffable forms, in order to sigh now and say, "Ah, finally, he's signaling through the flames"?

Chaikin, for his part, is serene, Buddhistically at ease with a condition that over one million people in the United States experience as a frustrating debility. "It's a real privilege," he says, adding, "I like the name . . . aphasia . . . I like the word . . . it sounds." For obvious reasons, *Night Sky*—the play he is currently directing at the Women's Project, about a female astronomer who becomes aphasic after a car accident—is as much a matter of public education as of art for him. The moment I enter the rehearsal room he hands me a glossy pamphlet printed by the National Aphasia Association, of which he is a board member, his eyes sparkling with merriment. Does he know that he is the really interesting topic here? The more I watch him work the more I think not, but that doesn't make the questions about him any less pressing.

How will the founder of the Open Theater—which relied so much on his articulateness and charisma—function from a position of infacility, incapacity? Will his famed talent for distilling complex ideas abandon him with so many words lost, or "hiding," as Anna the fictional astronomer puts it? Will the aphasia actually help him, lead him to new insights and previously unimaginable distillations of thought? ("Clov: There are so many terrible things. Hamm: No, no, there are not so many now.") And what will happen to the old ideal of collective collaboration in rehearsals that require the most earnest efforts of concentration, sometimes strain, for the simplest communication?

The first full day of work provides the more practical answers at once. Chaikin is like a theatrical head of state, surrounded constantly by loyal supporters and enablers. Longtime friend Susan Yankowitz, who wrote *Night Sky* at his request and to his broad specifications, is his foreign language interpreter. She sits beside him and paraphrases his more fragmentary comments, explaining: "He has a poor sense of time, and he has a problem with numbers, like page numbers—anything to do with abstractions. So certain types of questions are better directed to me." Stage manager Ruth Kreshka, who also worked with Chaikin before the stroke, is his secret service agent. She clears and secures the way, her voice unusually strong in arranging the daily schedule and in moving rehearsals along from event to event. "I mean, if I say to go on and he's not ready, he's got no problem telling me so right away," she says, attempting to minimize her role.

The deeper mystery begins with Joan MacIntosh, the actress playing Anna, who, like Yankowitz, often seems to understand statements of Chaikin's that I cannot decipher even after listening to them several times on tape. "We've known each other since '67," she says, "and I still sense, I think, what exactly is on his mind, what he's trying to communicate. And he always was unique in his expression. He's never been like everybody else, anyway. He always had a very precise, direct, simple way of expressing what he wants." The only difference between Joe then and Joe now, she says, is that "the words he uses are different. He doesn't worry about the peripheries of a thought. He goes right to the core of it, even if he doesn't speak all the words, so you get it."

Chaikin to MacIntosh on Anna's relationship with a colleague after the accident: "Different . . . the realm . . . because . . . you're both . . . working . . . different . . . really truly . . . because our . . . just sports . . . like a . . . tennis . . . sports . . . but not sports you . . . you're . . . each of them . . . out of the mind . . . of the planets . . . and stars . . . planets . . . planets." In response, the actress simply nods and paraphrases: "So we're joined in our minds. The planets and the stars join us." Chaikin explains a line that reads in the script, "E, eef, eef, fuh . . . fuh-fuck!": "It's worst word . . . worst . . . small privilege . . . like small . . . a room . . . gonna talk . . . it's good idea . . . good." Again MacIntosh nods: "So she's not necessarily swearing. Maybe it's just what comes out."

Far from being ruffled by the fact that the play is being directed by someone who speaks like Beckett's Lucky, MacIntosh seems animated by it. Depending on your point of view, her situation is either a Stanislavsky wet dream or a nightmare: creating an aphasic character in the presence of an aphasic director who happens to be an old friend. She has ideal access to a research source, but will she find it difficult later on to separate from him and his mannerisms, forming an inner image truly her own? "First of all," she says, "I'm going to be meeting other aphasic people, patients at the Rusk Institute, and two doctors who work with aphasic people, to have more sources of input. Secondly, I'm not acting Joe Chaikin in this play, and it's not a question of avoiding that. His presence keeps me honest. It keeps me in line, in the right parameters, keeps me from straying too far in one direction or another."

Doubtless her concern with straying comes partly from knowing that her performance will be the hub and spokes of this production, the five other actors forming a vital but relatively unobtrusive rim. With immense compassion, Yankowitz has written what a drama hawk I know calls a Children-of-a-Lesser-Elephant-Man play, structured around the painful but ultimately heroic recovery (or reconciliation) of a central character faced with a major affliction. If *Night Sky* has another level of interest, it's because its affliction has to do with the relationship between language and thought—a topic of spirited debate and speculation since Leibniz. There is a touch of Handke's *Kaspar* in this work, since the audience will be asked not only to cheer Anna on but also to witness how the acquisition of speech delimits her imagination.

Why does thought gather around words, and what if it didn't? That, ideally, will be the central question raised by MacIntosh's performance, and knowledge of it doesn't make rehearsals any easier. "This has actually been, in a way, harder than anything I've ever done," she says. "I mean, I've done enough plays where I know how to understand by charting the progress of the beats in a scene. With this, I have to ask the playwright on every line,

'What was the intention here?' because it's in poetic shorthand. The first day we got on our feet, I never felt so helpless in my life. I had no idea what to do, absolutely none, which is exactly what Anna feels when she comes out of this accident."

MacIntosh is also acutely aware that the play all but assumes that the lead performance will eventually rise out of its naturalistic frame and become enlarged, an advertent tour de force, but she's uncomfortable talking about that at the stage where "all I'm concentrating on is getting it right." Nor does she feel that Chaikin's recent performance in the one-man double bill *Struck Dumb / The War in Heaven* can provide much succor for her: "Watching him is always helpful, watching him talk, watching him behave, his struggle to find words, but in those performances he was acting. His facial and vocal expressions were heightened."

I don't argue with that statement, but as she goes on to describe a peculiar torment she's felt over the past week, I begin to have doubts. "Since I've started working on this play things happen to my mind which I haven't noticed before. I'll just lose something and won't be able to get it back, or I feel in chaos and totally disoriented, or I don't remember things, or I don't speak in full sentences." The obvious differences between *Night Sky* and *Struck Dumb* understood, won't her achievement as Anna be at least partly a factor of how committed she becomes to exploring and making use of this torment? Many people came away from Chaikin's performance disturbed at the idea of real disability having been packaged for theatrical effect; the spectacle of the invalid, it seems, must be reserved for the freak show, not employed with dignity as metaphor for the spectacle of the actor in extremis. If MacIntosh succeeds in producing the hoped-for tour de force, won't it be precisely because she provokes something of that disturbance and conveys something of that dignity?

These are heady questions for the first week of rehearsal, when most of the actors are busy with fundamentals—which, for those meeting him for the first time, include learning how to listen and talk to the director. Chaikin, meanwhile, is signally, strangely buoyant at nearly every moment. "Good . . . good . . . the logic!" is his most frequent refrain on the days I visit. Even for an outsider, there is something, well, ethereal about him, sitting there at the end of a long table, bolt upright in his diminutive roller-stool, boyish parka hanging off the back, head cocked to one side, his "new words" spurting out in a breathy, high voice without a trace of embarrassment.

"I don't know . . . why . . . don't know exactly . . . why," he says, responding to a follow-up question after stating that he sees things since his stroke that he couldn't see before. "It's like . . . born again . . . not born again . . . but similar . . . colors . . . colors . . . to me . . . new colors . . . meshing with . . . cause anything to me . . . but settle more . . . new colors . . . blue and red. . ." Grain upon grain, one by one, and one day, suddenly, there's a heap, and we're speechless.

(May 14, 1991)

Two Teapot Tempests

We Keep Our PR Ready

We Keep Our Victims Ready, by Karen Finley, and *Rameau's Nephew*, by Denis Diderot, American Repertory Theatre

How benighted we've been all these years, overlooking the manifest affinities between Karen Finley and Denis Diderot! Not so Robert Brustein, though, who opened his season at ART this fall with a repertory festival entitled "Lighting the Way: Two Centuries of Revolutionary Self-Expression." The contents: Finley's newest one-woman show, *We Keep Our Victims Ready*, and a 1988 adaptation of Diderot's *Rameau's Nephew*. It smelled suspiciously like PR exploitation of the NEA flap, but I went anyway, half hoping to debunk some hype, half curious about the pairing. As it turned out, the events had a brilliantly ironic coherence that neither Brustein nor anyone else could possibly have foreseen.

Unfortunately for her and us, the NEA affair has now effectively become Finley's definitive cultural context. It surrounds her work like a thick piece of gauze, preventing her from moving freely and us from seeing clearly. The rescinded grant: it's the thing people know about her if they know nothing else, and since the American media thrive on depictions of scapegoat gods, that isn't likely to change in the near future. Put yourself in her place—an artist who woke up caged one morning, trapped against her will by a juggernaut of voyeuristic, if well-meaning, attention. It could make you scream and rant in convulsive, rhythmic wails—which is what she always did in her art, anyway, and what she ought to continue doing.

Contrary to hype, the juggernaut has mostly come not from the right wing but from the mainstream, that host of half-conscious co-opters who come see each "next wave" of avant-garde art in order to say "we know" and then surreptitiously inquire about prices—in other words, typical regional theater subscribers. Finley faces a tough dilemma if she's going to exercise her new options and play gigs like the white liberal intellectual temple of ART. She must either consent to her own co-optation—which, true to the inexorable logic of the "banned in Boston" syndrome, means possibly making a mint— or she must fight like a demon to keep her soul honest and her art dangerous. From the look of things, bless her heart, she's working hard at the latter, maybe too hard, and failing.

The structure and content of *We Keep Our Victims Ready* are no surprise to anyone who's seen Finley before. Many of the stories of rape, homelessness, victimization, and violence of all sorts have been previously heard or published, and she recites them in her trademark breathy manner while smearing herself with viscid substances (now it's chocolate). As usual, some lines make you want to embrace her, chocolate and all: "I hate postmodern, nonfeeling art. I hate bank art. [She spits]. . .I want dependency." And others make you want to stand up and cheer: "I hope George Bush and Cardinal O'Connor come back to life as pregnant 13-year-olds working at McDonald's and about to be chopped up by a doctor who's not a real doctor." [Quotes are from my notes.]

This time, though, she's not concentrating on her texts as she has in previous shows such as *The Constant State of Desire*. Instead, she interrupts (and *distracts*) herself repeatedly in order to issue half-hearted chastisements to spectators—"You can read the program after the show"—and make pissy, pseudopersonal cracks about "any rich cooters out there" and "any dramaturgs among you." When, in the middle of the poem "The Black Sheep," she kicks someone out of the house for coughing, her misplaced prima donna act has utterly alienated the audience. From the mouth of a woman in the lobby afterward: "Lady, you're just as much of a fucking fascist as any of those fucking people you're talking about." So much for the smarty-pants liberals going around with the misapprehension they were on her side.

What would Diderot have thought of this performance manque? Hard to say, but *Rameau's Nephew*, his strange, posthumous masterpiece written largely in dialogue around 1762, certainly provides tools to sort out some thoughts about it. The title character might be described as someone who makes his living from a private, ongoing "Gong Show" he has invented, based on calculated lies. Rameau ("He"), nephew of the famous composer, is a full-time sponger who—despite extraordinary creativity and intelligence—flatters and clowns for wealthy people in order to earn his meals and pocket money. As the action opens, he has recently lost the good will of his benefactors, due to an ill-considered jest, and is in a particularly forthcoming and truthful mood. He and the philosopher-narrator ("I") meet in a cafe and pursue a conversation that rivals "Don Juan in Hell" for unflinchingness in the face of uncomfortable questions such as: is our species ultimately even capable of morality?

In this Andrei Belgrader/Shelley Berc adaptation—a very stage-worthy text, played successfully at CSC two years ago and also marvelous in production here—the focus is squarely on Rameau as the artist misunderstood and mistreated by a philistine society. That may not have been precisely Diderot's point, but at ART such quibbles seem far less important than the fact that Tony Shalhoub's splendid performance in the role offers illuminating parallels to Finley. He even looks a little like her in his disheveled, 18th-century-style mop, and when he beats his chest and repeats a line at one point, explicitly imitating her, he gets a big laugh of recognition. His Rameau is a shyster, a glad-hander, a sycophant, but one who is so candid about his nature that we gather a slow, grudging respect for his virtuosity at inane, "useless" activities such as coughing arias and mimed instrumental solos. The all-important point is that he convinces us he holds the pretense separate from the virtuosity; we must be sure *he* knows which is which in order to care about what he says.

   With a giant grin, at the end of one story about duping prospective music pupils into believing he is a teacher in great demand, he raises his arm and declares, "That's advertising!" If only Finley knew as much about her efforts to be badder than even ART audiences could bear.

(October 2, 1990)

After its run in Cambridge, *We Keep Our Victims Ready* played at the Joyce Theater in New York and was reviewed by Michael Feingold (*Voice*, Oct. 9, 1990), who wrote that "if it hadn't been for Jesse Helms, I would not have gone to see Karen Finley—for the first time"; Feingold generally avoided solo performance, finding it "self-indulgent," he explained. Comparing her to an ancient Greek solo mime ("Finley is preclassical, going back to the roots of theater in ritual sacrifice"), he continued: "A commentator is not necessarily an artist, and in a certain sense Finley does not make art, which

*Jeremy Geidt and Tony Shalhoub in Denis Diderot's **Rameau's Nephew**, adapted by Andrei Belgrader and Shelly Berc, American Repertory Theatre, Cambridge, MA, 1990.*

might mislead people who come expecting to see a presentation from which the artist retains some distance. (It seems to have misled Jonathan Kalb, and some audience members at the Cambridge performance he chronicled in last week's *Voice*.) Rather than creating a work of art, Finley becomes one, turning her body, her voice, her presence, her transaction with the public, into an object at the service of what she wants to communicate." The following reply appeared on Oct. 16, 1990.

Finley Forever

In the spirit of a type of criticism that aims not at armchair judging, but at engaging performers and readers in constructive dialogue, I want to clarify my reaction to Karen Finley's performance at ART. Michael Feingold uses the idea that I "didn't get it" as a rhetorical flourish in what is essentially a lionization of her. He seems to believe that, because he is seeing her for the first time, everyone else must write as if they are too, repeating once again those same old verities about head- versus belly-reactions and blurred distinctions between life and art.

My point, lest it get lost in polemic, is that, at the performance I saw, the NEA affair seemed to have changed Finley's work, affected it for the worse.

Here's an example from 1989: her performance of *The Constant State of Desire* at the Quartier Latin in Berlin. Finley enters, lets out a giggle, touches her finger shyly to her lips, and says, "I'm just gonna enter again, okay?" She does so, then chats a while about how nervous she is, performing for the first time in front of "the coolest people in the world." I'm worried. Is this sincerity or sloppiness? It soon becomes clear, however, that the vulnerable suburban girl demeanor is a lure, leading us to expect something far less committed, raunchy, and raw than what actually happens. That opening *had* to be followed by an utterly schizophrenic transformation or it'd never have worked, and in the end the banter (which also continued between pieces) was believable, even indispensable. Had she played only the angry, raging woman, she would have lost her audience after ten minutes. It was the frame of humility and vulnerability—which suggested that she was "really" a thoughtful, probing person—that forced the audience to think about the performance as a consciously crafted, fully "controlled" expressive act. No matter whether it really was; she made us think of it that way.

At ART, on the other hand, her performance was so flooded with misdirected anger it swamped itself. Finley's shows are always circumstance-specific, she always pitches them to the given time and place, and here she miscalculated. She was so busy policing the audience for coughers and program-rustlers she couldn't concentrate on her texts, and few spectators were willing to give her the benefit of the doubt and assume she once could. Now, I've seen her calculate performances before with a precision Tristan Tzara would have admired, adjust herself to the ebb and flow of anger and release, playing moment to moment so expertly that it seemed like orchestration. I've seen her handle a house full of jeering, whistling men so you could actually hear them growing more and more self-conscious and uncomfortable as she screamed her stories and faced them down with her sticky, egg-splattered, naked body until even they couldn't help seeing it as a mockery of the sort of glitzy female they so badly wanted to paw.

The problem at ART wasn't that people were offended, but that they were *only* offended. What is usually most powerful in Finley's work was on this occasion weakly and diffidently presented, which is why I speculated about her feelings performing in white liberal Cambridge. For me, far more disturbing than her passing cracks, or those of audience members, was the impression that her performing had been adversely affected by the challenge of playing in her new "establishment" circumstances. I left that theater with the sad thought that her notoriety could prove her undoing, as it so often does when the limelight goes sour, and that in a backassed way Jesse Helms might indeed win.

In the Jungle
of Second Guesses

In the Jungle of Cities, by Bertolt Brecht, New York Shakespeare Festival

Directors with the courage to take on Brecht's shamelessly romantic early works have always been rarer than those ready to peddle his ideological wares, and Anne Bogart deserves a hosanna or two for trying to stage *In the Jungle of Cities* in a way that resists its romanticism. At a time when the artistic Left is more or less in crisis over how the fall of the Berlin Wall ought to affect its posture of permanent rebellion, we look all the more closely at confident, pugnacious work such as Bogart's, searching her deconstructions for fresh, credible values. Sad to say, her monstrance is empty this time, her approach to this seldom produced play dominated by driftless gestures of elusion. It's as if she was so busy avoiding the Scylla of ideology and the Charybdis of sentimentality that she ended up sacrificing clarity and meaning altogether.

The text of *Jungle* is the product of a grittier and more playfully iconoclastic mind than the one that produced all the brilliant theory in the 1930s and '40s. Still full of youthful enchantment with the Rimbaud-Verlaine affair, Brecht is unafraid of appearing "antisocial" (his buzzword later on) and uninterested in explaining his characters' motivations beyond subtextual hints about homosexual love. He barely offers a "why" in this play, which bewildered its first audiences even with a relatively accommodating director

(Erich Engel), confining himself to showing a "what" and leaving further speculation to others. Once upon a time in an imaginary Chicago, a librarian named Garga and a Malaysian lumber dealer called Shlink struggled to the death in "an inexplicable wresting match." *Schluss.*

The plot details—how family, friends, careers, and property are drawn into the fray—exist in order to disappoint. Fix your eyes on the finish, says the poet, in stark contrast to one of his later maxims. The attraction is in the language, a mixture of laconic keening and half-credible blustering, and in what he calls the pure pleasure of "sport." Some lines do betray an underlying theme, though, such as Garga's last: "It's a good thing to be alone. The chaos is spent. That was the best time." (Unforgivably, no translator is credited; much of it sounds like the Gerhard Nellhaus version, slightly altered.) Isolation, urban anonymity, existential angst: as a dramatist Brecht would never again begrudge himself even a controlled gush on such matters.

Bogart, for her part, seems to think he begrudged himself too much, placing the play in danger of oversimplification and misunderstanding at every turn. Hence, her job becomes maneuvering it around all the possible logical motivations for the "wrestling match" like a vehicle on an obstacle course. Does greed seem too easy a crutch? She'll have the actors brandish fistfulls of cash so frequently and ostentatiously that the audience loses track of where it came from and why. Are racial issues in danger of seeming primary? She'll solve that with cross-race casting: Fred Neumann as Schlink has silver hair but no Oriental makeup, and Garga's sister and girlfriend are played by black women (Fanni Green and Karen Evans-Kandel) while the rest of the Garga family is white. Even the homosexuality is effectively annulled, so few sparks of any kind flashing between Neumann and Mario Arrambide (Garga) that the line "I love you" in the penultimate scene is a non sequitur.

It wouldn't be such a shame if there weren't so much squandered talent on the stage. Gabriel Berry's wonderful thrift-store aesthetic—the costumes feature garish plaids, ugly stripes, and loud flowers in matched and unmatched outfits—almost succeeds where the direction fails in achieving style by way of avoiding it. Ruth Maleczech stands out as usual both as Garga's mother, Mae, and as a chorus who speaks poems and stage directions between scenes, but that's partly because the choral role, played in a plain raincoat while lurking about the loading-dock set in dramatically lit positions, gives her what no one else in the cast has, breathing space to act. The regrettable fact is that the production *is* interestingly cast (Green as Mary, Neumann as Schlink, Greg Mehrten as Worm were all good ideas), but the breakneck pacing and pomo-gimmick overkill keeps the performers from doing all they can with their parts.

Bogart comes off in this production as the Mike Dukakis of the avant-garde: sure, she's smarter than everyone around her but a few lessons in playing the crowd wouldn't hurt, even for a provocateur. Her "corrective" second-guessing extends to simple issues of accessibility; the two-hour, intermissionless action is so rushed it's impossible to tell who half the characters are. And when the audience realizes it's being excluded to that degree it grows uncurious to learn the wrestling outcome or anything else. Applause opening night was sluggish and cool. To put so much energy into preventing modes of access is eventually to create an impenetrable fortress. Hard to imagine a model for the theater less Brechtian than that.

(November 12, 1991)

On Dec. 3, 1991, the *Voice* printed a second review of *In the Jungle of Cities*, "Sleaze & Rage" by Richard Schechner, which vigorously defended the production. Assailing "embittered critics who don't know a good thing when they see it" and "homo- and gynophobes" whose "angry and snide reviews hurt the box office," Schechner wrote that the production was "admirable" in that it "reeked of discomfort, the inability to make things cohere" as well as "uncompromisingly vile sleaziness, violence, and rage," turning a clear mirror on "today's not-so-mythical New York." He explained: "Like Brecht's drama, the Bogart-Mabou production was confused, brutal, and violent; loud, lyrical, threatening, and improbable. It was loaded with strong, sharp acting squeezed flat up against the far wall of the theater room. What's wrong with confusion? Does theater have to be 'unified,' 'harmonious,' and 'beautiful'? Bogart's wild yet true-to-Brecht production rips political, social, psychological, and sexual fabrics." The following reply appeared on Dec. 24, 1991.

Thinking Makes It So

In his review of Anne Bogart's production of *Jungle of Cities*, Richard Schechner seems to advocate a Theater of Confusion. "What's wrong with confusion?" he asks. Well, I'll tell him. And my definition of "wrong" doesn't come from Aristotle ("Does theater have to be 'unified' 'harmonious' and 'beautiful'?") but rather the author of this play.

As Schechner knows, we are living through a quiveringly dangerous historical moment, sitting around waiting to see which easy, horrendous ideology (David Duke's? Igor Hasselbach's?) will rush in to fill the vacuum, and he rightly compares the moment to late Weimar. Nothing is more important in tinderbox times than good, clear thinking. Nothing. And it isn't a question of valuing thought above feeling or excluding beauty from the equation but rather of recognizing that beauty and feeling don't have a rubber's chance in Boston these days without lucidity: the ability to see the larger picture, not only historically, culturally, or psychologically, but in comprehensive (dare I say interdisciplinary?) terms. Though the '60s generation has never wanted to believe it, Brecht's most enduring legacy to the theater is not his playwriting. It's his theory, which argues that knowledge can't be excluded from art, that thinking, preferably the dialectical kind, is a moral imperative in a world where complex institutions and sociopolitical forces exert such thoroughgoing control over our lives.

Schechner the rebellious wunderkind now belongs to a new Father Generation that has a lot at stake in writing history in a way that makes its efforts and experiments seem unique. His validation of confusion amounts to a denigration. His blithe use of "confusion" recalls the way *October's* critics use "postmodernism" to refer to an art that can't hope to reach beyond spark-shooting. Postmodernism, a once promising concept, has lately become the Father's favorite way of insulting the next generation, implying that it isn't capable of perceiving, achieving, or appreciating the sublime. We're too damaged by the depredations of technology and history, the theory goes; the assault on the psyche led to permanent mass brain damage right after, say, *Dionysus in '69*, so it's naive and futile even to raise the question of meaning today. Indeed. I wonder what Bogart, an unusually intelligent director, thinks of the idea that her production was good because it accurately reflected confusion.

To her everlasting credit, Bogart didn't simply throw up her hands on this score. "Embittered critics who don't know a good thing when they see it" aside, I might well have written an "angry and snide" review had she done so. I could see her thinking the whole time. My problem was that too much of her thought was wasted on negatives, gimmicky devices designed to avoid various obsolete and discredited meanings. The cynicism of the '80s, which caused all meaning to devolve into irony or parody, is being supplanted by fresh imagery from artists formerly kept out of the mainstream, and these artists allow us to ask such questions as, "What positives are to be preferred?" My disappointment in Bogart's *Jungle of Cities* had everything to do with my counting her among them.

Rambo's Nephew

1991 (A performance chronicle of the rediscovery of America by the Warrior for Gringostroika), by Guillermo Gómez-Peña, Brooklyn Academy of Music

(A French cafe on Flatbush Ave.)
EL: So you wanna write about me, gringo?
YO: *I got fifteen column-inches and a mission. Whadya got?*
EL: Two hours at BAM and a MacArthur.
YO: *No fair odds, but hell, let's party.* Vate, *fire first.*
EL: What's with the French paradigms? You're not Diderot and I didn't

agree to write half this review. You some sort of Eurocentric neocon. This is "border culture." The terms are San Diego and Tijuana.

YO: *This is* El Este, *citadel of the New York intelligentsia. The illegal aliens our cultural border patrol chases come from France. The terms are money, fame, and death.*

EL: Don't give me that humanist bullshit. You're trying to melt me down, erase Otherness and Difference. See, now you got me doing it!

YO: *Worse, I'm imposing a new character on you: Rambo's Chicano nephew, celluloid warrior for Pax Americana and against Gringostroika. The nephew didn't inherit the family muscle tone, kept skipping gym, and ended up in graduate school. Now he's bent on killing you, his brothers, and provoking intellectual civil war through clowning.*

EL: Look, what are you saying?

YO: *Your piece is structured as a journey of discovery. You assume a dozen different bizarre disguises—all tested on U.S. officials at the Mexican border, you say—in the process of rediscovering a land that has presumably lost itself, partly due to ignoring people like you.*

EL: It's multicul. . .

YO: *Multiculti schmulticulti. My point is only that one of the sights along the way is yours truly, another kind of outsider who doesn't carry around a lot of guilt about (1) abetting the pernicious historical processes that led to that ignoring, or (2) not feeling as if his subjectivity is multiple or exploded. How does politically aggressive art like yours take root in minds that lack the fertilizer of guilt?*

EL: That's not my problem. I'd never insist that you or anyone assume the critical missionary position. As I've said before, my identity is "not a monolith but a kaleidoscope," and if I speak with many different voices it's not "mere postmodern theory" but "a quintessential feature of the Latino experience in the U.S." Now answer me something. Did you like my show?

YO: *(two weeks later) Yes. How can you dislike Coco Fusco in queenly regalia crowned with a carabela wrapped in hair, velvet paintings in the elevators and lobby beside a TV-shrine decked out with kitschy chatchkas, a flabby, mustachioed man dancing around in a zoot suit, ceremonial Aztec armor (my favorite) and a mariachi costume? I felt excluded, though, prevented from enjoying the silliness, and it wasn't because of the Spanish, the Spanglish, or the invented tongues. There was something exclusive, maybe even stiff, in your demeanor, and too many of the purportedly spontaneous touches shrunk from real-time spontaneity: colored cards and printed instructions passed out to segregate the audience according to "language skills and racial background" but no enforcement of those rules, empty threats to stop the action and engage spectators as actors. . .*

EL: You know what? I think you're saying you were intimidated.

YO: *I certainly got the message I was supposed to be.*

EL: Well, that's a start, *hermano*. That's a start.

(October 29, 1991)

"Resisting" Müller

Among the many thorny questions American theater people tend to ask about Heiner Müller's dramatic texts, with their apocalyptic tones, densely poetic language, and ambivalently messianic Marxism, one always seems particularly pressing: how the hell do you direct them? It may be perversely reassuring to learn, then, that the Germans have no idea either. That, at last, was my impression early this summer at Experimenta 6, an enormous theater festival in Frankfurt dedicated solely to the work of this author who has come to represent the immortal Teutonic hope that an effort of intellect can keep people from repeating their history: eighty-five events over seventeen days, including thirty-five full productions of twenty-four plays invited from both Germanys. I didn't attend everything—no one person could have—but I saw enough to become convinced that the sort of director capable of providing Müller's texts with "resistance"—his word for the quality of "reading" necessary to make any literature live onstage—is exceedingly rare in all countries.

The Germans, of course, try more often than anyone else, as the size of Experimenta 6 demonstrates, but they're ultimately no more successful than others at avoiding reductive and overly literal productions. Though many directors strive to maintain textual fidelity, which some critics are forever exhorting, Müller's work in effect rejects that loyalty, making it look like laziness and evasion; no one, it seems, can play Alan Schneider to this author's Samuel Beckett. Müller once called his technique "a dramaturgy of holes," by which he may have meant that it is as much concerned with absences, logical and temporal gaps designed to provide opportunities for fruitful critical exchange, as it is with lapidary statement of persuasive opinions and images. For him, as for Brecht, the ideal director brings original ideas to the text in order to challenge it, and incites spectators to do the same.

Unfortunately, things rarely work out so neatly in practice, partly because Müller's theatrical milieu forces him to fight many of Brecht's battles all over again. In the 1987 East Berlin Volksbühne production of *Gundling's Life Frederick of Prussia Lessing's Sleep Dream Scream*, for instance—which Müller says he never saw, although it was the GDR premiere—a perfectly viable text dealing with Prussian paternalism and the perversion of Enlightenment values was made to seem instantly old-fashioned by the same hallowed process that emasculates plays in American regional theaters. Perhaps in reaction to the ten-year ban on *Gundling's Life* in East Germany, directors Helmut Strassburger and Ernstgeorg Hering exalted it as a "classic," a clearly profound, historical parable whose meaning they were hell-bent on explicating. Of course, the work wasn't nearly so straightforward, may not even *be* a parable, and their plethora of asides and other gimmicky imitations of alienation effects ultimately read as compensations, apologies for the production's political inefficacy.

"What you can't kill, enshrine!"—the Communist Party's old byword has also applied for many years to the Berliner Ensemble, which brought two productions to the festival: Christoph Schroth's 1989 version of *Volokolamsk Highway*, a five-part dramatic poem dealing with Russian and German experiences during and after World War II, and Fritz Marquardt's 1989 GDR premiere of *Germania Death in Berlin*, a pastiche of scenes about violence and national identity in German history and myth. Both these directors strained their technical resources to the utmost, attempting to serve Müller by fabricating concrete corollaries for each and every fantastic image in his hyperbolic, occasionally dreamlike texts. The result was a collection of limply heavy-handed images devoid of humor: why do we need the satirical dialogue, for instance, when the bloodthirsty Nibelungen warriors in front of us are already wearing standard Wagnerian costumes and speaking in cliché gruff voices, or when the stodgy bureaucrats in nondescript suits are already sitting in rows behind plain desks with telephones? Hardly new or particularly edifying inadequacies: what's new is that the texts in question won't tolerate *any* form of cookbook treatment—not even once, in a premiere.

For those who wondered whether the West Germans were any more adept at "resisting" Müller, the festival offered abundant disappointments as well. A 1988 Bochum production of *Germania* directed by Frank-Patrick Steckel and a 1990 Frankfurt production of *The Battle* directed by Alexander Brill both turned out to be slick variations on the Berliner Ensemble approach: if it doesn't work as psychological realism, play it as exaggerated realism, then trick it up with bloody Nazi uniforms, phony limbs and eerie Day-Glo paint. To be fair, Brill did have one moment of inspiration in his ending: after a scene about German-German betrayal in 1945, the point of which was that the spoils went to the turncoats, the actors ran across stage with Eastern European flags minus the communist party emblems, drawing a direct parallel with 1990. It was too little too late, though: a single superimposed idea does not an effective Müller production make.

Nor did the festival justify any paean to director's theater, despite the fact that that is the most common response among German critics to the problems I've been describing. Those directors whose primary decision was to dismiss Müller's texts, or their apparent meanings, didn't fare any better than the would-be loyalists. A four-and-a-half-hour 1986 staging of the relatively conventional early play *Construction*, directed by Frank Castorf, was so thoroughly and aggressively arbitrary (the euphemism is "deconstructed") it prevented anyone who hadn't read the text from following the action.

To be sure, there were enjoyable moments in Experimenta 6. Several productions, including some already mentioned, were memorable for acting that sometimes eclipsed the limitations of the directing: Michael Abendroth and Martin Schneider in a 1989 Nuremberg *Philoctetes*, or Elke Lang in a 1987 Frankfurt *Quartet*, for instance. The only substantial clues to resolving the general directing dilemma, however, came from Müller himself, who also directed two festival productions. In his Deutsches Theater stagings from

1988 and 1990, *The Scab* and *Hamletmachine*—both of which have been written about extensively in theater journals—the author gave lucid examples of what he means by "resistance." He cut or reordered substantial passages and added newly written dialogue and text from his other plays; his settings included collages of paintings and other prominent, loaded items not mentioned in the published scripts; the acting was at all times self-consciously artificial even though the dialogue was occasionally naturalistic. In other words, directing is, for him, an act of playwriting, a fully engaged form of collaborative authorship.

Or is it? The trouble is, he denies in interviews that his published texts are in any way incomplete. He's a slippery fellow, this Müller, always trying to play both sides of theater's perennially controversial issue. It's as if he's committed a sort of provisional suicide, disclaiming authority in the production process like a good post-Artaudian corpse but cherishing the thought that privileged subtexts do exist in his work and will be discovered by future generations. Whether we accept his death notice or his self-canonization (or both, or neither) remains to be seen.

(September 4, 1990)

The Play of Laughter and Forgetting

Jacques and His Master, by Milan Kundera, The New Theater of Brooklyn

A 19th-century critic once called Denis Diderot "an intellectual acrobat." The epithet didn't quite fit: impressed yet distressed by Diderot's extraordinary eclecticism, his merry peregrinations of mind, the critic was unsure whether it was seemly to take him seriously. At the risk of being ridiculed by some knowing 21st century critic, though, I think this is precisely the right epithet for a self-styled *Diderotiste* of our era, Milan Kundera.

Even if you admire Kundera's novels, as I do, you have to admit that his technique is problematic. There's a certain circus-like quality in his plots and formal structures that borders on gimmickry, even dilettantism. Ostensible political content aside, only the strength of his observations on human nature saves him; for his digressions and multiple points of view, so often touted as the source of his originality, are really shameless borrowings from Sterne, Diderot, and others. He doesn't have Diderot's breadth of literary-historical knowledge, but he thinks he does, and somehow manages to turn that deep delusion into a naive charm. The paradox of Kundera is that he writes as if he were the first modern . . . and gets away with it.

Trying to do that with drama, especially when your expertise is in the novel, is an even greater risk, and indeed Kundera's play *Jacques and His Master*, a "variation" on Diderot's novel *Jacques le Fataliste*, is disappointing from its opening curtain. Jacques, the servant-hero, saunters on and addresses the audience directly: "All right then, what do you want to know? Where we came from? Back there. Where we're going? Which of us knows where we're going?" We may accept this as endearing from Diderot's narrator, but onstage it sounds immediately like half-digested Pirandello—and the truth is, any author with more than passing experience in the theater would have known that. "The theater has never had its Laurence Sterne," writes Kundera in the introduction to *Jacques*; maybe the Büchner translations in French are just too unbearable to read.

What do you do, as a director, with this would-be Rabelaisian mock-journey that is continually interrupted by would-be bawdy tales from the characters' pasts, this ream of clichés and catchall phrases that tries and fails miserably to become a pensive reflection on human freedom? Well, if you're Susan Sontag, who directed the American premiere in Cambridge four years ago, you salt it with a set modeled after one of Piranesi's fanciful-yet-architectonically-precise engravings and wait for the pot of 18th-century allusions to cook up into dramatic soup. If you're Deborah Pope—who lacks Sontag's intellectual-acrobatic credentials but has a theatrical horse sense that Sontag lacks—you set it on plain wooden planks that read "country inn" and play it for every old gag it's worth.

This New York premiere is something of a revelation; it demonstrates that, facile philosophizing notwithstanding, the play's low comedy can be funny if the actors milk the laughs and maintain eye contact in a small, intimate house like TNT's. It's a very actorly production that circumvents clichés through time-tried tricks: a trap door that adds amusement to banal, predictable entrances; a knowing look at the audience from Jacques when someone says, "One swallow does not make a summer." The cast isn't uniformly talented, but several first-rate performances establish a breezy median tone—chiefly Ray Virta as Jacques and Robin Tate as Saint-Ouen, the Master's rival—and it's clear that most of the others will come into their own as the production runs.

The major obstacle, aside from the play itself, is the new translation by Simon Callow, which is so full of jangling anglicisms ("chum"?) and colloquialisms ("spud"?) that the actors sound as if they'd prefer to be speaking French. If only Diderot were here to savor the irony of his thoughts being twice juggled, and twice mangled.

(November 7, 1989)

Unpolished Brass

Once in a Lifetime, by George S. Kaufman and Moss Hart, River Arts Repertory

Anne Bogart's adaptation of *Once in a Lifetime* isn't always extraordinary, but there's never any question that the ambition is extremely lofty. Bogart's work is generally characterized by startling collisions of style and substance, and the choice of a 1930 Kaufman and Hart comedy as a venue for her highly physical, expressionistic direction, strange as it may seem at first, makes perfect sense when seen as a rich source of incongruities. Like other Bogart productions, however, this three-hour *Once in a Lifetime* gives a sense of being willfully, almost pugnaciously, avant-garde, as if the director thought her efforts would lose all credibility if even one staged moment were left to communicate in the relatively conventional style of the original comedy. The excess implies diffidence—an impression reinforced by the fact that the production is neither all that funny nor technically very polished.

Once in a Lifetime, Kaufman and Hart's first collaboration, is a lightning-paced satire about Hollywood's transition to the talkies. Three unemployed vaudeville actors head out to L.A., hoping to strike it rich by opening a school for actors' voice training. Eventually, after numerous arbitrary and absurd quirks of fate, the two clever ones, May Daniels and Jerry Hyland, are bypassed in favor of the simpleton, George Lewis, who is placed in charge of operations at Glogauer Studios. The shticks are old, but the satirical targets are timeless: incompetence is rewarded, competence punished, and sycophancy, obsequiousness, and cronyism reign.

Bogart has placed this heightened reality into an even more heightened frame. A pianist (Nicky Paraiso) breaks up the action with sundry show tunes, which he plays and sings so beautifully I wished the director had let them stand alone. Instead, Paraiso doubles as a narrator, speaking stage directions aloud and commenting on the action sardonically, which is both redundant—the play itself is sardonic enough—and a source of confusion: the actors don't seem to know whether to react or ignore him. Playing mostly on a low, bare checkerboard platform the performers are all dressed formally, women in long dresses, men in tuxedos, and every movement is choreographed in the jerky, highly stylized manner that has become Bogart's trademark: a quick round of "patty-cake," a single tap-dance step, a line of players laughing in unison.

This manner fits some actors far better than others. Tom Caylor, who plays Jerry, is ideal, mostly because he's an accomplished comedian in his own right; it's hard to imagine a more fitting complement to Bogart's broad aesthetic than his particular studied insanity. Kristine Nielsen as May comes closest to matching his energy, taking numerous big risks while maintaining an inscrutable seriocomic demeanor; her character is a kind of street-wise doll. John Fistos as George occasionally rises to meet this hyperbolic manner, and when he does the show achieves a certain stride, only to slow down soon after with the return of less externalized playing. Fistos generally relies too much on wide-eyed facial expressions to communicate his character's naiveté, which makes his acting seem alternately more robotlike and more naturalistic than Caylor's and Nielsen's. And, to varying degrees, these same types of discord occur with almost all the other cast members.

Even with a completely balanced cast, I suspect there'd still be a discordant note or two. The original play actually contained some of the qualities Bogart's hyperactive "new vaudeville" context works so hard to provide. Kaufman and Hart's dialogue, much of which is upstaged by her movement, isn't only sarcastic but also mock-sarcastic; the characters already slip into caricature. Mr. Glogauer, speaking of his competition: "Everything comes to those Schlepkin Brothers! This fellow Lou Jackson—sings these mammies or whatever it is—he comes all the way across the country and goes right to the Schlepkin Brothers." How, then, are we to interpret Bogart's addition of yet another ironic layer? What does it mean to caricature caricature?

At times her approach does succeed in what is usually called "Brechtian fashion," keeping the audience at a healthy distance from coercive emotional attachments that might inhibit its thinking about the play's social meanings. Too often, though, it makes us wonder about whether American actors and directors have simply lost the knack of doing this type of brassy repartée "straight." Regardless of whether you agree that the original performance style is dated, Kaufman and Hart's dialogue is so clever and polished that Bogart needed to superimpose something equally polished onto it. Most likely that's what we she wanted, but the execution was less than perfect. The show is thoroughly disordered, not to say chaotic, and I'd guess nothing less than another several months' rehearsal could bring all its new "bits" up to the level of the old ones.

(*July 26, 1988*)

More Revenge on Objects

An Evening of Performance and Film, by Stuart Sherman, La Mama E.T.C.

Invert Anouilh's well-known description of *Waiting for Godot*—"The music-hall sketch of Pascal's *Pensées* as played by the Fratellini clowns"—and you have a passable description of Stuart Sherman's performances. The one-man "Spectacles" for which Sherman first became famous were like Fratellini clown acts performed by a formidable intellectual with a mystical bent, a jittery latter-day Pascal harried by an inexplicable pressure to express his thoughts in ridiculously short intervals, with the aid of toy props. Some critics frowned upon Sherman's aloofness in those early "Spectacles," assuming that his perfunctoriness really papered over "truer" feelings underneath. For me, they always seemed to demonstrate a great deal of emotional investment, even a certain spirituality, at least regarding objects.

Sherman once described his work as his "revenge on objects," and when his repertoire broadened to include films and short plays, the centrality of objects continued to assert itself. This is certainly true of the thirteen pieces now at La Mama. The evening is a potpourri—the trademark solo playlets together with miniature portraits of places and famous literary works, and plays in dialogue which do not include his characteristic fidgeting with props. All are well worth seeing, though the different modes don't all serve his aesthetic equally well.

"To Catch a Fish, or 'Cheese,' " "To Sneeze or Not to Sneeze," "To Eat an Apple," and "$?" are classic Sherman: the performer in tennis shoes behind a suitcase full of treasures and a folding table. In one, a mousetrap chases a toy mouse to the sound of chattering teeth, the trap catches a plastic fish instead, and then the table and props are covered with plastic wrap and basted. In another, Sherman "auctions off" dollar bills tied to various parts of his body, and after each sale he spears the bill on a pencil like a cashier dispensing with a check. All these pieces have in common the sense of vital, unresolved issues between Sherman and things, issues fraught with a desperation that is amplified by his deadpan demeanor. And, ironically, it's exactly that deadpan that makes them more than mere solipsistic diversions. As in Beckett's *Act Without Words I*, the torment of objects—the mouse in the trap—reads immediately as a cosmic question since all "normal" uses for the objects are summarily dispensed with.

Sherman's frumpy nonchalance is also what makes the playlets funny, which becomes all too apparent when other performers join or replace him in short plays like "The Man in Room 2538," "Our Love is Here to Stay, or Kiss (A Play for 8 Lips)" and "Chattanooga Choo-Choo (Für Elise)." Some of these are better acted than others; particularly memorable is the one in which a recently bereaved woman, who soothes herself by playing "Für Elise" on an imaginary piano, is interrupted by a neighbor crooning "Chattanooga Choo-Choo." In general, though, Sherman pushes his usual rough improvisational performance style too far in these works, where the absence of his anomalous props has enervated the action to begin with.

The gem of the evening is "But What is the Word for 'Bicycle'? (A Play in 3 Speeds)," in which Sherman plays a mute mechanic and John Hagan plays a "cyclist" who walks around two bicycle wheels while holding handlebars in front of him and telling disconnected stories. Hagan provides exactly what most of the other non-solo pieces are missing: an actor who can make the text resonate beyond what even the playwright might have imagined. Here the text is not only well-spoken but is also accompanied by the kind of stage business Sherman does best: manipulation of familiar objects, or in this case parts of them, in ways that make them thoroughly unfamiliar. This piece and a few others make up for the rough spots in the program. Go see Stuart Sherman, and shake up your old encrusted ideas about *bicycles* and other monstrous things.

(June 14, 1988)

Home, Fuge!

The Tragical History of the Life and Death of Doctor Faustus, by Christopher Marlowe, La Mama E.T.C

Nothing would please me more than to be able to attribute the deficiencies of this *Doctor Fastus* to some interesting cause, such as a miscast leading actor, a poorly designed set, or the director's sudden conversion to fundamentalism. The fact is, all the actors are miscast, the set is well designed but poorly utilized, and the production offers no coherent ideas about the play's action, religious or otherwise. Indeed, it offers little exercise for the mind of any kind.

Leonardo Shapiro has chosen a classic text that he feels is particularly timely—"With whose blood have we signed the materialistic contract which has divorced us from the interconnected spiritual life of the natural world?"—only to cut it down to an intermissionless eighty minutes dominated by a collection of predictable, toothless effects. And he has chosen actors for this "first great theatrical poem of the English language" who cannot speak Marlowe's verse to save their souls, and who are in any case often drowned out by the effects. The action is both noisy and listless, and sitting through its hopeless attempt to gather momentum is a lot like being stuck in traffic.

The structure of *Doctor Faustus* is simple, as Shapiro says: it's a morality play in which the scholar Faustus becomes fascinated with "necromantic books," sells his soul to Lucifer for twenty-four years of worldly pleasure, fails to heed heaven's admonitions to repent, and is ultimately damned. What has made it age so much more gracefully than its medieval forebears, however, is its poetry, which is wholly in the Renaissance spirit—a poetry of longing for new worlds ("From thence to Venice, Padua, and the East,/In one of which a sumptuous temple stands,/That threats the stars with her aspiring top") and new experiences ("let me an actor be,/That this proud Pope may Faustus' cunning see"). The verse reveals that Marlowe loves every sinful word his hero utters, but there is no such atheistic wink in Shapiro's production because there is no intelligible poetry. The director seems to think the stodgy, moralistic frame of the work is urgent and contemporary, but he lacks the skill to construct even a lucid modern morality play.

The set consists mainly of a raised, cruciform platform extending backstage behind a low curtain—a fine, spacious construction with far more possibilities than Shapiro discovers. The Chorus's prologue speeches are delivered from there, occasional conjuring occurs in a magic circle at the "crossing," and un-frightening spirits sometimes enter along the "nave," but generally the platform is neglected in favor of cramped scenes near the curtain and gratuitous gymnastics on the Annex's seating tiers.

Something of the production's conceptual muddle can be seen in the very first scene, when the Good and Bad Angels who periodically visit Faustus pop out, cuckoo-style, from two painted clocks near the ceiling, and the *good* one turns out to be naked except for a rhinestone harness around her breasts. Shortly, Mephistophilis, played by Regina Taylor, the one cast member who doesn't brutalize the iambic pentameter, implores Faustus so convincingly to reconsider his pact with the devil that, for the rest of the action, she seems kind and benevolent.

The production is filled with low comic bits that are bungled to the point of embarrassment: the Bad Angel's bat wings get caught on the sides of the cuckoo clock; actors playing "keep away" accidentally drop the object they are tossing. Then there's the subtle contemporizing: after signing his contract, Faustus changes from a medieval doctor's robe to a modern business suit; the dancing devils wear skeleton outfits with Nazi accessories; Faustus wears an astronaut's suit during his tour of the heavens. Imagine, gentle reader, all this combined with a plethora of annoying loudspeaker effects and a musical score that resembles a radio receiving two raunchy stations at once, and my advice to anyone contemplating a visit to this *Tragical History* will be as clear as God's warning on Faustus's arm: *Homo, fuge!*

(April 26, 1988)

Chez Ubu

Being at Home with Claude, by René-Daniel Dubois, Ubu International Festival

To come across a substantial playwriting talent during Ubu International—a festival planned to introduce New Yorkers to French-speaking dramatists that consisted largely of mediocre writing—was a delight and a relief. *Being at Home with Claude*, by René-Daniel Dubois, of Quebec, would stand out in any collection of new plays. This is the first American production of any play by this author, who has written a dozen since 1979 and has earned a considerable reputation in France and Quebec, and if it's at all typical, he deserves much wider recognition.

Set in a judge's office at the Montreal Courthouse during the summer of 1967, when thousands of tourists were visiting Expo, the action of *Being at Home With Claude* consists of the last ninety minutes of an interrogation that has been going on for over nine hours. After slitting a man's throat, a young male prostitute named Yves called to turn himself in, insisting that the police meet him at this office. The police cannot establish a connection between Yves and his victim, a well-educated, middle-class student named Claude, and admit they'd never have tracked him down themselves. They are thus at loose ends trying to understand why he called them and why he is threatening to create a scandal by telling reporters—waiting outside the door for a scoop to please the tourists—how he got the judge's keys. Why has he gone to all this trouble? What does he really want? When the play opens, the Inspector has one hour to find out.

Just another detective story, right? Well, no, and that's the surprise. What's interesting about this play is that it raises narrative expectations, only to imply that they're not where the important action is. Something is weird about this interrogation, about the barely concealed hysteria of the cop and the evasiveness of Yves's answers; after a very short time the focus shifts onto a kind of Strindbergian power struggle between the two men. Even the Inspector's touching confession, near the end, of his own homosexual leaning doesn't *explain* things, because by then it's already clear that the tension is too knotted to be undone by sudden revelations. The action is really driven by Yves' attempt to heal his own psyche after his terrible act.

The play places its audience in a position similar to that of the Inspector, who barrages Yves with short, factual questions in order to determine "when," "where," "how," and especially "why." It's that question of motive that most bothers the cop, whom Michael B. Littman plays at such a high pitch of agitation you'd think *he* was the trapped murderer—the parallel is with our expectations in conventional naturalism. Neither the Inspector nor the audience is about to learn "why" in the way they want, because Yves is neither able nor willing to try to tell anything "short and sweet." "Why do you insist on putting all the pieces together? Somebody was killed. It's your job to find the murderer? You got him. What more do you want?" says Yves. His object in this struggle of wills is not to avoid explaining his crime but to exhaust his opponent enough so he can explain it *his* way, and indeed he does prove the stronger, ultimately narrating his passionate act in a thirty-minute monologue. He needs to confess, but confession is worthless to him unless it occurs on a certain scale.

I cannot imagine a more intelligent production of this intelligent play, which Achim Nowak has directed as precisely what it is, a dance marathon. The action begins at a feverish pitch, with both actors shouting. Rusty W. Laushman, a tall, gaunt, long-haired actor with a vein in his forehead that's perfect for the latently violent role of Yves, has a certain equanimity in his voice even in the upper registers that seems to infuriate Littman's Inspector and make him try all the harder to be intimidating. Littman plays a man who has long since lost his patience and with it his civility, interrupting everyone at every turn, even his colleagues who wander in and out, and the fact that the hysteria never lets up is what first clues the audience in that the play isn't fully realistic.

Soon there are more overt hints, which provide variation and a much needed dose of irony. At one point during the constant cacophony of speech and interruption—the details of the dialogue are only sporadically intelligible—the Inspector stands on a chair while Yves lies on his back on the floor, kicking; then, ten minutes later, Yves is standing on the desk while the cop lies on the floor, kicking and twitching. The two men periodically run in place next to one another, Yves punching the air like a boxer in training. It doesn't take too many examples of this kind to realize we shouldn't be looking for meaning only in the elusive story. Instead of playing the realism and trying to make every word understood, Nowak literalizes the subtext, making it a physical and psychic contest.

At times this is a bit overdone, uncontrolled; the judge's function in the plot, for instance, is so unclear in this production that it never even gets a chance to exert dramatic pressure. In general, though, I think the externalization is exactly right for a play that ends with thirty minutes of relentless talking about what the character himself admits cannot be put into words. Yves, who killed Claude during the act of lovemaking, tries and fails to describe his feelings of love—"I know that sounds corny and that pisses me off. It's like the words . . . the words . . . refuse . . . Just hot air. Empty."—and the play literally traps us in his inability to be articulate about what was, for him, an epiphany. It's because the play rises to this level of intensity that its few concessions to sentimentality are conspicuous, e.g. the cop's admission of the obvious about himself, or some images in Yves' monologue ("I could feel his sex, like a tree, exploding"). These are quibbles that the play's merits far outweigh, though, and this production of *Being at Home With Claude* deserves to be mounted again on its own.

(April 12, 1988)

Hypothetical Madmen

The Hypothesis, by Robert Pinget, and *The Diary of a Madman*, adapted from the story by Nikolai Gogol, La Mama E.T.C.

That twenty-two years elapsed before the first American production of Pinget's *The Hypothesis* is, to be charitable, embarrassing. The "new novelists" were mostly just that, and not playwrights, but one of them did write a play as innovative and disturbing as *Krapp's Last Tape*, with which it is sometimes compared. Unfortunately, though, you are not likely to see in this stiff American premiere why the work has been so highly praised.

The Hypothesis remains the only play Samuel Beckett ever directed that he didn't write. It is also one of the few plays not by Beckett that might be mistaken for his. Like Lucky's speech in *Godot*, most of Pinget's text is a long, unpunctuated monologue that flows in a torrent but nevertheless makes sense in the end if you listen carefully to the syntax. A well-dressed man, Mortin, speaks aloud the contents of a fat manuscript on the desk in front of him, as if he were an actor drilling lines, occasionally checking a word or phrase when his memory fails him. He tells a story about a writer who may or may not have thrown his manuscript down a well, "instead of himself." Because he reached a state of "complete prostration"? Or perhaps because of his "inaptitude to assume the impedimenta of existence"? Which hypothesis you accept is, of course, up to you.

Like the narrators in Beckett's novels, Mortin suggests rather than asserts the events in his story; characters appear and disappear, adopt one personality and then suddenly another, at the whim of the petulant speaker. Because this is a play and not a novel, however, the whimsical narrative eventually comes to seem less important than the situation onstage. We wonder about ludicrous anomalies, such as why the character would want to memorize such an absurdly digressive text, or why anyone, Mortin included, would take seriously the main hypothesis that the fictional writer, the real subject, is someone other than Mortin himself. In the end, frustrated by the recurrence of film clips of his own face interrupting and contradicting him, Morton throws his manuscript into the stove—which is not a well, but the parallel is clear.

This production's problem is that Pinget's text is treated as if it were indeed a novel, relying primarily on language to hold audience interest and failing to develop urgency in present time. Ryan Cutrona portrays a self-confident, thumbs-in-the waistcoat author, who, despite getting carried away at times by his own story, ends up a monotonous bore. Cutrona tries to vary his vocal delivery, but that's not enough; he never shows any consciousness that, as Pinget suggests, the play is really "a game."

To illustrate: when Mortin considers briefly the hypothesis that no fictional author exists, Cutrona pauses, genuinely troubled. The problem is, however, that much more's at stake in this moment. Pinget is not just hinting at the revelation that the story is really about Mortin; he is disclosing the sardonic underpinnings of the entire drama. In fact, Mortin is aware of everything—of his verbosity, of the unprovability of all hypotheses—and he is playing with us impishly, just as the film clips play with him.

Director Liz Diamond made some similar misjudgements when she worked with Cutrona on Beckett's prose texts, *Fizzles*: the actor also tried to speak the words musically, but neither his delivery nor the setting managed to communicate the peculiar plural nature of what Beckett calls his "voices." Unlike *Fizzles*, however, *The Hypothesis* has a stage history, and Diamond could have looked into how Beckett and others solved certain problems. (Perhaps she did and rejected it.) Beckett, for example, had Mortin drop pages of his manuscript on the floor throughout the action, which left him in the end rustling noisily through paper and holding only one sheet when the time came to toss the pile into the stove. Melodramatic artifice was asserted only to be undermined, and the manuscript-cum-author was both burned and not burned. Diamond decided to cut the stove, perhaps in an effort to avoid melodrama, but the melodrama arrived, alas, anyway as the play became a tale of a writer's would-be-tragic fall from certainty to uncertainty.

The irony of this double bill is that the less substantial text, *Diary of a Madman*, is the more satisfying experience. *Diary* is overdone, having had at least fifteen productions in New York alone since its English-language premiere in 1964, but Gogol's tale of a government clerk driven to distraction by, among other things, unrequited love for "the Director's daughter" is always a good showcase for a talented actor. Ismail Kanater, a Moroccan performer with a thick French accent, which he uses to advantage, performs his own adaptation with gruesome conviction. He is funny, versatile, and able to create highly specific caricatures of the story's numerous personalities. The play itself is relatively straightforward—a movement from sanity to madness that the actor may understand in more or less realistic terms. Too bad that a work as sophisticated as *The Hypothesis* has been pressed into the same mold.

(January 5, 1988)

Notes

BERLIN BY METAPHOR

* Unless otherwise noted, all financial statistics on the German theater, here and elsewhere in this collection, are quoted from the "operational data" periodically published in *Theater heute*. The August 1990 number was particularly helpful. All translations are mine unless otherwise noted.

GERMAN THEATER AFTER THE *WENDE*

1. Both the bureaucracy and the marvels are presumably teaching aids for use in the enduring Schillerian project to enlist theater as the Great Educator of the middle class, but they also invariably become new capitulations to that class's age-old desire to see mirror-images of itself—in this case, its love of gimmickry and institutions—in art. A book could be written about the myriad ironies this situation caused in the East German theater, which often competed with perceived technical "advances" beyond the Wall.

2. Contrary to the claims of many journalists during the current "crisis," capacity houses were not always assured in the GDR. In *Theatre in the Planned Society* (Chapel Hill: Univ. of North Carolina Press, 1978), 148, H.G. Huettich writes:

   > By 1968, the GDR stage, as represented by the contemporary topical drama, had become that "moral institution" envisioned by the SED [the ruling Communist Party], which resembled German classicism of the late eighteenth century. But as it fulfilled its social-political role to the greatest extent, it also confronted its greatest crisis. For by 1968, there was a dearth of plays, a dearth of authors, and even more critical, a waning audience.

3. *Theater heute*, Aug. 1990, 5. The situation hardly improved in the following few years; eighty percent of the spectators at the former East German theaters were Westerners in 1992.

4. *Theater 1990: Das Jahrbuch der Zeitschrift "Theater heute"* (Zürich: Orell Fussli + Friedrich Verlag, 1990), 130. All page numbers in parentheses, here and in the text, refer to this volume. Others have been harsher than Brasch. Author Frank Sporkmann, for instance: "We (by that I mean myself and some other GDR colleagues) are children with damaged imaginations." (143) Playwright Georg Seidel, who died in June, 1990: "We've all necessarily worked our way more and more into metaphors, I'd say, into an elevated slave-language, in order to be able to write anything at all. . . . The hermetic quality of our literature naturally has to do with the fact that we lived in a state that was dictatorial, established itself absolutely, and constantly employed notions of eternity. That's also why the writers here searched more strongly than those in the West for an absolute literature. We've probably written a little too much for eternity." (*Theater heute*, Mar. 1990, 22)

5. For a discussion of the Koerbl and Latchinian productions, see Franz Wille, "Über die Haut der Prothese," *Theater heute*, Mar. 1990, 20-26.

6. Quoted from *Theater heute*, Aug. 1990, pp. 4-5. The interview originally appeared in *Neues Deutschland*.
7. *Theater der Zeit*, which was founded three years before the GDR in 1946, struggled to stay alive after the *Wende* under the editorship of Martin Linzer and ceased publication in March 1992. It reappeared in May 1993, under private sponsorhip, declaring that its "most important aspiration" was "to help the new theater ferret out and foster a new time."
8. The following are two examples of directors' comments on differences among actors.

> Actors 'over there' [in West Germany] are a great deal faster—I'm talking about qualified people, always—at producing something like a nervous breakdown, exhibiting themselves. The way of the actor in the West is shorter in that way. On the other hand, with us the way to the spectator is shorter—what you do on the stage gets transported out there faster. . . . It's a triangle-relationship. The actor has his partner on the stage and his partner in the audience. Theater in the GDR was for decades a substitute for the media, and we took ample advantage of that.
>
> —Wolfgang Engel (48)

> The difference consisted in having to be on your toes. In the GDR we learned always to observe the milieu, the day, the surroundings, the politics, very closely—an element I've noticed much less with western actors. They're more inclined to admire themselves in the mirror, observe themselves. . . . I was always struck by a certain courteousness in the West German actor; when I came to the GDR, a much coarser wind blew around my ears from the direction of the ensemble. I always had to assert myself much more severely. Naturally, my being received differently also had to do with the fact that they couldn't be fired. Sure. This sort of independence and maturity didn't arise out of nowhere but was a result of particular conditioning factors.
>
> —Thomas Langhoff (44)

A CONVERSATION WITH BECKETT

* When this essay first appeared in *Theater Three*, it was accompanied by this prefatory note:

> The following text, written December 1986-January 1987, has lain unpublished for four years because of my desire to respect Samuel Beckett's aversion to publicity and encomium. As is well known, Beckett generally requested that he not be quoted by those who met with him, partly due to being stung repeatedly early in his career by journalists of dubious integrity. Though he made an exception in my case, allowing me to use some quotation in my book *Beckett in Performance*, I didn't want to risk embarrassing him with this piece and decided to suppress it indefinitely. In the months since his death, however, numerous colleagues and friends have urged me to change my mind, arguing, first, that the question of the author's embarrassment is now moot and, second, that the text has intrinsic value. Bowing to those arguments and to a feeling that my original impulse to share the experience was valid, I offer it now as a posthumous tribute.

IN SEARCH OF HEINER MÜLLER

* Several months after this interview was published, Bonnie Marranca, Müller's American publisher, told me she had never had the conversation with him he describes here. It would not be the first time Müller had turned out to be forensically unreliable, nor is it the only example in my interview. He insisted three times, for instance—twice verbally, once when checking the transcript—that Wilson had directed *Hamletmachine* at Columbia University, not NYU, in which case I made the correction (with hesitation). I have strong suspicions about other points as well, but lack verfication of them.

OUTTAKES: FRAGMENTS FROM AN INTERVIEW WITH HEINER MÜLLER
* The poet Inge Müller committed suicide in 1966.

A COUPLA WHITE GUYS SITTIN' AROUN' TALKIN'
* This interview was one of three assigned by theater editor Ross Wetzsteon for the *Village Voice*'s annual Obie Supplement for 1992. Alisa Solomon, Marc Robinson and I were asked to speak with (in Wetzsteon's words) "the three senior statesmen of American drama criticism," Eric Bentley, Richard Gilman and Stanley Kauffmann, about "what enduring contributions Off- and Off-Off-Broadway have made to our theater, and what contributions they can continue to make."

THE MEDIATED QUIXOTE
1. Samuel Beckett, *Disjecta*, ed. Ruby Cohn (NY: Grove Press, 1984), 106.
2. Ibid, 145.
3. Robert Coover, "The Last Quixote," *New American Review* 11 (1971), 139.
4. Unless otherwise noted, all Beckett quotations are from Samuel Beckett, *Collected Shorter Plays* (NY: Grove Press, 1984).
5. See Martin Esslin, *Mediations: Essays on Brecht, Beckett and the Media* (NY: Grove Press, 1982) and Clas Zilliacus, *Beckett and Broadcasting* (Abo: Abo Akademi, 1976).
6. John Fletcher and John Spurling, *Beckett: The Playwright*, revised ed. (NY: Hill and Wang, 1985), 44.
7. Zilliacus, 37.
8. Ibid, 50.
9. Esslin, 131.
10. Chabert, 25.
11. Zilliacus, 56.
12. Quoted in Zilliacus, 3.
13. Samuel Beckett, *Three Novels* (NY: Grove, 1965), 192.
14. See Zilliacus, 103.
15. Everett Frost, "Fundamental Sounds: Recording Samuel Beckett's Radio Plays," *Theatre Journal* 43:3, Oct. 1991, 374-5.
16. Quoted in Zilliacus, 114.
17. Quoted in Jonathan Kalb, *Beckett in Performance* (Cambridge: Cambridge Univ. Press, 1989), 233.
18. Deirdre Bair, *Samuel Beckett: A Biography* (NY and London: Harcourt Brace Jovanovich, 1978), 204.
19. Linda Ben-Zvi, "Samuel Beckett's Media Plays," *Modern Drama* 28:1, Mar. 1985, 31.
20. See Schneider's apologia, "On Directing *Film*," in Samuel Beckett, *Film* (NY: Grove, 1969), 63-94.
21. See Zilliacus, 60.
22. Ben-Zvi, 30.
23. Vincent Murphy, "Being and Perception: Beckett's *Film*," *Modern Drama* 18:1, Mar. 1975, 47.
24. Sylvie Debevec Henning, "'Film': A Dialogue Between Beckett and Berkeley," *Journal of Beckett Studies* 7, Spring 1982, 99.

25. Alan M. Olson, "Video Icons & Values: An Overview," in *Video Icons & Values*, eds. Alan M. Olson, Christopher Parr, and Debra Parr (Albany: SUNY Press, 1991), 2.
26. Beckett to Israel Shenker in 1956, quoted in: Lawrence Graver and Raymond Federman, eds. *Samuel Beckett: The Critical Heritage* (London: Routledge & Kegan Paul, 1979), 148.
27. See Kalb, 95-116.
28. Ben-Zvi, 36.
29. James Knowlson, "*Ghost Trio/Geister Trio*," in *Beckett at 80/Beckett in Context*, ed. Enoch Brater (NY and Oxford: Oxford Univ. Press, 1986), 199.
30. Ben-Zvi, 35.

KRAPP AT THE PALAST

1. The Palast der Republik, variously disparaged by locals over the years as *Ballast der Republik* (burden of the republic), *Palazzo Prozzo* (ostentatious palace), and *Honeckers Lampenladen* (Honecker's lamp store), stood empty for three years after the end of the GDR as German officials debated what to do with it. In March 1993 it was condemned to razing.
2. S.E. Gontarski, *The Intent of Undoing* (Bloomington: Indiana Univ. Press, 1985), 61.
3. Pierre Chabert, "Beckett as Director," *Gambit*, Vol. 7, No. 28 (1976), 44.
4. "Beckett's Letters on *Endgame*," *The Village Voice Reader*, ed. Daniel Wolf and Edwin Fancher (Garden City: Doubleday, 1962), 183.
5. Kalb, *Beckett in Performance,* 215.
6. Chabert, 45.

MAYAKOVSKY'S TRAGIC COMEDY

1. Bertolt Brecht, *Poems: 1913-1956*, ed. John Willett and Ralph Manheim (NY: Methuen, 1976), 319.
2. Edward Brown, *Mayakovsky: A Poet in the Revolution* (Princeton: Princeton Univ. Press, 1973), 335; Vera Alexandrova, *A History of Soviet Literature* (Garden City: Doubleday, 1963), 65. Very little serious criticism on *The Bathouse* exists in English, French or German, the languages in which I am qualified to research. A noteworthy exception is Angelo Maria Ripellino, *Maiakovski et le théâtre russe d'avant-garde* (Paris: L'Arche, 1965).
3. Obviously, many of the specific references mentioned in the script (e.g., P.S. Kogan, L. Friedland, the Dnieper Power Plant, the Izvestia skyscraper) had for 1930 audiences a direct effect that probably cannot be regained. In a contemporary production, especially one outside the former Soviet Union, some of those references would have to be cut or changed. A surprising number of them, however, can remain unaltered. For example, Chudakov's interpretation of the coded letter announcing the Phosphorescent Woman's arrival:

> VELOSIPEDKIN. . . . "R-V-1-3-2-24-20." What's that, the telephone number of somebody called Comrade Arvey?

> CHUDAKOV. It's not just the letters *r* and *v*, it's "arrive." They write in consonants only, which means a saving of twenty-five percent on the alphabet. The numbers 1, 3, and 2 show the sequence of the vowels: A, E, I, O, U: "arrive." See? The figure 24 means the 24th day of the month—tomorrow. And 20 indicates the hour. He, she, or it will arrive at eight o'clock tomorrow night.

His speech satirizes the orthographical reforms that had tried to do away with unnecessary letters in the Russian alphabet, but it is also funny in context because of the improbable speed with which he grasps the code. It is worth pointing out that both *The Bedbug* and *The Bathhouse* were popular successes when they were revived in the Soviet Union during the Malenkov "thaw" of the early 1950s. (In an important 1952 speech, Politburo member Georgi Malenkov had sanctioned satirical criticism in socialist literature.) Comments on Valentin Pluchek's 1953 production of *The Bathhouse* may be found in Ripellino, 247-249, and in Marjorie Hoover, *Meyerhold: The Art of Conscious Theater* (Amherst: Univ. of Massachusetts Press, 1974). *The Bathhouse* also had several popularly successful productions in East Germany, the earliest in 1959. See the review by Friedrich Luft, *Stimme der Kritik: Berliner Theater seit 1945* (Hannover: Friedrich Verlag, 1965), 289-291. A recent American version by Paul Schmidt entitled *The Bathtub* (published in *Theater* 22:2, Spring 1991) demonstrates what may be accomplished with the play in the hands of an inspired adaptor.

4. The 15th Congress of the Soviet Communist Party had in 1927 declared a campaign against bureaucratic waste. James Symons, *Meyerhold's Theatre of the Grotesque* (Coral Gables: Univ. of Miami Press, 1971), 186.
5. Victor Terras, *Vladimir Mayakovsky* (Boston: Twayne, 1983), 35. Terras also quotes Mayakovsky's suicide note, written in April: "Tell Ermilov that it is too bad I took down the slogan, ought to have fought it out."
6. Meyerhold's production emphasized these divisions in many ways; for example, the workers all wore coveralls and moved with acrobatic agility while the bureaucrats wore business suits and sat about in armchairs. Descriptions of the production may be found in Konstantin Rudnitsky, *Meyerhold the Director* (Ann Arbor: Ardis, 1981) and Edward Braun, *The Theatre of Meyerhold* (NY: Drama Book Specialists, 1979).
7. All quotations from *The Bathhouse* are from *The Complete Plays of Vladimir Mayakovsky*, trans. Guy Daniels (NY: Washington Square Press, 1968).
8. See Henri Bergson, *Laughter: An Essay on the Meaning of the Comic*, trans. Cloudesley Brereton and Fred Rothwell (NY: Macmillan, 1917), 10.
9. For one thing, Mayakovsky depicts as would-be heros workers alienated from their labor due to impediments in socialist, not capitalist, society, which emphasizes the pathos of the individual over the glory of his or her self-sacrifice for the sake of the nascent socialist ideal. It is precisely because of the temptation to write "fatalistic" plays like *The Bathhouse* that the rules of Socialist Realism became so rigidly codified and enforced in the first place.
10. Eugène Ionesco, *Notes and Counter Notes*, trans. Donald Watson (NY: Grove Press, 1964), 27.
11. Northrop Frye, *Anatomy of Criticism* (Princeton: Princeton Univ. Press, 1957), 224.
12. Another interpretation of Act III may also help to explain its tentative sense of hope: since the fiction onstage now represents real life, the Director's actions represent manipulation of real life, the very thing that was impossible in Acts I and II.
13. R.C. Elliot, *The Power of Satire* (Princeton: Princeton Univ. Press, 1960), Ch. 1.
14. Though biographical speculation is usually idle, the proximity of *The Bathhouse* to Mayakovsky's suicide makes it hard to resist asking whether the author himself was fully aware just how shattered his faith appeared in this script. Did he intend, for example, that the characters' leaving, their dismissal of their world, be so easily readable as a callous rejection of the Soviet system and the propagandist notion of "struggling to build it"? Was it his purpose to depict a metaphorical bathhouse in which people wash their hands of the iniquitous environment so thoroughly that they scrub away the future? In light of such questions the boilerplate Soviet defense of the play (see, for instance, Peter Yershov's *Comedy in the Soviet*

Theater (1956)), that Mayakovsky did not feel that the problems were faults of the Soviet system but of people like Pobedonosikov, strains belief even with the most sympathetic hindsight.

15. According to Konstantin Rudnitsky, one of Meyerhold's initial reactions after reading *The Bathhouse* was to compare it with Molière (*Meyerhold the Director*, 448-449), and that comparison illuminates the ending from yet another perspective. Since Molière never violated the neoclassical rule of consistency of character, his dramaturgy is based on an assumption that characters cannot change: all reversals in Molière are of plot, not character. One result of such a reliance on plot reversal is that endings can be very strange: e.g. in *Tartuffe*, where the characters speak as if they have changed (after all, there's been a catastrophe) even though they are exactly the same; or in *Le bourgeois gentilhomme*, where Molière does not manage a plot reversal and resorts to pure theatricality, providing closure but no ending. In *The Bathhouse*, too, the characters are types and cannot change, so the plot must effect change, which it does in the form of the Phosphorescent Woman. As a deus ex machina, however, she carries too much irony to resolve the play unambiguously, so Mayakovsky resorts to theatricality as a final gesture that emphasizes the uncertainty while providing closure.

Rudnitsky, an actor in Meyerhold's production, says that Mayakovsky originally planned another, more spectacular ending that was changed due to budget considerations, to the cast's dismay.

> The time machine was to have thrown out the bureaucrats, headed by the chief high leader Pobedonosikov, and that would have put a period on the finale. But this was not contained in the prop design. Everyone went upward somewhere on the construction, with suitcases and bags, and the spectator could not understand what was happening. This was a great omission. (464)

As should be clear from my discussion, I think the new ending, less straightforward in moralistic terms and hence richer thematically, was by far the better choice.

WHY I WRITE FOR THE *VILLAGE VOICE*.

1. "Crritic" was the rubric of an occasional series of articles by members of the theater community that ran in the *Voice* during 1991. The series began with an article by Ross Wetzsteon (*Voice*, Jan. 29, 1991) that described certain problems with the current practice of theater criticism and called for contributions.

2. This article was written before I was offered my current academic job.

Index

Acknowledgements

The author is grateful to the editors of the following publications for permission to reprint.

"Berlin by Metaphor," *The Threepenny Review*, Fall 1990.

"Notes on the Last Cold-War Theatertreffen," *Performing Arts Journal* 35/36, Winter 1990.

"2 Stücke/2 Gegenstücke" and "Krapp at the Palast," *Theater,* Summer/Fall 1990 and Fall/Winter 1987.

"A Conversation with Beckett" and "Out-Takes: Fragments from an Interview with Heiner Müller," *Theater Three* 9, Fall 1990 and 8, Spring 1990.

"In Search of Heiner Müller," "Kroetz in America," "The Other Avant-Garde" and "One Thing After Another," *American Theatre* (published by Theatre Communications Group), Feb. 1990, Feb. 1991, May 1992 and May 1990.

"The Mediated Quixote," *The Cambridge Companion to Beckett,* ed. John Pilling (Cambridge University Press, 1993).

"Gender and the Void," *The Michigan Quarterly Review,* Spring 1992.

"Mayakovsky's Tragic Comedy," *Before His Eyes: Essays in Honor of Stanley Kauffmann* (University Press of America, 1986).

Some of the above first appeared under different titles. All pieces not listed here originally appeared in *The Village Voice*.

About the Author

Jonathan Kalb, who lives in Brooklyn with his wife, Julie Heffernan, and their young son, Oliver, has been a theater critic for *The Village Voice* since 1987. He is a professor of theater at Hunter College of CUNY and the author of *Beckett in Performance* (1989). He is the youngest person ever to be honored with the George Jean Nathan Award for Dramatic Criticism, which he won in 1991.